Classroom Research

K. PATRICIA CROSS

MIMI HARRIS STEADMAN

Classroom Research

Implementing the Scholarship of Teaching

JOSSEY-BASS PUBLISHERS ▪ San Francisco

Substantial discounts on bulk quantities of Jossey-Bass books are available to corporations, professional associations, and other organizations. For details and discount information, contact the special sales department at Jossey-Bass Inc., Publishers (415) 433–1740; Fax (800) 605–2665.

For sales outside the United States, please contact your local Simon & Schuster International office.
Manufactured in the United States of America
Interior design by Gene Crofts

Brandt, R. "Punished by Rewards? A Conversation with Alfie Kohn." *Educational Leadership*, Sept. 1995, pp. 13–16. Reprinted with permission of the Association for Supervision and Curriculum Development. Copyright © 1995 by ASCD. All rights reserved.

Excerpt in Chapter Two from *Statistical Power Analysis for the Behavioral Sciences* by J. Cohen, 1988, Hillsdale, N.J.: Lawrence Erlbaum Associates, Inc. Copyright 1988 by Lawrence Erlbaum Associates, Inc. Reprinted with permission.

Hutchings, P. *Using Cases to Improve College Teaching: A Guide to More Reflective Practice.* Washington, D.C.: American Association for Higher Education, 1993. Permission granted by the American Association for Higher Education.

Library of Congress Cataloging-in-Publication Data
Cross, K. Patricia, (Kathryn Patricia), date
    Classroom research : implementing the scholarship of teaching / K.
Patricia Cross, Mimi Harris Steadman. — 1st ed.
       p. cm. — (The Jossey-Bass higher and adult education series)
    Includes bibliographical references and index.
    ISBN 0–7879–0288–8 (cloth : acid-free paper)
    1. College teaching—United States. 2. Case method. 3. College
teaching—Research—United States. I. Steadman, Mimi Harris.
II. Title. III. Series.
LB2331.C766 1996
378.1′25′072073—dc20   96–10108

FIRST EDITION
PB Printing 10 9 8 7 6 5 4 3 2 1

The Jossey-Bass
Higher and Adult Education Series

CONTENTS

PREFACE   xi

THE AUTHORS   xxi

CHAPTER 1   Introduction to Classroom Research   1

CHAPTER 2   "The Leslies"   29
Learning Issues: Prerequisite Knowledge;
Metacognition and Learning Strategies;
Self-Confidence and Motivation

CHAPTER 3   "The Captive Audience"   93
Learning Issues: Learning Goals; Deep and
Surface Learning; Student Ratings of Instruction

CHAPTER 4   "But Is It Working?"   161
Learning Issues: Peer Learning; Intellectual
Development and Critical Thinking

CHAPTER 5   "The Challenge"   207
Designing Your Own Classroom Research

NOTES   231

REFERENCES   235

INDEX   253

PREFACE

This book is about Classroom Research—and also about far more than that. It is about creating a climate on campus for the serious discussion of teaching and learning, and it is about meeting the intellectual challenges of teaching through continuing study and investigation. It is written for college faculty members engaged in the scholarship of teaching and for graduate students planning to teach and work in higher education.

As teaching moves to a place of priority on college campuses, there is an urgent need for materials about classroom teaching written specifically for college teachers, who are usually disciplinary specialists with experience and interest in teaching but without a knowledge base in their common profession of teaching. We agree with Ann Lieberman's observation that "what everyone wants for students—a wide array of learning opportunities that engage students in experiencing, creating, and solving real problems, using their own experience, and working with others—is for some reason denied to teachers when they are learners" (1995, p. 591).

In addition to practicing what we are preaching by trying to engage the readers of this book in "solving real problems, using their own experience, and working with others," we are mindful of the enormous contribution that classroom teachers can make to the practice of teaching (especially their own but also that of their colleagues) by using their classrooms as laboratories for the study of learning. Scholarship involves both continuous learning and productive contributions to knowledge. This book is one effort to implement the widespread interest in the "scholarship" of teaching sparked by the report of The Carnegie Foundation for the Advancement of Teaching (Boyer, 1990).

Goals and Purposes

We have three major goals for this book: (1) to engage teachers and prospective teachers in collaborative problem-based discussions about teaching and learning, (2) to integrate their firsthand teaching experience with recent research and theory on learning, and (3) to introduce them to the purposes and methods of Classroom Assessment and Classroom Research for use in their own classrooms.

To accomplish those purposes, we have devised a unique format. First, to give teachers a focus for group discussions of common teaching problems, we present four separate cases, four stories about classroom learning situations, written by experienced college teachers from a variety of academic disciplines. The incidents presented in the cases will be easily recognized by experienced teachers, but not easily solved. They will provoke discussion and encourage teachers participating in the discussions to exchange ideas and interpretations about the case.

Second, to integrate teachers' experience with research and theory, for each case we present a brief review of the recent relevant research on learning, followed by an annotated list of further readings. Third, for each case we suggest ways teachers can further study the learning issues through their own Classroom Assessment and Classroom Research. The outline, then, of the case study chapters is as follows: (1) presentation of the case, (2) case analysis, including formulation of some possible hypotheses about learning problems, (3) review of the research literature relevant to each hypothesis, (4) recommended readings relevant to each hypothesis, (5) illustrations of Classroom Assessment, and (6) suggestions for Classroom Research relevant to each hypothesis.

This format is designed to bring teachers and potential teachers together in a teaching community for sharing insights and experiences; to illuminate their wisdom of experience with the knowledge of research and theory; and finally, to encourage their continuing study of teaching and learning through Classroom Assessment and Classroom Research. In short, we treat teachers as lifelong learners and potential scholars in the exploding field of knowledge about human learning.

Audience

We have written this book with some particular learner groups in mind.

Individual readers. Because reading is basically an individual activity, any book has to be relevant and interesting to the solitary reader. We hope, however, that the stories and ideas in this book will make readers want to engage others in discussions about it.

Graduate classes on teaching and learning. It is our hope that this book will be an ideal textbook for classes and seminars on teaching and learning in higher education. We designed it to be provocative—encouraging students to engage in discussion—and academically sound—presenting the latest research and theories about learning.

Formal instructional or faculty development groups. By formal groups, we mean those organized by a faculty development specialist. We believe that the unique format of this book provides special opportunities for faculty members to participate effectively in such activities as orientation for new teachers, teaching workshops, semester-long teaching seminars, and similar events.

Teaching assistant programs. Increasingly, universities are offering coordinated programs for the training of graduate teaching assistants (TAs). These programs need challenging materials for these potential college teachers who are knowledgeable in their disciplines but weak in their knowledge about how to teach those subjects to undergraduates. We hope this book will serve as a resource for both centrally organized campuswide TA programs and those directed from within academic departments.

Informal collegial groups. In community colleges, especially, collegial groups of faculty are meeting regularly or occasionally to talk about their common interests in teaching. This book offers a structured curriculum of study for such groups, who might welcome the discipline of focused study but lack the time to develop it.

Discipline-based faculty groups. These groups differ from instructional or faculty development groups in that they are usually organized by someone whose expertise is in a discipline—for example, a department or division chair—rather than someone who specializes in improving instruction. The resources in this book are especially appropriate for intelligent and dedicated teachers who nevertheless lack knowledge about learning and research in education.

Classroom Assessment and Classroom Research groups. Many existing Classroom Assessment groups were initially formed to learn about and practice Classroom Assessment in semester-long or yearlong study groups. They then continued on informally, with or without a facilitator, because the members appreciated the forum for sharing Classroom Assessment projects and results. Because many of these ongoing groups have been in place for some time, their members have developed a substantial level of trust and comfort in experimenting with collaborative case discussion, case writing, and Classroom Assessment and Classroom Research projects. This book may be used by these groups to deepen their discussions and enrich their projects.

Overview of the Contents

This book is about learning rather than teaching. The centerpiece of the book, as described earlier, consists of four cases (Chapters Two, Three, Four, and Five) that are classroom scenes illustrating a variety of *learning* issues. Learning case studies are not common in higher education, where most cases are *teaching* cases, in which some critical incident occurs in the classroom (a student makes a sexist remark, for example) and the question for discussion is, What should the teacher do next? The purpose of the discussion in teaching cases is reflection and an exchange of ideas with other experienced teachers.

Learning cases are different because they show students in the process of learning, and they illustrate student problems and perceptions. The questions for discussion in a learning case are these: How are students perceiving what is going on in this class? What are some hypotheses about what is interfering with their learning? What might research on learning tell us about this student or this group of students? And how might we find out more about these learning issues? Moreover, whereas teaching cases usually examine a single incident, learning cases tackle long-term issues. The question is not usually, What should the teacher do next? but rather, How can the teacher make the class more productive for students' learning?

The experienced college teachers who write the four learning cases presented in the book represent different disciplines and different types of colleges. In Chapter Two, the case is written by Jerry Evensky, associate professor of economics at Syracuse University, and it concerns Leslie,[1] a student who is thinking of dropping economics because she does not understand what is going on. In Chapter Three, the case is written by Priscilla Laws, professor of physics at Dickinson College. The scene is a physics laboratory in a required course for premeds, who are not really interested in learning physics. In Chapter Four, the setting is a history classroom at a city college, observed by Pat Hutchings, director of the Teaching Initiative at the American Association for Higher Education. Hutchings collected some fascinating data on the class in preparation for writing her case. Thus, readers have an opportunity to hear what the teachers say they are trying to do and then to observe students' reactions to the teachers' efforts. We wrote the final case, presented in Chapter Five. It is a compendium of all the learning issues that appeared in previous chapters. It is our challenge to you, the readers. We ask you to identify the learning issues in the case and to integrate your teaching experience with your learning experience as readers and active participants in the activities suggested in this book.

Using Cases to Engage Teachers in Discussions About Teaching

There are several reasons for using cases to create opportunities for teachers to come together to talk about teaching. First, as we suggested earlier, is the need to develop a *teaching community*. Hutchings observes that "there's a growing recognition that what's really needed to improve teaching is a campus culture in which good practice can thrive, one where faculty talk together about teaching, inquire into its effects, and take collective responsibility for its quality" (1993, p. v).

Ironically, teaching, the common mission that is shared by all colleges and universities, is a strangely private affair, often practiced behind closed doors without much opportunity for discussion with one's professional peers. Many teachers have opportunities to participate in research communities or to serve on committees addressing concerns about governance, but few have any reason to come together in thoughtful conversations about teaching. Thus it is that one of the goals of this book is to provide substantive issues for discussion via cases.

A second reason for engaging teachers in case discussions about teaching is to enrich and challenge their individual thinking through engaging them in group problem solving. Cases as currently used in faculty development rely almost entirely on teaching experience; there is usually no "right" answer, but thoughtful discussion of the questions involved leads to constructive thinking that may not occur to individual teachers, isolated in individual classrooms. Hutchings writes that useful cases "depict teaching and learning incidents that are deliberately open to interpretation—raising questions rather than answering them, encouraging problem solving, calling forth collective faculty intelligence and varied perspectives, and promoting more reflective practice" (1993, pp. 2–3). Harvard case writer, Abby Hansen, writes in the same vein, noting that "each case is a kaleidoscope; what you see in it depends on how you shake it" (1987, p. 57). The cases in this book are intended to be shaken by teachers with a variety of experiences and from many different disciplines.

Integrating the Experience of Teaching with the Scholarship of Research

Although we believe bringing faculty together to talk about teaching from their wealth of experience is the first step in creating a climate for good teaching, we also believe that in these times of very active research on cognition and learning, experience is not enough. Teachers need some exposure to what research has to say about how students learn—an exposure lacking for teachers whose preparation for college teaching usually stops with mastery of the subject matter. Although some fifty disciplinary teaching journals are beginning to bring knowledge about pedagogy to the attention of discipline-oriented faculty members (Weimer, 1993), many teachers do not know what exists in the way of research on learning or even where to look for it. Thus, our second step in developing this book has been to bring relevant research into teachers' discussions about teaching and learning.

We do this through the presentation of brief syntheses of research relevant to each case. Each case in the book is followed by a case analysis that includes some hypotheses about the question, What is going on here?—the common query that opens case discussions. For example, a common problem for first-year students without much experience in or vocabulary for the study of a particular discipline is that there are huge holes in the knowledge they need to understand the "language" of the discipline. In research on cognition, such a network of knowledge is known as a *schema*—a term not even familiar to most college teachers. Thus, in this book, each hypothesis for student learning is followed by a synthesis of research and theory on that hypothesis, plus an annotated list of readings appropriate for further study. For example, the first case—about Leslie, the student who is thinking about dropping economics because she does not understand what is going on in class and, despite conscientious study, fears she will do poorly in the course, suggests several hypotheses that could explain her fear of remaining in the course. One is that she lacks the prerequisite knowledge to understand the language of economics. That is, her schema for economics is not sufficiently well developed to permit her to make the connections between the new information presented in class and what she already knows. Because we believe it is important to understand whatever researchers know about the role of schemata in learning, we synthesize briefly what is now known through research and cognitive theory about the importance of previous learning to new learning. This synthesis provides both an overview of the important concepts and also an entrance into the vocabulary of cognitive psychology. An annotated list of references, especially selected for their appropriateness for a general reading audience, is then provided for further reading.

Encouraging Classroom Assessment

Finally, because we believe that the creation of a climate for teaching is more likely to involve the continuing search for knowledge than the finding of answers, we attempt to further engage the intellectual curiosity of teachers by presenting some examples of Classroom Assessment and Classroom Research that can be conducted rather simply but effectively in any college classroom by teachers across a variety of disciplines.

This book evolved in part from the interest and support generated by college teachers who are using the Classroom Assessment Techniques (CATs) described in *Classroom Assessment Techniques: A Handbook for College Teachers* (Angelo and Cross, 1993) in their own classrooms. The purpose of Classroom Assessment is to make both teachers and students more aware of the learning that is taking place—or perhaps not taking place—in the classroom; it is an assessment of learning in process, during the semester, in a given classroom.

This book assumes reader access to *Classroom Assessment Techniques*. Although we give enough information about the CATs we discuss that the reader can follow the discussion, we try not to repeat detailed instructions that are easily accessible elsewhere. We appreciate that many of the readers of this book will be experienced users of Classroom Assessment.

Each case study, plus its attendant hypotheses and synopses of relevant research, is followed by some examples of how CATs might be used to investigate the hypotheses and to collect further information. In the first case, for example, the teacher might wish to answer such questions as, How many other "Leslies" are there in the class? What is the students' general level of background and experience in dealing with quantitative relationships? How well do they understand the concepts of economics? Can they analyze the pros and cons of an explanation? How much time are students spending studying for this course? And is their study time productive? These are all questions for Classroom Assessment, providing information to teacher and students alike about how students are responding to the challenge of learning in a particular class.

Classroom Assessment typically answers questions about *what* students are learning and how well, but it often raises questions about *how* students learn. Those questions lead teachers to Classroom Research.

Introducing Teachers to Classroom Research

This book is our first effort to define Classroom Research and provide helpful guidelines for its practice. Chapter One provides the definition of Classroom Research—what it is and what it is not—and the rationale for it. Classroom Research is not traditional research conducted in or on classrooms. It is a specific methodology designed for discipline-oriented teachers without training or experience in the methods of educational research. It is most simply defined as ongoing and cumulative intellectual inquiry by classroom teachers into the nature of teaching and learning in their own classrooms. Inquiry into a question about how students learn typically leads to new questions and thus to continual investigation through Classroom Research.

The purpose of Classroom Research is not to report findings but rather to deepen teachers' understanding and to promote their continuing intellectual interest in the challenge of teaching. Moreover, we believe that in order to effect substantial change in college teaching, the involvement of discipline-oriented college faculty members in research on teaching and learning is necessary. Teachers who know their discipline and the problems of teaching it to others are in the best position to make systematic observations and to conduct ongoing investigations into the nature of learning and the impact of teaching upon it.

For each hypothesis emerging from the analysis of a case, we present some ideas for Classroom Research, posing questions that might be addressed and modest designs for study. Our suggestions are illustrative rather than prescriptive. Our intention is to spark ideas, encouraging teachers to be creative in the questions they pose as well as the inquiries they design.

Awareness of Diversity

We have made a special effort to illustrate diversity in students, subject matter, types of institutions, teaching methods, and learning issues. The cases include one from the social sciences, one from the physical sciences, one from the humanities, and one from the professions. The campus types are a research university, an independent liberal arts college, an urban institution, and a state university. Students come in all varieties and are generally representative of today's diversity. The location of the cases is likewise diverse; they take place in a teacher's office, a science lab, a classroom using small-group meetings, and a typical classroom discussion. We have tried to include some discussion on most of the major learning issues on which there is substantive research and a base of knowledge. Learning issues addressed include memory, motivation, deep and surface learning, metacognition, learning strategies, gender issues, intellectual development, and critical thinking.

Acknowledgments

We would like to acknowledge our appreciation for the support of the David Pierpont Gardner endowed professorship in higher education at the University of California, Berkeley, which provided the financial support for the preparation of this book. Our grateful appreciation is also extended to Jerry Evensky and Priscilla Laws for permission to use their case studies as the foundations for Chapters Two and Three. Pat Hutchings gave generously of her expertise and time in writing the case used in Chapter Four and in making available to us her extraordinarily rich files of research on the case.

We are also indebted to our academic colleagues whose wealth of expertise and experience in matters related to teaching and learning greatly enriched our work. Colleagues who took time out from busy schedules to review, in various stages of development, one or more chapters of the book include Thomas A. Angelo, director, AAHE Assessment Forum; Dennis Chowenhill, Scott Hildreth, and Carol Lyke, instructors at Chabot Community College; Elaine El-Khawas, vice president for policy analysis and research, American Council on Education; George Kuh, professor of education, Indiana University; and Erika Nielsen Andrew, director, Urban Schools Network, National Center for Research on Vocational Education. Finally, we wish to thank the dedicated teachers, in all kinds of colleges and universities throughout the land, whose insights and experiences have constantly challenged and inspired us.

We hope that this book will challenge teachers to use their classrooms as laboratories for the continuing study of learning. We hope that teachers will join together to share experiences and insights and to collaborate on Classroom Assessment and Classroom Research. Most of all, we hope that this book will heighten the intellectual challenge of teaching, serving teachers as a tool to implement the scholarship of teaching.

Berkeley, California   K. Patricia Cross
July 1996   Mimi Harris Steadman

THE AUTHORS

K. Patricia Cross is the David Pierpont Gardner Professor of Higher Education at the University of California, Berkeley. Cross has had a varied and distinguished career as a university administrator (assistant dean of women at the University of Illinois and dean of students at Cornell University), researcher (distinguished research scientist at the Educational Testing Service and research educator at the Center for Research and Development in Higher Education, University of California, Berkeley), and teacher (professor and chair of the Department of Administration, Planning, and Social Policy at the Harvard Graduate School of Education and professor of higher education, University of California, Berkeley).

The author of eight books and more than one hundred and fifty articles and chapters, Cross has been recognized for her scholarship by election to the National Academy of Education and receipt of the E. F. Lindquist Award from the American Educational Research Association, the Sidney Suslow Award from the Association for Institutional Research, and the Howard Bowen Award from the Association for the Study of Higher Education. Past president of the American Association of Higher Education, she has also received a number of awards for leadership in education, among them the 1990 Leadership Award from the American Association of Community and Junior Colleges and the 1990 award for outstanding contributions to the improvement of instruction from the National Council of Instructional Administrators.

Cross serves on the editorial boards of six journals of higher education, both national and international. She has lectured on U.S. higher education widely in the United States and in England, France, Germany, the Netherlands, Sweden, the former Soviet Union, Japan, and Australia. Her interests lie primarily in the changing college student populations and the improvement of teaching and learning in higher education. Cross received her B.S. degree in mathematics from Illinois State University and her M.A. and Ph.D. degrees in social psychology from the University of Illinois.

Mimi Harris Steadman is a research specialist at the National Center for Research in Vocational Education at the University of California, Berkeley. As a 1993 fellow in the National Center on Adult Learning practitioner-based research program, she conducted dissertation research on the implementation and impact of Classroom Assessment Techniques in California community colleges. During her graduate study, she completed a higher education internship at the Western Association of Schools and Colleges and worked in institutional research, student development, and instruction. She has taught adults, adolescents, and children, in subject areas from psychology to sailing.

Her interests focus on improving teaching and learning in higher education and on designing meaningful learning opportunities for all teachers. Steadman holds a B.S. degree from Cornell University and an M.S. degree from the University of Rhode Island. She received her Ed.D. degree in higher education administration from the University of California, Berkeley.

Classroom Research

CHAPTER 1

Introduction
to Classroom Research

The richness of faculty talent should be celebrated, not restricted. Only as the distinctiveness of each professor is affirmed will the potential of scholarship be fully realized. Surely, American higher education is imaginative and creative enough to support and reward not only those scholars uniquely gifted in research but also those who excel in the integration and application of knowledge, as well as those especially adept in the scholarship of teaching. Such a mosaic of talent, if acknowledged, would bring renewed vitality to higher learning and to the nation.

Boyer, *Scholarship Reconsidered*, 1990, p. 27

The Carnegie report titled *Scholarship Reconsidered* (Boyer, 1990) has received widespread interest, and many colleges and universities are especially interested in implementing its recommendation to give greater attention to the "scholarship of teaching." But what exactly is the scholarship of teaching? The Carnegie report gives scant attention to an operational definition, but it does say what good teachers do. They "stimulate active, not passive learning and encourage students to be critical, creative thinkers, with the capacity to go on learning after their college days are over." Further, "good teaching means that faculty, as scholars, are also learners. . . . Through reading, through classroom discussion, and surely through comments and questions posed by students, professors themselves will be pushed in creative new directions" (p. 24). Well, maybe.

We believe that the learning required for the scholarship of teaching goes considerably beyond the traditional classroom activities of reading, class discussion, and being "pushed in creative new directions" by the comments and questions of students. Just as students must be actively engaged in formulating their own learning questions and thinking critically about them, so teachers must be actively engaged in formulating their own questions about learning and the impact of their teaching upon it. Teachers have an exceptional opportunity to engage actively in the scholarship of teaching by using their classrooms as laboratories for the study of teaching and learning. Observing students in the act of learning, reflecting and discussing observations and data with teaching colleagues, and reading the literature on what is already known about learning is one way teachers can implement the scholarship of teaching. It is what we call *Classroom Research*.

Classroom Research may be simply defined as ongoing and cumulative intellectual inquiry by classroom teachers into the nature of teaching and learning in their own classrooms. At its best, Classroom Research should benefit both teachers and students by actively engaging them in the collaborative study of learning as it takes place day by day in the particular context of their own classrooms. Teachers are learning how to become more effective teachers, and students are learning how to become more effective learners. In the next section, we describe the specific characteristics of Classroom Research.

Characteristics of Classroom Research

Many of the characteristics of Classroom Research (specifically learner-centered, teacher-directed, context-specific, and continual, or ongoing) are shared by Classroom Assessment (see Angelo and Cross, 1993, pp. 4–6).

Learner-Centered

Classroom Research focuses the primary attention of teachers and students on observing and improving *learning*, rather than on observing and improving teaching. In Classroom Research, it is learner responses to teaching rather than teacher performance that is the subject for study. Through systematic and careful study of learning as it takes place day by day in the classroom, teachers are gaining insight and understanding into how to make their teaching more effective, and students are gaining the lifelong skills of assessing and improving their learning.

Teacher-Directed

Classroom Research is dedicated to the proposition that college teachers are quite capable of conducting useful and valid research on classroom learning. Although Classroom Research does not obviate the need for technically trained educational researchers, it does change the focus from teachers as consumers of research to teachers as active investigators, engaged in studies of learning in their discipline.

Collaborative

Classroom Research requires the active engagement of students and teachers. In most circumstances, students become partners in the research and share in the analysis and interpretation of the results. Classroom Research is also enriched by discussion and collaboration with teaching colleagues. Because the purpose of Classroom Research is to deepen understandings about how people learn, it benefits from full discussion and participation by all who have something to learn and something to contribute.

Context-Specific

Classroom Research is conducted to shed light on the specific questions of an identified classroom. It involves the teaching of a particular discipline to a known group of students. Although the results may be generalizable to other populations and other disciplines, Classroom Research does not require technical research skills such as sampling and making statistical inferences.

Scholarly

Classroom Research is intellectually demanding and professionally responsible. It builds upon the knowledge base of research on teaching and learning. It requires the identification of a researchable question, the careful planning of an appropriate research design, and consideration of the implications of the research for practice.

Practical and Relevant

The questions selected for investigation in Classroom Research are practical questions that the teacher faces in teaching the class. The primary purpose of Classroom Research is not to advance knowledge in general or to publish findings but rather to deepen personal understandings. Although Classroom Research projects may be related to theory and topics in the literature and may be published or otherwise shared with colleagues, the measure of the quality of the project is its contribution to the knowledge and practice of the teacher.

Continual

Classroom Research is ongoing. Frequently, a Classroom Research project will raise new questions, leading to cascading investigations, with new projects emerging from past investigations. Classroom Research is also continual in the sense that changes suggested by the research are treated as experiments requiring continual evaluation and modification. Classroom Research is more a process than a product.

Roots of Classroom Research

Because Classroom Research is just one of many efforts to improve the quality of undergraduate education, it may be best understood in the context of its relationship to four additional major efforts to improve teaching and learning in higher education: (1) the application of educational research to practice, (2) faculty development, (3) the assessment of student learning, and (4) the Carnegie proposals to broaden the definition of scholarship. All of these approaches to the improvement of teaching and learning exist in some strength today, but they were established in different times in recent history. In fact, each decade since the 1960s has featured a distinctive effort to improve teaching and learning.

In the 1960s, a huge and expensive effort was launched to create large federally sponsored R&D (research and development) centers to conduct research and engage in the development and dissemination that would make the research useful to educational practitioners. The 1970s were a decade of growth nationwide for *faculty development*, which usually meant the creation of an office of special consultants on campus to work with faculty toward the improvement of teaching (Centra, 1976). The 1980s, especially in the years following the publication of *A Nation at Risk* (National Commission on Excellence in Education, 1983), generated intense and widespread involvement in the assessment of student learning outcomes. The 1990s opened with the publication of *Scholarship Reconsidered* (Boyer, 1990). Its recommendation for recognition of the scholarship of teaching has met with widespread interest, and it promises to make the 1990s a decade (or perhaps more) of emphasis on the recognition and reward of good teaching.

All of these approaches have made, and continue to make, important contributions to the improvement of teaching and learning. A major problem for each of the first three approaches, however, is that they cast people other than teachers as the "experts" in teaching and learning. This means that major efforts must go into making the knowledge from the various experts available and useful to those who can use the knowledge to improve practice, namely teachers and students. One can picture a chasm with teachers on one side and various campus resources for the improvement of teaching on the other. Bridge building across this chasm has been difficult.

In the 1960s, major efforts went into building bridges between research and its application by practitioners through R&D. Every large educational research center had on its staff specialists in development and dissemination whose task it was to convert the findings of research into practice. The envied solution was the extremely successful agriculture extension model, in which discoveries in the laboratories of the universities were taken to the farmers in the field by agriculture extension agents. Unfortunately, in education we have never come close to matching the success of agriculture in demonstrating the usefulness of research and delivering it for implementation to teachers (Cross, 1988b). "Practitioners seldom read the research literature," writes Elliott Eisner of Stanford. "Even when they do, this literature contains little that is not so qualified or so compromised by competing findings, rival hypotheses, or faulty design that the framework could scarcely be said to be supported in some reasonable way by research" (1984, p. 258). Research on learning makes some advances with each passing decade of investigation, but despite the best efforts of R&D, discipline-oriented faculty remain largely unaware of—and sometimes resistant to—applying pedagogical research to their teaching practices.

Faculty development offices, often directed and staffed by experts knowledgeable about teaching practices, continue their efforts to get faculty involved, to educate faculty to the latest findings of research, and to coordinate efforts for the improvement of instruction on campus, but many such offices exist precariously on the edge of budget cuts, and in the most prestigious universities, they are sometimes advised to "keep a low profile" and "not make waves," lest they alienate faculty. The credibility gap between the pedagogical knowledge of the faculty development specialists and the disciplinary knowledge of the faculty has proved hard to bridge. Yet faculty development specialists have access to a rich network of professional colleagues and resources that are valuable in joining the "wisdom of practice" (Shulman, 1987) to the knowledge of research.

There are, in all institutions of higher education, clusters of faculty intensely interested in teaching. Peer review of teaching and the analysis of case studies are examples of currently popular activities for faculty who are sincerely interested in making constructive contributions to the improvement of teaching, but these activities often proceed without any knowledge input from the specialists in educational research, faculty development, and assessment. Under these circumstances, the interested faculty retain credibility with their colleagues but paradoxically, for educators, reject academic knowledge about teaching in favor of employing experience as their base of knowledge about teaching and learning. Their assumption is that experience alone will improve teaching, if that experience is widely shared. Without a doubt, college teachers can learn a great deal about teaching through experience—their own as well as that of their colleagues. But it is our contention that these well-motivated faculty groups have much to gain from—and much to contribute to—building bridges to reach academic knowledge bases of teaching and learning.

Finally, the recent emphasis on assessment has made a major contribution by focusing on the quality of *learning* as the ultimate criterion of good teaching. Assessment, however, is frequently left to the "measurement experts," who duly collect reams of data and then file them in institutional offices to fulfill the requirements of governmental and accrediting agencies. It has been a major problem to get faculty involved in the assessment process and to complete the feedback loop that would enable teachers to use these data to improve student learning.

These lessons from the past have powerful implications for Classroom Research. Classroom Research *starts* with faculty and students. Its purpose is to assist teachers to assess the quality of learning in the classroom and to provide feedback (assessment) to both their students and themselves, to conduct investigations into the nature of learning and to apply the results to teaching and learning (research and development), and to join with faculty colleagues in recognizing and improving teaching and learning throughout the campus (faculty development).

The premise of Classroom Research is that if faculty are encouraged to become active participants in the search for knowledge about teaching and learning, they will become interested in building bridges across the chasm that separates the practice of teaching from knowledge about assessment, research, and faculty development.

The remainder of this chapter defines Classroom Research further by describing its relationship to these other ongoing efforts to improve teaching and learning, concluding with a discussion of the relationship of Classroom Research to the present high interest in the scholarship of teaching.

Further Defining Classroom Research

It is, perhaps, important to state explicitly that Classroom Research is proposed as a supplement to and not as a replacement for any of the established approaches to the improvement of teaching and learning. It is derived from and indebted to work in assessment, research on teaching and learning, and faculty development, but it is critic as well as friend of these major efforts. As the character of Classroom Research continues to emerge and take shape, it is defined as much by its departure from established approaches to the improvement of instruction as it is by its heritage in them.

We shall begin with an analysis of the relationship of Classroom Research to assessment, because our development of Classroom Research really began with Classroom Assessment. Although our early work used the term Classroom Research as a generic term that included Classroom Assessment (Cross, 1986), we started with Classroom Assessment for pragmatic as well as logical reasons. The assessment movement was in full swing in the late 1980s, and people were eager to involve faculty more directly in the assessment efforts. Thus, it seemed practical to capitalize on the high interest in assessment by defining a form of assessment that was especially relevant to teaching faculty and for which we could devise some operational methods and instructions (Angelo and Cross, 1993; Cross and Angelo, 1988). Logically, it made sense to start with Classroom Assessment because it was more concrete and easier to define and illustrate than Classroom Research and because the methodology for Classroom Assessment could benefit from larger efforts to develop sophisticated assessment methods.

Although today the terms *Classroom Assessment* and *Classroom Research* are frequently used interchangeably, Classroom Assessment is the more limited concept. It is frequently a part of Classroom Research. Classroom Assessment usually addresses the "what" questions about classroom behaviors—*What* did students learn from the class discussion?—whereas Classroom Research is concerned with the "why" questions—*Why* did students respond as they did? Classroom Assessment describes what *is* happening; Classroom Research tries to find out *why.*

Relationship to the Assessment Movement

Classroom Assessment is intimately related to institutional assessment. It has its heritage in the fundamental notion that learning can and should be monitored and that feedback from assessment should lead to more effective instruction, with the ultimate goal of improved learning. But much of the distinctive character of Classroom Assessment lies in its departure from mainstream assessment.

Most people think of assessment as a *large-scale* testing program, conducted *periodically* at the *institutional or state level,* usually by measurement *experts,* to determine what students *have learned in college.* Classroom Assessment questions almost every working word in that image. Its contrasting definition is this: Classroom Assessment consists of *small-scale* assessments conducted *continually* in college *classrooms* by discipline-based *teachers* to determine what students *are learning in that class.*

The advantage of thinking small in assessment is that if the ultimate purpose of assessment is to improve teaching and learning, then the results of successful assessment must eventually bear directly on the actions of teachers in their classrooms. This means that the feedback from assessment must reach classroom teachers and be perceived by them as relevant to the way they do their jobs. Because classroom assessment was born partly in support of and partly in protest against what assessment was becoming, it is helpful to look at the characteristics and promise of its parent assessment movement, which swept the nation with remarkable speed and breadth considering the number of people affected and the decision-making mechanisms involved.

In the beginning of the assessment movement, much attention was given to the demonstration of the accountability of educational institutions to the society that supported them. Assessment-for-accountability is illustrated in this remark of Missouri governor John Ashcroft in his role as chair of the Governors' Task Force on College Quality: "The public has the right to know what it is getting for its expenditure of tax resources; the public has a right to know and understand the quality of undergraduate education that young people receive from publicly funded colleges and universities" (National Governors' Association, 1986, p. 154).

As the assessment movement matured, attention turned more heavily to the uses of assessment to improve the quality of education. The assessment-for-improvement perspective was expressed by William Turnbull, late president of Educational Testing Service, when he wrote, "The overriding purpose of gathering [assessment] data is to provide a basis for improving instruction, rather than keeping score or allocating blame" (Turnbull, 1985, p. 25).

Although ultimately the purpose of both kinds of assessment is to improve education, the most important distinction between assessment-for-accountability and assessment-for-improvement lies in what is done with the results of the assessment. Those who, by virtue of their positions, are interested in accountability usually have indirect responsibilities for teaching and learning. They are usually not on the campus or in the classroom and must use assessment results in whatever ways they can to influence the behavior of those who are in a position to affect teaching and learning directly. The further removed one is from the scene of the action in teaching and learning, the more one is dependent on manipulating reward and punishment to bring about desired ends.

Thus, motivation for improved teaching in accountability models usually takes the form of extrinsic rewards: increased funding for institutions; larger budgets or more positions for departments demonstrating accountability; promotion, tenure, or a "teacher of the year" award for good teachers; and usually, lack of reward (rather than punishment) for poor teachers.

Conversely, in assessment-for-improvement models, the results of the assessment go directly to those who can, through their own efforts, make the improvements indicated. For example, departments may collect data to show how their graduates perform on tests for graduate and professional schools, and they may directly change the curriculum when indicated. Classroom teachers are directly involved in instruction; through their *own* actions, they can change the quality of teaching and learning in the classroom. Reward systems in this model are usually intrinsic: teacher satisfaction in seeing students learn, stimulation of intellectual curiosity about the learning process, and increased professional knowledge and self-esteem.

The importance of the *feedback loop,* of getting the results of the assessment to those who can do something about it, can be illustrated through an analogy to learning archery. Imagine a group of people learning archery in a darkened room, where both the target and the feedback on hitting it are invisible. The learners might be provided with the best and most sophisticated equipment that money can buy; have one-on-one coaching from an expert who demonstrates effectively how to hold the bow, get the right tension in the string, and place the arrow; and have access to study materials on the dynamics of flight and the arc of the trajectory. Despite all this input, it is pretty clear that they are not going to improve their performance until they get some feedback on whether they are hitting the target. Herein lies the enormous contribution of the assessment movement. Targets are identified and the results of hitting them fed back continually to the archers.

Those of us in education do not pay a lot of attention right now to giving students feedback on their progress as learners. Almost all students get grades that tell them how they have done relative to their classmates, but that sort of information is not useful feedback on their progress as learners, nor does it help them develop the skills they need for self-assessment as lifelong learners. The assessment-for-accountability models do not address these learning issues either. The situation now in many institutional assessment programs is akin to turning on the lights in the target practice room after the students have left and reporting on the total number of hits to whoever is paying for the archery lessons. Turning on the lights after practice—as is beginning to be done with some of the educational outcomes assessments—is probably better than being left permanently in the dark. When the lights go on, the institution, at least, gets feedback on how well students did. The problem is that there is no useful information about what caused good or poor performance because the lights were off during practice. We might carry this analogy further to point out that if research showed that even a dim light in the room improved scores dramatically, then the message would be clear: it would tell institutions that they should turn on the lights during practice so students and teachers, not just institutions, can see what they are doing.

Although some faculty members are currently involved in designing or approving institutional assessment programs, they are acting as representatives of the collective faculty, which is a different role from assessing their own effectiveness as teachers. It is assumed in most forms of institutional assessment that if college teachers as a group are made aware that students lack knowledge or skills in areas considered important, the collective faculty will then take steps to correct the deficiency—usually through changing the curriculum or increasing requirements. The changes made are frequently *additions* of courses or requirements, leaving the impression that education is additive, that is that more requirements equal more learning. Virtually ignored is the fact that much of what is taught is not learned.

If teachers could reduce the gap between teaching and learning, they could not only increase the productivity of the present workforce but could also begin to visualize learning as transformational rather than merely additive. Learning, correctly understood, consists of new learning transforming what already exists in the minds of learners, leading them to deeper understandings and appreciations. In this view, learning is more than the accumulation and storage of knowledge; it is dynamic and interactive, constantly changing and evolving. Classroom Assessment operates on the premise that learning is constantly in process and that assessments must be conducted frequently and the results made available immediately to both students and teachers so that any necessary changes can be made while there is time to benefit from them.

In summary, Classroom Assessment has its roots in the assessment movement. Its assessment parentage is clearly visible in its search for valid measures of students' learning and in its systematic monitoring of progress. To its credit, assessment has come a long way from a decade ago when accountability models launched the movement. The departure of Classroom Assessment from that assessment heritage is most apparent in the changed locale of the power to directly influence the quality of teaching and learning. Whereas in accountability models the power usually resides in the experts who design the assessment and in the legislators and administrators who reward the performance, Classroom Assessment empowers teachers to design assessments that are meaningful to them and that can be used to improve their own teaching. Once again, the rewards of Classroom Assessment are more intrinsic than extrinsic.

Relationship to Traditional Educational Research

In much the same way that Classroom Assessment both parallels and diverges from the direction of the assessment movement, so Classroom Research is both allied with and critical of traditional educational research. It shares with educational research the broad goal of improving education through the systematic study of teaching and learning. But it questions the heavy dependence on the current "scientific method" as the only or most valid approach to knowledge. We believe that the experience and insights of teachers, their knowledge of the subject matter they are trying to teach, their continuing association with students in the process of learning, and their opportunities to observe both the struggles and triumphs of learning are just as important as the "scientific objectivity" of external researchers seeking generalizable knowledge about learning.

Research in the social sciences is undergoing slow but obvious change, generally away from the rigidities of scientism. (*Scientism* is defined in *Webster's New World Dictionary,* Third College Edition, as "the principle that scientific methods can and should be applied in all fields of investigation.") Educational research has many faces, and at this time, the research community is vigorously debating future directions for educational research and evaluation and their potential for improving education (Eisner, 1984; Guba, 1979; Keller, 1985; Lincoln, 1989; Mishler, 1979; Reichardt and Rallis, 1994). The meaning of Classroom Research can be further defined by tracing briefly the issues under discussion in traditional research and the position of Classroom Research with respect to each. Let us look first at the criticisms of educational research within the social science research community.

The "scientific method" is under attack primarily on the grounds that it has become a "virtual orthodoxy—*the* way of getting at the truth" (Guba, 1979, p. 268). Even though the assumptions of scientism have worked remarkably well in the natural and physical sciences, their application to inquiry in the social sciences remains problematic. The points of contention fall into two major categories: (1) The nature of the *questions* to be investigated and (2) the research *methods* to be used. Both these seemingly concrete issues, however, are embedded in larger philosophical or epistemological debates over positivism versus any number of emerging isms, including feminism, constructivism, and functionalism. Because today's literature consists largely of attacks on positivism, we shall attempt to present briefly the essence of the arguments for change launched by the critics of traditional research.

Yvonna Lincoln (1989), one of the outspoken critics of traditional research, has analyzed some of the criticisms of logical positivism as a basis for research in the social sciences, categorizing the criticisms into issues of "debate." Because it is important for Classroom Researchers to understand these criticisms in order to gain maximum benefits from their research, we shall review briefly those aspects of Lincoln's critique that have specific implications for Classroom Research.

- *The Exception Debate.* This is the term Lincoln uses to describe a cluster of criticisms directed at specific axioms of scientific inquiry. Positivism in science, for example, assumes that "truth" is "out there" and will be discovered as scientific investigation converges on that single reality. But generalizations about "truth" in human behavior are so problematic that a widely respected research scholar has suggested that in this field, it would be preferable to abandon the search for general truths in favor of "working hypotheses," to be tested in each new context (Cronbach, 1975).

Classroom Research is based on the premise that generalizations across classrooms are, at best, tentative hypotheses, to be tested within the specific context of a given classroom. Experienced teachers know that even when the same teacher teaches the same subject in the same classroom at the same hour of the day, the learning environment, or context, can differ greatly from one semester to the next. Classroom Researchers will ultimately build a base of knowledge about what works for them in their discipline with their students. A Classroom Research project is not a one-shot effort that is completed, published, and assumed to contribute one more brick to building the wall of truth. Rather, Classroom Research projects can be described as continual and cascading, the conclusion from one project suggesting the beginning of another.

- *The Exclusion Debate.* The conventional paradigm for science research is considered by many to represent a majority, male, and elitist view. Indeed, many of the descriptive terms most often applied to science and "scientific" research are also considered descriptive of males—objective, analytical, cool, and impersonal— as opposed to characteristics more often considered descriptive of females—sensitive, warm, caring, and personal. It is thus not surprising that the most vigorous criticisms with respect to the exclusion debate have come from feminist scholars—although people of color and other excluded populations have joined in the criticism that science is mobilized to defend the status quo by excluding researchers without the accepted training.

Until a few years ago, research on college students was conducted largely by middle-class white male researchers studying middle-class white male students, and according to critics, resulted in conclusions that are sexist, biased, misleading, and unreliable (Lincoln, 1989; Namenwirth, 1986; Stage, 1990). Women researchers, such as Gilligan (1982) and Belenky, Clinchy, Goldberger, and Tarule (1986) have demonstrated through their own research, that the male norm is not necessarily the human norm. Similarly, ethnic researchers and gerontologists have shown wide cultural departures from the norms of young white middle-class males. Because the student population today is diverse in almost every respect, and students who are not young, white, male, or middle-class are not only frequently found in college classrooms but often make up the majority in those classrooms—it is clear that Classroom Research cannot accept a science that excludes any aspect of student diversity.

Even more important to the concept of Classroom Research, however, is the axiom that research on teaching and learning in the classroom cannot exclude those who are most involved and most affected, namely teachers and students. Ironically, traditional educational researchers often reject teachers and students as investigators (on the grounds that they lack technical research skills and "objectivity") while these same researchers are struggling to gain teachers' and students' cooperation as subjects for research. Moreover, the subordination implied in the expert-subject relationship is not completely alleviated by placing teachers and students on "advisory" committees to inform the experts about investigations that would improve practice. Thus, Classroom Researchers support the argument that exclusion exists. Indeed, a science predicated on bringing into the classroom an outside expert to study what teachers and students know best is both exclusionary and inadequate. We do not intend to imply that educational research should not be done in and on classrooms. We do believe, however, that reliance on "scientific" research as the "best" or "most legitimate" source of knowledge about teaching and learning has failed to demonstrate its usefulness.

The major tenet of Classroom Research is that college teachers are capable of doing their own research on the questions that interest them. Classroom Research capitalizes on the talents and competencies that teachers bring to the systematic study of teaching and learning: knowledge of the subject matter, experience in teaching it to others, and an interest in gaining a greater understanding

of how students in their classrooms learn what teachers are trying
to teach.

• *The Whole Paradigm Debate.* One of the most basic axioms
of traditional research is that science can get at an understanding
of the whole through studying the parts individually. The common
practice of "controlling" some variables while studying others or,
in statistical studies, of "holding constant" some variables while
abstracting others out for intense study is coming under increasing
criticism in a variety of disciplines. The penchant for "context
stripping," which is a "key feature of our standard methods of
experimental design, measurement, and statistical analysis," says
Mishler (1979, p. 2), "treats context as though it were the enemy of
understanding rather than the resource for understanding."

Classroom Research welcomes the context of the classroom in
all its complexity as a resource for understanding. Certain types of
learning can be isolated for study in the laboratory, but teaching
never can be. Teaching is necessarily interactive; it requires a
teacher, a learner, and a context.

Because interaction is *the* important characteristic in the learning environment of the classroom, a science that in the interest of
rigor and neatness, attempts to separate this variable from its environment, is at best inadequate and most likely misleading. Classroom Research is interested in the interaction between teachers and
learners in the context of their natural environment.

• *The Impoverished Debate.* A major criticism of traditional
research based in a logical positivist framework is that its emphasis
on quantitative methods is impoverished. The inclusion of qualitative methods, it is argued, would add richness, texture, and greater
depth of understanding to investigations. Because it is hard to
refute the reasonableness of this argument, we would like to think
that the impoverishment debate is now moot. However, as the continuing debates over methods suggest (and is shown later in this
chapter), the issue remains alive—at least among career
researchers, who tend to develop high levels of expertise in either
quantitative or qualitative methods, and who therefore have a
vested interest in their use.

The indications that the debate between the "quants" and the
"quals" (Rossi, 1994) is still alive and vigorous are revealed in
Reichardt and Rallis's *The Qualitative-Quantitative Debate: New Perspectives* (1994). Their introduction comments that "the origins" of
their book "can be found in the long-standing antagonism between
qualitative and quantitative researchers in evaluation. This antagonism was part of the reason that the field of evaluation gave birth
in the 1970s to two separate professional organizations: the Evalua-

tion Network (ENet) and the Evaluation Research Society (ERS). When ENet and ERS decided to merge to form the American Evaluation Association (AEA) in the mid-1980s, the antagonism did not disappear, it was merely suppressed" (p. 1).

These suppressed hostilities surfaced in three successive conventions of the American Evaluation Association in the early 1990s (Fetterman, 1992; Lincoln, 1991; Sechrest, 1992), adding fuel to the charge that academic social scientists have devoted too much attention to methods and not enough to the formulation of meaningful questions for investigation. But that is not a new charge. "Historically," writes House, "methodology has been greatly overemphasized at the expense of content" (1994, p. 14). This was especially true in the heyday of behaviorist psychology, leading Chomsky to call behaviorism "a methodology without a subject matter" (1977, p. 46).

The problem of maintaining a constructive balance between methods and questions for study is captured by Donald Schön in his description of the dilemma of "rigor versus relevance."

> In the varied topography of professional practice, there is a high, hard ground where practitioners can make effective use of research-based theory and technique, and there is a swampy lowland where situations are confusing "messes" incapable of technical solution. The difficulty is that the problems of the high ground, however great their technical interest, are often relatively unimportant to clients or to the larger society, while in the swamp are the problems of greatest human concern. Shall the practitioner stay on the high, hard ground where he can practice rigorously, as he understands rigor, but where he is constrained to deal with problems of relatively little social importance? Or shall he descend to the swamp where he can engage the most important and challenging problems if he is willing to forsake technical rigor?
>
> There are those who choose the swampy lowlands. They deliberately involve themselves in messy but crucially important problems and, when asked to describe their methods of inquiry, they speak of experience, trial and error, intuition, and muddling through [1983, p. 42].

Classroom Research is not completely comfortable with either the "high, hard ground" of rigorous methods or the "swampy lowlands" of practical relevance. Classroom Researchers are most interested in building a bridge across the swamp, not necessarily to the high ground of rigorous methodology but at least to more solid ground, where teaching is subject to systematic investigation. Forced to choose, however, Classroom Research would opt for relevance over rigor, for two reasons.

First, if the question for study is not highly relevant to the real-life needs of the Classroom Researcher, then there is no point at all in doing the study. The purpose of Classroom Research is more to enhance the understanding of the researcher than to report findings to the research community.

Second, Classroom Researchers are, by definition, not methodologists with technical research competence in the social sciences. Their great strength as researchers lies in their understanding of the classroom context, their closeness to the learning problems, their experience in the practical realities of teaching, and their knowledge of the subject matter being taught. More often than not, Classroom Researchers will opt for careful observation, interviews with students, and understanding in the swamps of the natural environment over working on the high hard ground of experimental and statistical methods.

However much we might wish for a resolution to the "paradigm wars" (Lincoln, 1989), the conflict has a long history and, to many, a competitive present. Rossi, a self-identified quant, says, "In my home base discipline, sociology, the struggle between the quants and the quals is alive and well today, but it has been alive and well since sociology first turned away from being an armchair discipline and started to undertake empirical investigations" (1994, p. 24). Rossi argues that the quals and the quants have usefully different functions in today's evaluation programs. Large-scale well-funded projects using quantitative methods are generally feasible only for large research firms (dominated today by economists, significantly) and are most useful to policy makers, whereas small local projects dominated by people with "extensive practical and theoretical knowledge, further illuminated by a rich and intimate knowledge of the program in question and its ecology" (p. 32) are more appropriate for stakeholders. Although it is conceivable that Classroom Research might have some implications for policy makers somewhere in the future, it is specifically designed for stakeholders. Faculty and students are stakeholders in the academic enterprise.

One practical objection to the standard statistical methods employed by the quants is that they are most useful with large samples—fine for lecture classes numbering in the hundreds but of dubious value in the typical classroom of twenty to forty students. More serious, however, is that statistical analysis is based in probability theory. The question in statistical analysis is, What is the *probability* that the findings differ from chance? Although that is a useful question for policy makers, it is not an appropriate question for classroom teachers who are interested not only in how the majority confirm a hypothesis but also in why individual learners may depart from it. Indeed, understanding the exceptions in the classroom may tell teachers far more about the learning process than understanding the majority; teachers must be just as concerned with the 30 percent who do not change "significantly" as with the 70 percent who do. Classroom Researchers are not looking for a law of human behavior, an if-then formula to tell them that *if* they teach in a certain way, *then* a certain kind of learning will occur—or even that such learning will occur predictably in 62 percent of the students. Classroom Researchers are primarily interested in gaining the insights and understandings that will strengthen their base of professional knowledge about teaching. They want to know *what* works, of course, but they are even more interested in knowing *why* it works. They want to understand learning as a process, and they consider insights as important as findings.

It is extremely important that Classroom Researchers use the methods that will address their questions. They need make no apology for their lack of advanced study in methodology—either quantitative or qualitative. The tide is turning now to greater concern about the relevance of the research, and it would be hard to find researchers who are more relevant to the issues of teaching and learning than teachers and students. The strengths they bring to classroom investigations are different from, but at least as important as, academic methodological sophistication.

Classroom Research makes a point of encouraging a wide variety of research measures—quantitative, qualitative, or performance—whatever measure serves up information about what the teacher wants to know. Indeed, Classroom Researchers are encouraged to place no arbitrary restrictions on data collection and even to invent their own methods. Classroom Assessment Techniques (CATs), for example, are common sources of data for Classroom Researchers, and they come in a wide variety of forms: quantitative, qualitative, and performance measures and what might be called modest pedagogical experiments. Because the results of Classroom Research are frequently tentative and suggestive of further experimentation and development, data may consist of almost any sort of information that adds to a teacher's understanding of teaching and learning.

Again, although we have been critical of the current heavy emphasis on traditional research to ferret out the complexities of teaching and learning, our argument is not for the abolition or even diminution of traditional educational research. Rather, it is for the legitimate addition of Classroom Research. In the present academic climate, because Classroom Researchers are not well grounded in current methods of research, their efforts are still not considered quite legitimate. Classroom Research faces the same uphill battle that qualitative researchers faced ten years ago—and in many places still face.

Our argument is that Classroom Researchers bring to the study of teaching and learning in the classroom some particularly valuable talents and opportunities that educational researchers do not have—just as traditional researchers bring to their investigations background, experience, and training that classroom teachers do not have. We need both, and each should enrich the other. The more Classroom Researchers learn about the practical questions that interest them, the more appreciative and interested they will be in the knowledge of educational researchers. Likewise, the more educational researchers can learn about Classroom Research, the more specifics from that research will enrich their own investigations.

Relationship to Faculty Development

Classroom Research is an important form of faculty development. Its purpose, consistent with the broad purposes of faculty development, is to engage faculty in a program of continual learning about how to improve their own teaching. The assumption behind Classroom Research is that as teachers become involved in systematically inquiring into the impact of their teaching on students' learning, they will raise questions about their own teaching and seek further knowledge about it. Thus, Classroom Research serves as a motivator for faculty to take advantage of faculty development programs and to contribute to them.

As is the case with traditional assessment and research, Classroom Research is consistent with but different from traditional emphases in faculty development. Differences are most likely to take place over the actual program of activities and, most importantly, in the focus of attention. The direct goal of faculty development is to improve the performance of *teachers* by inculcating teaching skills and techniques, increasing the self-confidence and performance of teachers, and creating a supportive institutional climate that recognizes good teaching and is conducive to its growth. Classroom Research is also interested in effective teaching, but the attention of Classroom Research is on *students* rather than on teachers. The premise is that it makes no difference how perfectly a teacher is teaching if students are not responding in their learning.

Thus, the two stances are quite different. Faculty development starts with the fundamental assumption that through orientation, workshops, and the like, faculty can learn how to lecture, lead discussions, construct tests, assign grades, and use such varied techniques of teaching as collaborative learning, case studies, role-playing, and most recently, techniques employing technology and computers. (See the chapter headings in such popular books as McKeachie's ninth revision of *Teaching Tips*, 1994, and Davis's new

Tools for Teaching, 1993, for example). There is no denying that these are important teaching functions or that most faculty have had little or no exposure to them in graduate school. Thus, traditional faculty development programs are, without doubt, making an important contribution to the improvement of teaching. How much they contribute to the improvement of learning is an open question, but one that can be addressed by educational researchers as well as Classroom Researchers.

There are two major arguments for including Classroom Research in faculty development. One addresses the psychological advantage of focusing on student rather than faculty performance. A major hurdle for any faculty development program to overcome is the faculty perception that there is something wrong with the teaching of those who participate in faculty development—or worse yet in some cases, that an interest in improving teaching may mean that the faculty member is on the slow track in research. It is far easier in most faculty cultures to admit an interest in scholarly inquiry about student learning than it is to profess an interest in or a need for improving one's own teaching.

The second reason for suggesting that faculty development programs might be enhanced by the addition of Classroom Research is based in motivational and learning theory. Teachers, like students, need to be active learners in order to remain motivated. Just as a one-shot lecture to students may have little impact on their behavior, so a one-shot program on how to lead a discussion may have little impact on teaching practices. A profession, by definition, requires lifelong learning. If teachers are to remain motivated to learn how to teach, they need to be actively involved in formulating questions about how to teach and seeking the answers; they need continual feedback on how well they are doing; they need the support and encouragement of their colleagues. In short, learning for teachers has the same requirements that it has for students. Teachers are—or should be—lifelong students of the teaching-learning connection.

It is instructive to look at the concept of teaching as lifelong learning through the lens of the well-known seven principles for good practice in undergraduate education (Chickering and Gamson, 1991). The seven principles were devised by a task force of scholars and researchers brought together in July 1986 by Zelda Gamson and Arthur Chickering to identify the key principles of learning derived from decades of research on undergraduate learning. Those key principles have been widely distributed (150,000 copies ordered in the first eighteen months!) and are perhaps the most succinct, comprehensive, and respected research-based conclusions about learning to be widely distributed to discipline-oriented college teachers. Although the principles were derived from research on undergraduate learning, they are far broader than that, incorporating information about cognition and motivation that is useful with any age group. With only occasional paraphrasing, the seven principles can be applied to teachers as lifelong learners and can serve as a rationale for Classroom Research as a productive learning experience for both teachers and students.

1. Good Practice Encourages Student-Faculty Contact. A substantial body of research has concluded that students showing the greatest gains in intellectual commitment, personal development, and motivation report high contact with faculty in and out of class (Sorcinelli, 1991). The same appears to be true for faculty in their contacts with students. Wilson and his colleagues (Wilson and others, 1975), in a four-year research project involving eight institutions, found that teachers nominated by students and colleagues as especially effective teachers reported more interaction with students than those less frequently nominated.

Students, over some twelve years of schooling, have developed some well-honed practices for hiding their confusion or lack of knowledge from teachers. Teachers who rely on body language or eye contact are often greatly surprised when they ask students for their reactions. The more a teacher can gain understanding of and show interest in students' learning, the more both teacher and students are likely to gain from contact.

Significantly, one of Classroom Assessment's best-known and most frequently used CATs, the Minute Paper, came from a study of effective teachers on the Berkeley campus of the University of California (Wilson, 1986). When researchers interviewed teachers to find out what teachers *did* that resulted in an exceptional number of student nominations for effective teaching, one physics teacher described the way he asked students to take a few minutes at the end of the class session to write anonymously what they had learned from that day's lesson. (See Angelo and Cross, 1993 pp. 148–153 for a more complete description of the Minute Paper.) Students had rated him especially high on "knowing how well students are understanding," and he suspected that at least part of the reason was his use of the Minute Paper. It is reasonable to suspect that he probably *did* know better than most teachers how well students were understanding but also that students were aware of his concern about their learning.

Interpersonal rapport shows up on virtually every list of the characteristics of effective teachers (Cross, 1988a; Feldman, 1994), and Lowman (1984) has reduced the characteristics of good teaching to two essential dimensions—"intellectual excitement" and "interpersonal rapport," the latter of which includes sensitivity to how students feel about the material and its presentation. He claims that outstanding teachers excel in one of these two dimensions and are at least competent in the other.

Aside from the evidence that appears with some consistency in research on effective teaching, it does not take much stretch of the imagination to conclude that student-faculty contact increases the understanding about learning and its progress on the part of both teachers and students. Thus, the first of the seven principles of good practice applies to the learning of teachers as well as students. One way for a teacher to learn how to teach effectively—and to continue to do so throughout the years of teaching and changing student populations—is to learn to know students, and especially to monitor their progress in learning.

2. Good Practice Encourages Cooperation Among Students—and Colleagues. There is a great deal of emphasis today on the importance of encouraging faculty to work with faculty on the improvement of instruction. Hutchings notes that "there's a growing recognition that what's really needed to improve teaching is a campus culture in which good practice can thrive, one where faculty talk together about teaching, inquire into its effects, and take collective responsibility for its quality" (1993, p. v). For college faculty, much of the credibility of teaching improvement programs lies in faculty members' faith in the knowledge and experience of their peers. Faculty development offices today are encouraging faculty initiative, "ownership," and responsibility for cooperative endeavors. Maryellen Weimer advises that college faculty members must be put in charge of their own improvement because "better teaching cannot be done by one party to another. . . . It is the teacher alone who changes the teaching" (1990, p. 25).

Empirical research on student-centered methods supports the contention that working together on learning (and learning how to teach) has clear advantages. In their extensive review of research on instructional methods, McKeachie, Pintrich, Lin, and Smith concluded that, "the best answer to the question, 'What is the most effective method of teaching?,' is that it depends on the goal, the student, the content, and the teacher. But the next best answer is, 'Students teaching other students'" (1986, p. 63). And so it would seem with faculty. Increasingly, there is good information about human learning being supplied by researchers and scholars in education and psychology, but the research suggests that when it comes to motivation, concept development, and application, peer learning has most of the advantages (McKeachie, Pintrich, Lin, and Smith, 1986, p. 68).

One of the most important—and surprising—conclusions of our experiences in working with faculty members on Classroom Assessment and Classroom Research is that these activities are highly social. Initially, we had thought that one of the advantages of Classroom Research was that it could be done independently, without participating in endless committee meetings or seeking anyone's blessing or approval. And it can be. As it turns out, however, once teachers begin to observe and study the effectiveness of their own teaching, they have a strong desire to share their findings and questions with others (Angelo and Cross, 1993). Thus, the colleges where Classroom Research has made the strongest inroads as part of the faculty culture are places where faculty regularly come together to share experiences and learn from one another.

3. Good Practice Encourages Active Learning. Perhaps no principle of learning has received more attention in recent years than this one. The Study Group on the Conditions of Excellence in American Higher Education selected active involvement in learning as one of their three "critical conditions for excellence" in the quality of undergraduate education. The study group contends that "there is now a good deal of research evidence to suggest that the more time and effort students invest in the learning process and the more intensely they engage in their own education, the greater will be their growth and achievement, their satisfaction with their educational experiences, and their persistence in college, and the more likely they are to continue their learning" (1984, p. 17).

Clearly, if teachers are to experience satisfaction and achievement in their teaching, they must be actively engaged in learning all they can about the impact of their teaching on students' learning. Classroom Research requires active involvement in learning about teaching. Teachers must not only raise their own questions about their teaching but then they must devise appropriate ways of investigating those questions. Researchers on cognition today recognize this model of self-initiated inquiry as one of the most effective for learning.

4. Good Practice Gives Prompt Feedback. The importance of prompt feedback ranks right up there with active involvement as a basic and fundamental requirement for learning. Like active involvement, it has been given major attention in recent years and is the very foundation of the assessment movement in education. The authors of the influential reform report *Involvement in Learning* (Study Group on the Conditions of Excellence in American Higher Education, 1984) write that "the use of assessment information to redirect effort is an essential ingredient in effective learning and serves as a powerful lever for involvement. This is true whether the learner is a student, a faculty member monitoring the progress of students, or an administrator seeking to identify the educational strengths and weaknesses of a college and its academic programs" (p. 21).

Providing prompt and regular feedback is certainly an important if not the most important function of Classroom Assessment. Teachers need feedback on their teaching as much as students need feedback on their learning. Good teachers spend a lot of time grading papers, making comments, redirecting efforts, and in general providing feedback on student progress. But teachers themselves, often working behind closed doors, rarely get any feedback on their teaching other than student ratings of teaching, which usually appear only after the semester has ended, when both students and teachers have forgotten the specifics and teachers have little motivation to incorporate suggestions for improvement into their lesson plans.

Research on the usefulness of student ratings to improve teaching has so far been disappointing—although in a study at the nine campuses of the University of California, 78 percent of the faculty reported making changes in their teaching based on student evaluations (Outcalt, 1980). Centra, in reviewing the research on actual change as a result of student evaluations, terms the impact "modest" (1993, p. 10). But most student ratings of instruction are designed and used more for summative evaluation (making judgments) than for formative evaluation (making improvements). Faculty have little control over these rating instruments, and Centra (1993) and Weimer (1990) are in staunch agreement that unless the faculty member values the feedback and it has high credibility for him or her, it will most likely have little effect.

Classroom Research preserves the feedback so important to learning, but it leaves the design and control of the method of getting that feedback in the hands of faculty, thereby preserving value and credibility. Critics see this as a problem for Classroom Research, saying that poor teachers can fool themselves by asking only for feedback that they believe will be positive. Our experience, however, suggests that teachers are somewhat more likely to ask for feedback on their weaknesses than on their strengths. As Centra reminds us, "Whatever the source, the evaluation must be a balance between challenge and support or it will be perceived as a threat and provoke the same anxious and self-defeating reaction" (1993, p. 10). And even if a defensive teacher designs Classroom Assessment and Classroom Research projects that give an overly positive view of his or her teaching, that may not be all bad for teachers with few bright spots in their teaching day. With a boost to the teachers' self-confidence, they may be encouraged to investigate other aspects of their teaching. Nevertheless, as suggested in principle 2, colleagues can be extremely helpful in preventing isolation and helping one another develop a realistic and constructive approach to getting and using feedback.

The major function of Classroom Assessment and Classroom Research is to give feedback about students' learning. The purpose of Classroom Assessment, in particular, is to monitor student learning throughout the semester and to provide information to both teacher and students while there is still time to take corrective action.

5. Good Practice Emphasizes Time on Task. Although much of the writing on this principle is laden with the educational jargon of "time on task" and "academic learning time" (ALT) (Berliner, 1984), it should come as no surprise that research concludes that the more time students spend actively engaged in the learning task, the more they learn. Students recognize this; there are "consistently significant correlations between the effective use of class time and overall ratings of course, instructor, and amount learned" (Sorcinelli, 1991, p. 20). We do not know of any research that has attempted to relate time spent on teaching with amount or quality of student learning. But it takes no great leap of faith to conclude that time spent productively on the task of teaching results in better use of class time.

Research by Steadman (1994) found that one of the major problems for teachers using Classroom Assessment was the amount of time required. This sets up a conflict for teachers. Is it better to spend time on learning content or to assess how effectively learning time is spent? To the extent that time is taken from learning content to collect information from students on their learning progress, one could argue that doing Classroom Assessment and Classroom Research is not consistent with the good practice of emphasizing time on task. However, that argument assumes that class time is maximally effective and that if the teacher and students were not taking time to monitor learning students would be using that time to actively engage in the task of learning itself. Research shows, however, that teachers are not very good judges of their own effectiveness, and they are quite likely to overestimate how much students learn. In one study, teachers thought students would know 75 percent of the items on a final exam, when in fact they knew only 58 percent (Fox and LeCount, 1991). Thus, the counterargument is that time spent in Classroom Assessment checks the assumption of maximal effectiveness of the teaching and the learning. Research on cognition shows that monitoring learning makes an important contribution to learning; therefore,

Classroom Assessment also contributes to the lifelong learning skills of students in monitoring their own learning.

6. Good Practice Communicates High Expectations. Research documents the wisdom that teachers get from students about what they expect. Teachers who expect high performance will usually get it and, in the process, win the respect of their students. "The literature consistently shows, contrary to faculty belief, that students give higher ratings to difficult courses in which they have to work hard" (Sorcinelli, 1991, p. 21). Research on cognition and motivation, however, suggests that there is an optimal level of expectation; if expectations are set too low, students will do less than they are capable of; if expectations are too high, students will engage in any number of counterproductive ego-protective devices (Corno and Mandinach, 1983; Covington and Berry, 1976).

Classroom Research and Classroom Assessment communicate high expectations in the sense that they assume that both teachers and students take the business of education seriously and are mature enough to want performance feedback with implications for improvement. The trend today in teacher evaluation is to expect teachers to collect information about their teaching, preferably along with reflections about their teaching (Edgerton, Hutchings, and Quinlan, 1991). We have questioned the use of Classroom Assessment and Classroom Research data in portfolios that are to be used for making decisions about promotion and tenure, on the grounds that Classroom Research might be distorted, in both design and interpretation, to show only favorable results. However, the fact that a teacher is designing and using Classroom Assessment and Classroom Research for his or her own improvement might be quite relevant to high self-expectations and self-improvement. Thus, a teaching portfolio might well include information about how a teacher was engaging in the lifelong development of his or her teaching effectiveness.

7. Good Practice Respects Diverse Talents and Ways of Learning—and Teaching. Just as students have different talents and learning styles, so teachers have diverse talents and styles of teaching. Although research on learning has been rather negative about lecturing as a style of teaching, this does not mean that a brilliant and inspiring lecturer cannot engage the minds of students in active learning or that the talented lecturer should revert to discussion groups. Just as a teacher should respect diverse talents and ways of learning, so institutions should respect and reward diverse talents and ways of teaching.

The contribution of Classroom Assessment and Classroom

Research to respecting diverse teaching talents is that the assessment and research methods are highly diverse and flexible. Teachers across a wide array of disciplines may select from a large number of designs already available (for example, the fifty Classroom Assessment Techniques in Angelo and Cross, 1993) or may invent personal assessments and research studies to provide the kind of information most useful to their own style and talents. The rationale for Classroom Research is that it *must* be personally designed by the teacher in order to address the questions relevant to that teacher.

Relationship to the Scholarship of Teaching

As mentioned at the beginning of this chapter, The Carnegie Foundation for the Advancement of Teaching has launched what appears to be a very promising nationwide movement to combat the overemphasis on disciplinary research as the singular form of scholarship in academe. Ernest Boyer (1990) calls for the recognition of four separate but overlapping functions of scholarship—the scholarship of discovery, the scholarship of integration, the scholarship of application, and the scholarship of teaching.

The Carnegie proposals are widely interpreted to mean that teaching should be recognized as one of the four forms of scholarship. We heartily endorse the Carnegie proposals to recognize more varied forms of scholarship, but we also believe that teaching itself, if it is to be real profession, should involve *all four* forms of scholarship.

"The scholarship of *discovery,* at its best," says the Carnegie report, "contributes not only to the stock of human knowledge but also to the intellectual climate of a college or university. . . . The advancement of knowledge can generate an almost palpable excitement in the life of an educational institution" (p. 17). There should also be a palpable excitement in the life of a teaching institution. Should not all teachers and students be engaged daily in the excitement of discovery about how people learn? We are not talking here about casual discovery or the occasional but welcome "aha" experience, Classroom Research involves systematic and scholarly inquiry into the nature of learning—specifically into the nature of learning English, or math, or psychology, or any other subject in which faculty have become lifelong learners. Dedicated college teachers have much to gain—and much to contribute—to the advancement of teaching as a profession through the scholarship of discovery in teaching and learning. Teachers employ the scholarship of discovery when they use Classroom Research to inquire about the learning taking place in their own classrooms and their own disciplines.

The scholarship of *integration,* according to the Carnegie definitions, involves making connections across disciplines and making interpretations that fit research into larger intellectual patterns. The very purpose of a liberal education, say Pascarella and Terenzini, is "to foster the integration and synthesis of knowledge rather than learning discrete bits of information" (1991, p. 136). Richard Light, director of the Harvard Assessment Seminars, writes in his first report that early on in the seminars, he asked faculty members what single change would most improve their current teaching. "Two ideas swamped all others," says Light. "One is the importance of enhancing students' awareness of 'the big picture,' the 'big point of it all,' and not just the details of a particular topic. The second is the importance of helpful and regular feedback from students so a professor can make mid-course corrections" (1990, p. 35). Classroom Research can respond to both of these expressed needs of college teachers. Regular feedback from students to teachers is, of course, the linchpin of Classroom Assessment, and Classroom Research, at its best, is integrative scholarship in the sense that it studies learning as it occurs in students—assessing not individual bits and pieces of the lesson but how students integrate them into a meaningful whole.

The scholarship of *application,* according to the Carnegie report, addresses the question, "How can knowledge be responsibly applied to consequential problems?" Law, business, medicine, engineering, and all the professional and preprofessional programs are committed to the application of knowledge. But teaching, for the most part, has not applied what is known about teaching and learning to improve the profession. Most teachers teach as they were taught. If teaching is to become a true profession, then teachers must *apply* what is known about learning to the teaching-learning process. Classroom Research concerns the application of knowledge from each teacher's own research as well as that of others.

Finally, there is the scholarship of *teaching.* Teaching, says the Carnegie report, is "a dynamic endeavor involving all the analogies, metaphors, and images that build bridges between a teacher's understanding and the students' learning. Pedagogical procedures must be carefully planned, continually examined, and relate directly to the subject taught. . . . Great teachers create a common ground of intellectual commitment. They stimulate active, not passive, learning and encourage students to be critical creative thinkers with the capacity to go on learning after their college days are over. . . . Teaching, at its best, means not only transmitting knowledge, but *transforming* and *extending* it as well" (pp. 23–24).

It is encouraging that the Carnegie report has been so well received. Many colleges and universities are beginning to build into their promotion and tenure procedures a broader definition of scholarship. That is both desirable and necessary, but there are broader and deeper implications of the report that have not been addressed.

The Carnegie recommendations are important not only as a *correction* for the existing problem of too much emphasis on research and not enough on teaching but also as an *opportunity* for institutions to take leadership in the advancement of teaching as a profession by encouraging faculties to involve themselves in the *multiple* scholarships of teaching.

Conclusion

This introduction has examined the place of Classroom Research in the context of modern approaches to the improvement of teaching and learning. Classroom Research has its roots in all four of today's institutional efforts to improve teaching and learning. It borrows from all, but it has its own distinctive character. It is none of them and all of them.

CHAPTER 2

"The Leslies"

Learning Issues: Prerequisite Knowledge;
Metacognition and Learning Strategies;
Self-Confidence and Motivation

CASE STUDY

Date: Fri, 8 Mar 94 01:07:58 EST
From: jdoe@econ.edu
To: jeanne@chem.edu
Subject: "It's Greek to Me"
Hi, Jeanne:

Another e-mail from the tundra. (Though I suppose Milwaukee ain't exactly balmy today either.) It's been another quiet week in Lake Wobegon. I'm working on that Smith paper on ethics. I really believe that if my colleagues would reexamine the roots of their Classical Liberal logic they would see, as Smith did, the fundamental foundational role that ethics plays in the logic of a Classical Liberal model, but . . .

So how's the world of better living through chemistry? Saved any lives lately with brilliant discoveries of new chemical stuff? I guess that's not exactly what a laser bombardment of molecules is supposed to be about, huh? What is it supposed to be about, anyway?

What a classic question: "What is it supposed to be about?" That's a great way to describe the issue that has haunted me this week. I had a kid in my office, a young woman, who isn't getting it. We just finished the midterm, and she got a solid D. She claims that she's really working hard—and I believe her. As we talked, she

Note: Case study by Jerry Evensky, Syracuse University

showed me the reams of notes she has and the pages of writing she's done as she's looked up all the objectives (I give them 23 pages of detailed objectives) in the text. It's really very impressive, but it obviously isn't working. What is more, she says she feels like she's sitting in a class where the teacher is speaking Greek (actually she said German, but the ol' "It's Greek to me" phrase seems so fitting). Because she doesn't speak the language, and she doesn't know what it's supposed to be about, she hasn't got a clue as to what is really going on.

What a frustrating conversation. She's obviously a very intelligent young woman, 'cause she's doing well (or so she says, and I believe her—she's really very articulate) in all her other classes (she says she has a 3.2 GPA). Anyway, she wants to drop my class. I HATE THIS. This is the very student I want to reach: not a major, but intelligent and willing to work.

Part of the problem is obvious and we talked about it. I tried to demonstrate to her that her approach to the objectives is not productive. She's playing stenographer with the objectives—or maybe search and destroy is a better image. She reads the objective, then she finds the "answer" in the book and copies it down. In the eye and out the pen without a stop at the cerebrum. I suggested that if she used the objectives to frame the reading—review them first to prepare your mind, read, then try to work toward them without the book to identify what you've really mastered—then her study time would be much more productive. That all made sense to her (why she didn't hear this same speech the first day of class escapes me), but still she said she wanted to drop.

I asked her why she wouldn't give it another try with the new strategy. She said that she was afraid that if she didn't succeed she would end up getting a D or, God forbid, an F, and that she just couldn't afford to take the chance. And she didn't have faith in her ability to catch on 'cause she still didn't see how to solve the "Greek" ("German") problem. "How," she said to me, "can I hope to succeed when I look at the graphs and all I see is lines that have no meaning?" She went on: "I haven't had geometry since tenth grade. I did OK [she implied this meant survived] then, but that was a long time ago." (I thought, this kid has no conception of "a long time." For her, tenth grade was four years ago, for me it was . . . never mind.) Anyway, she just doesn't see the content of the graphs 'cause the graphs themselves mean nothing. Geometry is a language she hasn't spoken in years.

She went on to tell me that her Dad had always joked about the fact that math and she were not meant for each other. After surviving geometry in the tenth grade, she hadn't taken any more math, and her math SAT was not too hot, which confirmed in her mind that she was not meant to do math.

What a frustrating conversation. She was honest, she was articulate, and she was determined to drop. I could deal with the study habit issue, but I didn't know how to deal with the "Greek" issue. What could I say? That it will come to you? No, it won't come like an unexpected gift from *The Millionaire.* (Remember that old TV program? No you don't do ya? You're like Leslie [the undergrad], too young to remember anything interesting or to really know the meaning of "a long time.")

So, Jeanne, what the hell do I tell her? I asked her to give me until Monday to think about a solution that could help her succeed. But I have no solution. So I turn to you. Do you ever run into a similar problem in chemistry classes? If so, what do you do about it? If you don't have a solution I can offer Leslie, how do I avoid having this same conversation with another "Leslie" that comes into my office next semester? I've heard this story before. I think what got me this time was the articulate way she set the issue before me—it really impressed me and depressed me at the same time.

Hellllllllp!
me

Date: Sun, 10 Mar 94 11:23:47 EST
From: jdoe@econ.edu
To: jeanne@chem.edu
Subject: "I've Got a Vague Idea"
Jeanne,

Thanks for the quick reply. It was very comforting to know that you can relate to the problem. Misery loves company. I appreciate your thoughts on a solution, or the lack thereof. Yeah, I think I'll have to be supportive of Leslie's decision to drop, because I don't see any quick fix at this point either. As for your comments on the "future Leslies," you're right—that's got to be where I focus my attention, and if there is a solution, it has to be implemented very early in the course so that I don't have to have this conversation after the midterm.

The term you used, "prerequisite skills" (is it yours?), is very appropriate for the issue. I assume that the students have a basic knowledge of geometry when they come to my class. It is a large part of, as Leslie so aptly put it, the language of my class. I spend a lot of time "speaking" graphs. I assume the students speak my language, but in fact, many of them (many who fail or just disappear) don't. Leslie really did them and me a favor by articulating their concern. I can't save her, but I can (I hope) make life (or at least my course) more amenable for her successors.

I'm in a very rudimentary stage of thought on this issue, and I would very much appreciate your suggestions. All I am fairly certain of now is that if I am to solve this problem the solution must be implemented at the beginning of the course. There must be a way to make a student aware of my assumptions about prerequisite skills so that she or he can be forewarned.

Gotta run. I just came in to do some prep for Monday. Celia and Abby are waiting for me. We're going to see the new baby elephant at the zoo. Thanks again for responding so quickly to my plea. As always, keep those cards and letters coming, and help me out on this prerequisite skills stuff.

> Take good care,
> me

Date: Mon, 11 Mar 94 16:43:42 EST
From: jdoe@econ.edu
To: jeanne@chem.edu
Subject: "The Talk"
Hi Jeanne,

I had the chat with Leslie. What a nice young woman. I really feel good and bad. She did drop—that's a bummer. She did get my attention—that's good. We talked for a pretty long time. Mostly about why all this graph stuff is necessary. She sees math as a necessary evil—like sorority rush, ya just gotta get through it, and then it's over. I tried to convince her that math isn't a hurdle, it's a tool. I think she got the point thanks to her own analogy: language.

I asked her if she was taking foreign language. Turns out she's in a real advanced conversational French class (it's her minor) 'cause she's planning to do the DIPA (our overseas program) semester in Paris. Perfect entrée: "You said that math is 'language.' Today, for better of worse, most economists speak math. If you want to be a part of their conversation, you have to speak math, too." Bingo! That made perfect sense—and then Bam! just when I was feeling so smart, she draws out the logic with: "See, I'm just not meant for this course, because I can't speak math." To which I responded with a definitive yes and no. Yes, you're not ready for this course, but—you can do math.

I told her she most certainly can do math if she can do heavy-duty French. Unlike French (and English), math has few idioms or exceptions. Like French, it just takes faith in yourself and practice. I also tried to convince her to take on her math phobia, because for her to succumb to it is to allow herself to play out a stereotype of women, and that will come back to haunt her down the line when she's sitting in some conference room with a graph in front of her and her boss says, "Leslie, what do you think of this trend?"

So we agreed that she'll drop my course, and she said she'd go to the math department to find a course that would help her develop her confidence and abilities. She promised to return, empowered. If failure can be success, this was it.

But still I'm haunted by the next "Leslie." I don't want it to come to this, but I know that, whether I hear from an articulate source like this Leslie or not, others will face the same dilemma if I don't do something about it. Any brilliant suggestions?

Abby loved the baby elephant. What a trip to see the world through the eyes of pure wonder, surprise, and joy.

Hope all is well with you.

Take good care,

me

Date: Wed, 3 Apr 94 3:26:57 EST
From: jdoe@econ.edu
To: jeanne@chem.edu
Subject: "An Idea Develops"
Jeanne,

Just a quickie to pick your brain. I've been talking to the Center for Instructional Development (an excellent in-house shop) about my future "Leslies" problem. They suggested a pretest screen to determine whether the students entering my class have the "prerequisite skills" necessary for success. I like the idea in principle, but I can think of a lot of problems in practice, like creating the test, administration of the process, what to do with the information (should I make passing it a requirement?), and so forth.

Whadayathink? Suggestions?

me

CASE ANALYSIS

The case we just presented is especially rich in highlighting learning issues from the perspective of the learner. In his conversation with Leslie, the teacher draws out clues to a number of potential learning problems. Although the instructor concludes, quite logically, that Leslie's basic problem is her lack of prerequisite knowledge, there are other significant learning problems revealed in this case. The instructor portrayed here chose to focus on Leslie's lack of prerequisite knowledge for the course. The unwritten assumption of both Leslie and the instructor is that Leslie will take an appropriate math course, be successful in it, and return to economics "empowered." The instructor, however, recognizes—but does not deal with—other problems that may face Leslie later: for example, her lack of confidence in her math abilities and the stereotypes of women as "not meant for math."

All instructors have their biases, based on their experiences as teachers and as learners. Another instructor, for example, might have pursued a "math phobia" hypothesis, probing with Leslie why she had avoided taking math in high school. Yet another instructor might have pursued the ineffective study methods, trying more diligently than did the instructor in the case to help Leslie develop productive learning strategies, hoping that she would not have to drop the course.

In any event, sometimes the precipitating reason for dropping a course covers up more fundamental reasons. Leslie may find, for example, when she registers for the math course that is supposed to build skills and self-confidence, that her fears about her lack of ability to "do math" will surface as a problem to be dealt with.

The starting point for our analysis of this case is the facts one can gather from reading it. Case leaders often start off discussions by asking, "What's going on here?" What clues does Leslie give, as revealed in the conversations with this instructor, about her reasons for wishing to drop the course?

For our analysis, we will stick rather closely to what is said. In this case, the reader hears about the learner's problems through a double filter—what Leslie is willing and able to tell the instructor and how the instructor interprets Leslie's perspective. But the instructor feels that Leslie is "honest" and "articulate"—and the reader has the same feeling about this instructor's analysis of the learning problems.

In our reading of the case, at least three learning problems are introduced by Leslie's instructor in his electronic mail communication with his colleague. First, he reports that Leslie lacks prerequisite skills and knowledge for his course. The instructor summarizes succinctly what Leslie is telling him about her background for his course in economics; "she feels like she's sitting in a class where the teacher is speaking Greek. . . . Because she doesn't speak the language, and she doesn't know what it's supposed to be about, she hasn't got a clue as to what is really going on." Leslie verifies this interpretation when she asks, "How can I hope to succeed when I look at the graphs and all I see is lines that have no meaning? . . . I haven't had geometry since tenth grade." The instructor contrasts Leslie's background with his expectations when he says, "I spend a lot of time 'speaking' graphs. I assume the students speak my language, but in fact many of them (many who fail or just disappear) don't." The instructor concludes that a pretest might screen out future Leslies who lack the background skills necessary for success in his course.

A second problem identified by the instructor and recognized by Leslie herself is that her study methods are not working for her in this class. The instructor says, "She claims that she's really working hard—and I believe her. . . . She showed me the reams of notes. . . . It's really very impressive, but it obviously isn't working. . . . She's obviously a very intelligent young woman, 'cause she's doing well . . . in all her other classes." The instructor concludes that Leslie is intelligent and conscientious but that her study methods are inappropriate and unproductive.

The instructor describes Leslie's ineffective study methods as "playing stenographer," searching for the "answer" and copying it down without really learning concepts and how they relate to one another. Both Leslie and the instructor recognize that she needs to develop more effective learning strategies, and the instructor tries to help—"I tried to demonstrate to her that her approach to the objectives is not productive"—and he goes on to suggest procedures that would make her study time "much more productive."

Finally, the third problem area is revealed when Leslie provides several clues that suggest she lacks confidence in her ability to do well in the course. Leslie reports that her Dad jokes that she and math "were not meant for each other," a perception that she has apparently internalized in a cycle of lack of success in and avoidance of quantitative subjects. She "did OK" in (survived) her math courses, but she has taken no math since tenth grade and her SAT math score "was not too hot." The instructor is unsuccessful in persuading her to stay with the course because she is "afraid that if she didn't succeed she would end up getting a D or, God forbid, an F, and that she just couldn't afford to take the chance." Leslie really doesn't know if she has the ability to handle the quantitative analysis required for the course, and she is reluctant to put herself to the test in this realm.

Formulating Hypotheses

Using information gleaned from studying the case, we can formulate some working hypotheses for further study and investigation. In this case, we have narrowed the search to three broad areas, based on the clues that Leslie and her instructor have presented. (Of course, individual readers or Classroom Research groups may, we hope, generate and investigate additional hypotheses about this case.) The three working hypotheses that arise out of our analysis of the case are as follows:

Hypothesis 1: Leslie lacks the prerequisite knowledge and/or skills for understanding this course in economics.

Hypothesis 2: Although Leslie is intelligent and conscientious, her study methods are not productive.

Hypothesis 3: Leslie lacks confidence in her ability to do well in economics.

The purpose of formulating hypotheses is to have a guide for the following procedures: (1) a search of the relevant literature, (2) the collection of further information via Classroom Assessment, and (3) the development of research questions for Classroom Research. Hypotheses serve as bridges from the initial analysis of the case to the search for further understanding of the teaching and learning issues involved.

In the next section of this chapter, we investigate the three working hypotheses about the Leslies case with the help of literature on learning and the methods of Classroom Assessment and Classroom Research.

INVESTIGATING HYPOTHESIS 1 _____

Leslie Lacks the Prerequisite Knowledge and/or Skills for Understanding This Course in Economics

REVIEWING
THE LITERATURE

What Do We Know from Research and Theory About Schemata and the Role of Background Knowledge?

Introduction. Hypothesis 1 assumes a problem in the background knowledge that a student brings to a new learning situation. Therefore, it will be helpful to start the investigation with a review of what is known about prerequisite knowledge and how students connect new information to what they already know in order to create understanding. In the language of modern learning theory, Leslie's *schema* for incorporating new learning into what she already knows is not sufficiently well developed to provide a mental framework on which she can build. She lacks not only quantitative skills but also the understanding of relationships and connections among economic concepts that would enable her to relate new information to what she already knows. Thus, an appropriate literature review might delve into research and theory on the schema and the importance of background knowledge. The highlights of this research are presented later in this chapter.

Leslie describes her experience in economics lectures as "sitting in a class where the teacher is speaking Greek." Leslie explains that when her instructor uses graphs on the board to explain economics concepts, all that she sees are "lines that have no meaning." Leslie and her professor agree that her problem in understanding economics is due in large part to her weak background in math. But even students possessing the math skills that Leslie appears to be lacking struggle with learning new concepts in introductory economics. Students often report that introductory-level courses seem more difficult than upper-level courses. In courses like Economics 101, Psychology 101, or Geology 101, students must learn a brand-new vocabulary and set of basic concepts that will serve as a foundation for more advanced learning. In advanced courses, students already share a common language with the instructor and are able to build upon their background knowledge in the subject matter. Prior knowledge influences how well new information is understood and stored in memory.

The following review of the literature will describe the importance of schemata, the existing network of information stored in the learner's memory. To set the stage for a discussion of schema theory and to provide additional background for readers less familiar with cognition theory, the review begins with a brief introduction to current views of learning and memory.

Learning and Memory. According to modern theories of learning, human beings are active information processors who must act upon new information to construct meaning for themselves. Before the advent of cognitive views of learning, learners were viewed as passive players in the teaching and learning process, to be acted upon by teachers or instructional techniques. Now, as a result of the cognitive revolution in thinking about memory, "knowledge is no longer viewed as a reflection of what has been given from the outside; it is a personal construction in which the individual imposes meaning" by making connections between new information and existing knowledge or a schema (Resnick, 1985, p. 130). For later use and recall of new information, learners must transfer incoming information out of the limited capacity of the short-term memory and into long-term memory by building connections to what they already know (Kurfiss, 1988).

According to current views of learning, then, teaching is not a process of dumping information into the empty brains of the students. Rather, teaching involves figuring out what learners already know (including misconceptions about a given subject), building upon that existing knowledge, and helping learners make connections between new information and prior learning so that they can understand and retain the new material.

Obviously, people do not remember everything they read, see, or hear. Unless new information is actively attended to, it will not be stored in memory for later recall. Memory has been described as a continuum from short to longer term (Weinstein and Meyer, 1991). The capacity of short-term memory is quite limited; for example, there is consensus among investigators now that the number of digits anyone can store in short-term memory is about seven. Learners can compensate for short-term memory limitations with "chunking" strategies. For example, it is quite difficult to remember the number 2798432431, but it becomes easier when one chunks it into the area code 279 plus the phone number 843–2431. Similarly, we remember our nine-digit social security numbers in three smaller chunks, 000–33–1234. Advertisers take advantage of chunking by connecting numbers to meaningful groups of letters that are even easier to remember. For example, fans can purchase season tickets to Berkeley football games by calling 1–800-GO-BEARS, and travelers can get the Amtrak train schedule by calling 1–800-USA-RAIL.

Automaticity is another function that offsets limits to short-term, or working, memory. When tasks become routine and familiar, they no longer require as much attention or space in the working memory (Resnick, 1985). Although reading, for instance, is a highly complex skill, much of the activity becomes automatic after a time. Most English-speaking adult readers, as they read this sentence, will automatically recognize the pronunciation and meaning of each word rather than having to sound words out or look up definitions in the dictionary. Quantitative activities like reading graphs can also become automatic. Leslie, however, does not yet have the skill to quickly understand trends indicated by the slope of lines on a graph. Students who can understand graphs with some level of automaticity have a much better chance of following economics lectures because that ability leaves them with some working memory available to process other new information.

Schema Theory. Cognitive views of learning contend that new information is more easily understood and retained when it can be related to existing knowledge held by the learner. The knowledge structures that organize and store information in a learner's memory are referred to as schemata, or in singular form, schema (Bartlett, 1932). (For discussions of schemata that go beyond what is offered in this chapter, see Anderson, 1985; Gagne and Dick, 1983; Hirsch, 1987; Norman, Gentner, and Stevens, 1976.) These structures might be compared to networks of facts, ideas, and associations formed around related concepts. People have schemata for events, places, procedures, and persons. A person's schema for a place such as a university, for example, might include such concepts as its geographical location and climate, the characteristics of the student population, the style of the campus architecture, and the reputation of the basketball team. Leslie's schema for her university, from her perspective as a student, probably differs from the schema of her instructor, a faculty member at the same university.

Consider a possible schema for a historical event such as the assassination of President John F. Kennedy. A prominent feature of the schemata of adults who are in their thirties or older would probably include a memory of what they were doing when the assassination was announced, vivid images from news footage as well as details from the tragedy's aftermath. The schemata of people in their twenties or younger, who were not yet born in 1963, are probably quite different. In their schemata, developed through historical accounts rather than firsthand experience, different elements would stand out as most salient, perhaps culled from the blend of history and conjecture in television specials and films like Oliver Stone's *JFK*.

Crawford and Chaffin summarize three assumptions about the way schemata work. First, "mental representations are not 'copies' of original events or statements." People do not remember information exactly as they received it. Second, "schemata are generalized knowledge structures that provide the framework for and determine the nature of understanding." That is, they provide a lens through which new information is filtered. "Third, schemata allow the understander to go beyond the information actually given," by providing him or her with background knowledge from which to make inferences (1986, p. 6).

Consider further that the first assumption of schema theory is that *memory does not record exact copies of information* in the world around us. Research on people's recall of stories and information suggests that knowledge is stored in memory as abstract and reorganized representations. For example, in studies where people were told the events in a story in a mixed-up order and then were asked to recall the story, they often reorganized it in a more logical fashion (Crawford and Chaffin, 1986).

People remember the gist of new information rather than remembering it in the exact form in which it was presented. A simple experiment demonstrates the process. Subjects were shown the sentence "The window is not closed" and then asked to recall that sentence, given the following options:

The window is not closed. [Correct.]

The window is closed.

The window is not open.

The window is open. [Preserves the gist.]

The subjects chose "The window is open" more often than any other incorrect choice, thus preserving the meaning of the sentence, if not the precise wording. Later experiments showed that meaning is made "at the time a sentence is understood, not later in recognition or recall" (see Hirsch, 1987, p. 37).

Thus, if the learner had no mental image of what an unclosed window is, his or her only recourse would be to memorize the exact wording of the sentence. This theory helps teachers understand why students who lack an adequate schema for getting the gist of a lesson resort to desperate attempts to memorize the wording of new information even when they cannot understand it.

For an everyday example of how people remember the gist of new information, consider someone reading the morning newspaper to keep current on world events. Later on in the day, the reader remembers key issues from several articles, but not the articles word for word. Cognitive views of learning do not value a photographic memory, which imprints the text of an newspaper article into the reader's mind. Instead, they state that new information must be processed and connected to existing knowledge in the learner's schemata for successful use and recall at a later time.

The second assumption of schema theory is that *existing knowledge structures provide a framework for understanding new information:* "The more prior knowledge we have in an area of a field of study, and the more this knowledge is organized and integrated, the more we can make sense of new information that we are trying to learn, and the more connections we can build between it and what we already know" (Weinstein and Meyer, 1991, p. 16).

For example, if the newspaper reader mentioned earlier were a Russian history major, she would have background knowledge to facilitate her understanding as she read an article about border disputes among small republics in the former Soviet Union. Imagine that an equally bright student but a math major were to read the same article. Because he lacks information about Russian language and geography in his existing knowledge base, he might have trouble making sense of and recalling the names and relationships of the significant people and places in the article.

Research consistently indicates that what learners already know, their existing schemata, greatly facilitates the comprehension and remembering of new information (Crawford and Chaffin, 1986; Hirsch, 1987; Pintrich, 1988b). For example, studies of recall among baseball fans found that persons who already had a significant knowledge base of baseball facts and statistics were more successful at learning new baseball trivia, presumably because they had existing knowledge with which to integrate new information (Chiesi, Spilich, and Voss, 1979).

Research by de Groot (1966) that compared novice and expert chess players' ability to memorize the layout of chess pieces also demonstrates the role of existing knowledge structures in new learning. Chess players of different skill levels were shown the game pieces on a chess board for a few seconds, then were asked to recall the position of the pieces. The novice players were only able to place five or six pieces correctly, but the experts could re-create nearly the whole board. However, when these players were shown the pieces placed randomly on the board (rather than positions from a real game), novices and experts performed about the same. The experts could re-create real games that fit with existing schemata for patterns in chess games, but were no better than novices at memorizing random placements. (For a summary of de Groot's research, see Chi, Glaser, and Rees, 1982, or Hirsch, 1987.)

A classic study by Bransford and Johnson (1972) demonstrates how activating appropriate schema helps encoding, comprehension, and recall of new material. The following excerpt is from a passage that people were asked to read and recall:

> The procedure is actually quite simple. First you arrange things into different groups. Of course, one pile may be sufficient depending on how much there is to do. If you have to go somewhere else due to lack of facilities that is the next step, otherwise you are pretty well set. It is important not to overdo things. That is, it is better to do too few things at once than too many. In the short run this may not seem important but complications can easily arise. A mistake can be expensive as well. At first the whole procedure will seem quite complicated [cited in Crawford and Chaffin, 1986, p. 7; Hirsch, 1987, p. 40].

As written, this passage is rather confusing, and the main ideas would be difficult to recall a day later. However, set the passage in a context with the title "Washing Clothes" and it becomes much clearer. A reference to washing clothes activates the reader's existing schema about doing laundry, and the elements of the passage make sense in light of what the reader already knows about washing clothes. If the passage had been titled "Writing an Essay," the reader might have only remembered those aspects that fit with the reader's essay-writing schema. Perhaps the reader would have interpreted the "piles" as notes for writing and "going elsewhere" as going to use word-processing facilities, but other elements of the passage would not make sense and would therefore probably be more difficult to remember.

Our existing knowledge base is the Velcro of the mind to which new information sticks. However, in the same way that lint can keep Velcro from sticking, misconceptions in a schema can interfere with connecting new information to existing knowledge. For example, people who have studied several foreign languages report that learning a third and a fourth language comes easily once they have acquired some basic structures for language learning. Occasionally though, knowledge of words from one language can interfere with the learning of new words in another language that sound the same but mean something different.

The third assumption of schema theory is that *background knowledge enables learners to make sense of information beyond what is explicitly stated.* The Russian Studies major probably understands newspaper analyses of events in the former Soviet Union on a deeper level than the math major because her background knowledge in the subject enables her to place current events in a larger historical context.

Learners' background knowledge helps them to read between the lines of what they see or hear. For example, shared schemata allow friends and colleagues with common experiences to get the meaning of each other's inside jokes. Or consider the following sentence: "Leslie fished her ID card out of her backpack and presented it to the lab monitor in exchange for French tapes and earphones." A reader trying to understand this sentence would be helped by the knowledge that Leslie is a college student majoring in French, that her backpack is a book bag rather than hiking equipment, and that ID cards are the main currency on college campuses, used to get dinner in the dining hall, to check out library books, and to borrow equipment in the language lab.

To understand any text, a learner must use an existing schema to make inferences about its unwritten meaning. Hirsch describes written text as "the tip of an iceberg of meaning; the larger part is below the surface of the text and is composed of the reader's own relevant knowledge" (1987, p. 34). For example, scholarly journal articles in economics may refer to a concept like "price elasticity" or "marginal utility" and expect the reader to know and understand the concept's definition although a basic economics textbook might devote several paragraphs to defining those terms.

College faculty have been heard to complain that students today cannot read. Hirsch and his colleagues conducted an experiment on the reading comprehension of community college students in which students read a passage about Robert E. Lee's surrender to Ulysses S. Grant at the end of the Civil War. The readers did not have any trouble decoding the words and understanding vocabulary, but their comprehension was weak because they lacked background information about who Grant and Lee were. Hirsch concluded that reading skills of community college students—"their memory capacities, eye movements, basic vocabularies, and reading strategies"—were not deficient but that they lacked significant background knowledge to help them make inferences from the text and place the passage in the context of the Civil War history (1987, p. 47).

Naveh-Benjamin, McKeachie, Lin, and Tucker (1986) studied the relationship between the organization of students' schemata and their academic performance. Students were presented with concepts from a class and were asked to arrange them in an "ordered tree" according to the relationships among the concepts. The researchers then inferred the organization of students' cognitive structures from how they arranged the course concepts. The researchers found that these college students' knowledge structures were related to their grades and success on a final exam. Students whose schemata were organized in a fashion similar to their teachers' were more likely to perform well in a course.

Leslie is lacking skills for graph reading and other quantitative procedures, and because this is her first economics course, she is also lacking schemata or knowledge structures for economic terms and concepts. Her probability for success in the course is further limited because her study methods are to record and memorize rather than to build connections for deeper understanding. What can the instructor do to help this Leslie and future Leslies?

Current theories of learning emphasize that learners are ultimately responsible for their own understanding through active construction of meaning. However, the importance of the teacher's role has in no way diminished. Although "instruction cannot simply put knowledge and skills into people's heads" (Resnick, 1983, p. 30), teachers can facilitate learning by presenting new information so that it is related to students' existing knowledge and by modeling active processing of new information for students. The literature reviewed here stresses the role that prior knowledge plays in learning, understanding, and remembering new information. Thus, the implications of schema theory for improving teaching and learning include recommendations for teachers to take into account how students' learning of new concepts will be supported or thwarted by their background knowledge. In addition, cognitive theory advocates instruction that explicitly encourages learners to construct meaning for themselves by building connections to existing knowledge and organizing information for later retrieval.

To assist you to build upon the introduction to schema theory and the role of background knowledge provided here and to expand your own analysis of the case, several supplemental readings are suggested in the next section. These may be read on your own or shared and discussed with a Classroom Research group on your campus. Following this bibliography, the investigation of this case continues with Classroom Assessment Techniques and Classroom Research designs that may be used to assess the background knowledge of Leslie and her fellow students.

RECOMMENDED
READING

Schemata and the Role of Background Knowledge

Carey, S. "Cognitive Science and Science Education." *American Psychologist,* 1986, *48*(10), 1123–1130.

This article, targeted at science teachers, addresses the challenges of integrating new scientific information with students' existing misconceptions. Even students who have taken a year of college physics still make errors based on their naïve notions about the forces of motion. Thus, it is clear that students' incorrect background knowledge complicates science teachers' efforts. Carey's discussion promotes helping students shift from novice toward expert organization of concepts through knowledge restructuring.

Crawford, M., and Chaffin, R. "The Reader's Construction of Meaning: Cognitive Research on Gender and Comprehension." In E. A. Flynn and P. P. Schweickart (eds.), *Gender and Reading: Essays on Readers, Texts, and Contexts.* Baltimore, Md.: Johns Hopkins University Press, 1986.

Crawford and Chaffin provide a thorough introduction to and overview of the tenets of schema theory, supported by examples from research. In addition, their chapter contains an important discussion of the implications of gender and sex-role stereotyping for differences in individuals' schemata and comprehension.

Hirsch, E. D., Jr. "The Discovery of the Schema." In *Cultural Literacy.* Boston: Houghton Mifflin, 1987.

Although Hirsch's *Cultural Literacy* has met with considerable controversy, Chapter Two of his book provides an excellent introduction to schema theory. Hirsch presents his own and others' research, with detailed explanations of several experiments, to support the existence of schemata.

McKeachie, W. J., Pintrich, P. R., Lin, Y.-G., and Smith, D.A.F. *Teaching and Learning in the College Classroom: A Review of the Research Literature.* Ann Arbor: National Center for Research to Improve Postsecondary Teaching and Learning, University of Michigan, 1986.

The review of knowledge structures in Chapter Three of McKeachie and colleagues' comprehensive review of the literature on teaching and learning in higher education includes explanations of knowledge structures in different domains, research techniques that have been used to assess knowledge structures, and suggestions for developing students' knowledge structures through instruction.

Norman, D. A. "What Goes on in the Mind of the Learner." In W. J. McKeachie (ed.), *Learning, Cognition, and College Teaching.* New Directions for Teaching and Learning, no. 2. San Francisco: Jossey-Bass, 1980.

Norman describes learners as theory builders who build upon incomplete evidence. He introduces different theories about how people learn and makes recommendations for teaching, including the suggestion that teachers supply prototypes or models to improve student learning.

CLASSROOM
ASSESSMENT

Collecting Further Information

Introduction. Classroom Assessment may be used to collect information about students' knowledge, skills, backgrounds, attitudes, and reactions to instruction. It is used only rarely to gain insights into the problems of an individual learner, but Leslie of course stands for a generic learner, a proxy for all the learners that might be having trouble in economics for any number of reasons, and Classroom Assessment is used with such generic groups. The purpose in using Classroom Assessment is to see how prevalent certain problems are among members of the class and to gain an understanding and insights into the learning profile of the class.

The use of this book assumes access to—and preferably familiarity with—its predecessor, *Classroom Assessment Techniques: A Handbook for College Teachers,* by Thomas A. Angelo and K. Patricia Cross (1993). Although we hope that this section on Classroom Assessment can be read with some understanding by college teachers, their application of Classroom Assessment will be greatly enriched if they can refer to the more detailed descriptions of Classroom Assessment Techniques presented in that handbook.

Collecting Further Information About Hypothesis 1. The next step in the investigation of hypothesis 1 (Leslie lacks the prerequisite knowledge or skills to understand this course in economics) might be to collect information from other students in the class. The assumption in this case is that there are more Leslies in this class and will be yet others in classes to come. Indeed, the problem for the teacher in the case study is not so much the present Leslie who, sadly enough, has departed from this teacher's concerns, but the future Leslies. Thus, an obvious question for investigation is, How many students in the class share Leslie's problem as stated in hypothesis 1? How many lack the appropriate background knowledge and skills? Can the instructor get some accurate information about the background skills of students in the class and perhaps a better picture of the schemata they have for incorporating new knowledge into existing knowledge?

Through the use of Classroom Assessment Techniques (CATs), instructors can collect data that will give them further information about the math backgrounds of the students in their classrooms. The two sample CATs to be discussed here, the Background Knowledge Probe and Concept Mapping, are examples of how any college teacher might assess the learning backgrounds of his or her students.

Example 1: Background Knowledge Probe. (See CAT 1 in Angelo and Cross, 1993, pp. 121–125.) Background Knowledge Probes (BKPs) are simple pretests designed to collect specific feedback about students' prior learning. They are often used to help teachers determine the appropriate level for instruction and sometimes to pinpoint particular problem areas that the teacher knows from experience are likely to be troublesome. Over a period of several semesters, a BKP might also provide promising items for the construction of a more formal prescreening test, should the instructor or department conclude that certain prerequisite skills are critical for success in the course.

The BKP is extremely flexible. It may be given at the very beginning of a course or to introduce a new unit or used as a pre- and posttest to determine students' accomplishments in the unit or course. It may consist of a few items or many, in multiple-choice, short-answer, or problem-solving formats. It may be scored immediately by students themselves or scored out of class and used for planning the next lesson.

Constructing an appropriate Background Knowledge Probe is not simple. It requires experience (Where have students stumbled in the past?), knowledge of subject matter (What is the proper sequence of knowledge?), and careful attention to the construction of the BKP items. The BKP is most likely to be successful if it is introduced not as a test or quiz (responses should be anonymous) but rather as a diagnostic instrument that will inform students about their readiness for the course.

The case study shows that the instructor and Leslie have both discovered that reading and understanding graphs is a necessary skill for success in the course. Thus, an appropriate BKP would include some items calling for the interpretation of graphs. If this were an upper-level economics course that required calculus or statistical regression methods, items requiring those skills would be included as well. The BKP would also include other items that sampled background knowledge deemed important to the understanding of introductory economics.

The results of BKPs not only serve as guides to the instructor but also indicate to students how well prepared they are for the course. When feedback from the BKP in this economics class is given to students—as it always should be—students who really had no idea how to go about reading the graphs would have known that they were in big trouble. Leslie, for example, might have discovered early on that she needed more background in the language of graphs before she could hope to succeed in this course. Other students might have missed the right answer on the BKP but when shown the right answer might have known right away what they did wrong and might have concluded that they just needed to brush up a bit on their math skills. Yet others might have sailed through the BKP with ease and have been reassured that they had the necessary math background for the course. Used in this way, the BKP serves to inform both teacher and students whether students possess the prerequisite skills for success in the course.

Information about the levels of prior knowledge that students bring to his economics course will enable the instructor to plan the level, pace, and organization of his lectures. Although the BKP may not "save" the Leslies of the world, it may save them time, frustration, and blows to their self-esteem, and for the instructor, it may screen out, on a voluntary basis, students who have little chance for success. More important, the Leslies who are on the borderline of being prepared for this course and who chose to stay will be prepared to do some math review or to seek out extra assistance from the teaching assistants or the university learning center.

Example 2: Concept Maps. (See CAT 16 in Angelo and Cross, 1993, pp. 197–202.) A Concept Map is a drawing or diagram that represents a student's schema for a given topic. It shows the mental connections that the student makes among concepts. When assigning a Concept Mapping task, the instructor asks students to create a diagram that organizes what they know about a topic in a way that demonstrates relationships and hierarchies among concepts and ideas. The maps offer instructors a peek inside students' heads by representing students' knowledge structures on paper. The contents of some students' Concept Maps will closely resemble the instructor's schema for the topic whereas other students' Concept Maps will be so sparse or show such misconceptions that the schemata will be judged inadequate for purposes of integrating new information into existing understandings.

A Concept Map for our analysis of the Leslie case might look like Figure 2.1. This map illustrates the interrelationships among the learning issues present assumed to be related to Leslie's decision to drop economics.[1] A Concept Map also shows, sometimes better than words can convey, the interrelationships among concepts. For example, Leslie's lack of prerequisite skills is related to

Figure 2.1.
Concept Map of Leslie's Decision to Drop Economics.

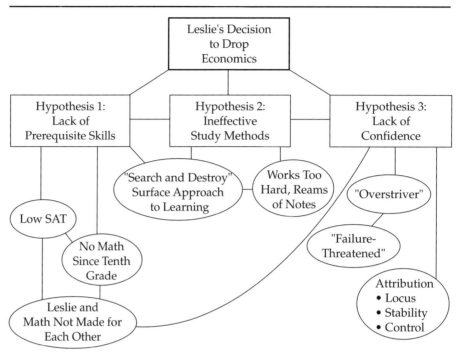

her failure to take any courses in math since tenth grade, which also probably contributed to her low SAT scores. These factors are both cause and effect in Leslie's suspicion that maybe she and math were not meant for each other, contributing to her lack of self-confidence as well as to her ineffective study methods.

Following a related train of thought, this Concept Map suggests that Leslie's lack of math skills contributes to her behavior in the class as an overstriver, who takes "reams of notes," and to her surface learning approach to reading economics assignments, because she is faced with the threat of failure (see the discussion of surface learning on pages 122–124, and threat of failure on pages 82–84). Once the instructor has identified the possible interrelationships among concepts, a diagnosis of learning problems becomes possible.

A Concept Map might also be used by the instructor in this case not to uncover inadequate prerequisite skills (for example, geometry) but rather to identify misconceptions regarding economics that might interfere with further learning or to get a picture of students' prior knowledge about topics that students are likely to have some exposure to, for better or for worse, outside of class. One economics professor, for example, during the first week of class asked students to draw a Concept Map representing their understanding of "free trade" (see Angelo and Cross, 1993, p. 200).

His diagnosis of students' understandings helped him to prepare the unit on free trade, and when he showed the class his Concept Map, it highlighted for students critical concepts that should get special attention as they studied.

Concept Maps can be used in a variety of ways throughout a course: to show the development of a schema, to organize a lesson, as a diagnostic tool to identify misconceptions, and as a pedagogical device to encourage students to visualize interrelationships.

The previous CATs—Background Knowledge Probes and Concept Maps—are provided simply as examples of how further information might be collected in this case. Teachers are encouraged to formulate their own needs for a particular type of information and to invent useful CATs to collect the data. These data may raise further questions that can be investigated through additional Classroom Assessment activities or may assist instructors to formulate Classroom Research questions like those introduced in the following sections.

CLASSROOM
RESEARCH

Explorations for Understanding

Introduction. Classroom Research differs from Classroom Assessment on the one hand and from traditional educational research on the other. We shall try to illustrate both those differences in this discussion of Classroom Research for the Leslies case. The immediate question that pops to mind in this case is this: How is prerequisite course experience related to success in economics? This type of research question, simple though it appears on the surface, has several design issues embedded in it. First is the shaping of the hypothesis. From reading the Leslies case, it looks as though the instructor believes that a fairly recent course in geometry is an important prerequisite for success in economics. Thus, he might simply compare the final economics grades of students who had taken a recent course in geometry with the grades of students who had not.

Another hypothesis for possible investigation is that the *grade* received in geometry is the most relevant predictor. Even though this is a quite reasonable hypothesis, it has two practical problems. One is that asking students to report past grades to an instructor is a dubious procedure, because students may suspect that this knowledge would influence their grade in economics. The desire to do Classroom Research should never violate the trust or compromise the integrity of the student-teacher relationship. The second problem is the age-old problem of causality versus association. Is a high grade in geometry *responsible* for a high grade in economics, or do generally bright students tend to make high grades in both geometry and economics? In other words, would a high grade in chemistry—or French—be an equally good predictor?

Still another possible hypothesis is that mathematical sophistication is the relevant variable, in which case, the teacher might be interested in correlating the *number* of math courses taken with the final grade in economics. This too, however, raises the question of causation versus correlation. It might be that generally bright students tend to take more math and that it is general ability rather than prerequisite knowledge that is responsible for the high grade in economics.

Clearly, formulating the hypothesis is the first important step in conducting research. It determines the design of the research and the confidence in the interpretation of the results.

It seems reasonable, as well as practical in this case, to formulate the hypothesis as one of prerequisite knowledge, that is, to theorize that the ability to read and interpret graphs and deal with relationships among numbers is a necessary skill for understanding economics.

The next step is designing the study, and in order to illustrate some very important differences between traditional educational research and Classroom Research, we will go into some detail to show how each type of research project might be conducted.

Traditional Educational Research Approach. A simple traditional design to test the prerequisite knowledge hypothesis might consist of sorting students by final grades in economics and by whether or not they had taken a course in geometry within the last four years. Let us assume that we have data for 100 students. The tabulation might look something like this:

Final Economics Grade		Took Geometry Recently	
Grade	*N*	*N*	*Percent*
A	15	15	100
B	30	20	67
C	40	20	50
D	10	4	40
F	5	1	20
Total	100	60	

If the instructor's grade distribution looked like this, it would be clear that those students taking a recent course in geometry have a consistently better chance of making a good grade in economics. All of the students making an A had taken geometry recently, compared to 50 percent of the C students, compared to 20 percent of F students. The percentages decline consistently with poorer grades. Although we rarely find such clear relationships in human learning, a grade distribution such as this would confirm the hypothesis that taking geometry and making good grades in economics go together.

Another way to look at these data would be to group "good" students (A or B grades) and compare their geometry background with poor students (D or F grades). Of the forty-five students making good final grades in economics, thirty-five, or 78 percent, had taken geometry; of the fifteen students making poor grades, only five, or 33 percent, had taken geometry. Is the difference between 78 percent and 33 percent significant? Is the instructor who gets such data safe in concluding that a recent course in geometry is associated with success in economics?

There are statistical techniques to determine whether findings are statistically significant, that is whether they depart from what might be expected from chance alone. The larger the sample, the more confidence one can have that there is a real difference. If eighty people out of one hundred show a given characteristic, for instance, one can be far more confident that the result is not simply a chance finding than one could be if four out of five people show the characteristic. In another sample of five people, for instance, three or even only one person might show the characteristic. Thus, the level of confidence that the researcher can have in his or her findings depends on the size of the sample and the size of the finding. The problem for Classroom Research is that most classes are likely to have small samples (often thirty students or fewer), inconsistent findings, and small differences, because human learning measures are rarely as consistent as those used in our hypothetical example.

The most practical and sensible discussion of statistical significance in traditional educational research that we have seen is presented by Harvard professors Light, Singer, and Willett in a small, well-written, authoritative book titled *By Design* (1990, pp. 187–210). They approach the question of sample size by asking how large an effect is worth your time? In most cases, Classroom Researchers are not interested in a statistical significance so small that only through statistical procedures could they be sure that the difference existed at all. Usually, Classroom Researchers want to be able to see a difference by eyeballing the data. In their discussion, the Harvard authors present some helpful guidelines on statistical significance originated by Jacob Cohen (1988), who provides the following rules of thumb:

A *small* effect is undetectable by the naked eye: a difference of .20 standard deviations between two group means, a correlation of .10 between a predictor and an outcome, or the difference between 50 and 45 percent. A small effect corresponds to the mean difference in heights between fifteen- and sixteen-year-old girls—two groups that differ, but not by much.

A *medium* effect is large enough to be detected by the naked eye: a difference of .50 standard deviations, a correlation of .30, or the difference between 50 and 35 percent. A medium effect corresponds to the mean difference in infant mortality between blacks and whites in the East South Central states.

A *large* effect would not be missed by even a casual observer: a difference of .80 standard deviations, a correlation of .50, or the difference between 50 and 25 percent. A large effect corresponds to the mean difference in height between thirteen- and eighteen-year-old girls.

Classroom Researchers should, in most cases, plan for medium to large effects. Medium effects can be seen in groups of between one hundred and two hundred students and large effects can be seen in groups of twenty-five to seventy students. Such group sizes are feasible if an instructor has multiple class sections or is part of a cooperating team of Classroom Researchers, but we have argued (see Chapter One) that the whole point of Classroom Research, for a number of reasons, is to use methods other than those that work in traditional quantitative research. Traditional models can be used, and there are ways around the technical problems encountered. However, our reasons for defining Classroom Research as quite different from traditional educational research are illustrated in the contrasts between the very simple traditional design we have just presented and the design of the Classroom Research project that follows.

A Typical Classroom Research Design. Let us assume the same data used in the previous illustration. The Classroom Researcher might begin by putting the data in the four-way matrix shown in Figure 2.2.[2]

Quadrant 1 represents the thirty-five students who made an A or B in economics and who took geometry within the past four years. Quadrant 2 represents the ten students who made A or B despite the fact that they had not taken geometry recently. In quadrant 3 are the ten students who made poor grades (D or F) and who did not take geometry; in quadrant 4 are the five students

Figure 2.2.
Four-Way Matrix.

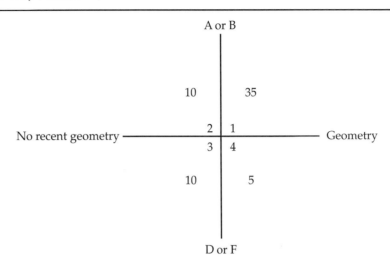

who made poor grades despite the fact that they had taken geometry. The students represented in quadrants 1 and 3 are performing as expected by the hypothesis: those who took geometry did well; those who did not performed poorly. Because the results come from a fairly large sample of students ($N = 60$), it is quite clear, just looking at the matrix that the hypothesis is confirmed. Thus, this teacher might conclude that in general, it would be well to advise students that a recent course in geometry is helpful. (The teacher, of course, must remain mindful of the possibility, pointed out earlier, that correlation does not prove causation.)

However, the really interesting research questions for classroom teachers lie in what traditional researchers call errors—the students in quadrants 2 and 4 who did not perform as predicted. Having labeled these data as errors, traditional researchers ignore this valuable information. Classroom Researchers, however, are very interested in such data. How did the ten students who performed well in economics do so without the presumably appropriate prerequisite of geometry? Interviews with these students might turn up some interesting themes. Perhaps they studied with a classmate who did have the appropriate background. Maybe they just worked extremely hard. If so, what were the motivating factors? Perhaps they found a way to demonstrate quantitative relationships that did not depend on geometry.

Similarly, interviews with students falling in quadrant 4 have a high potential for revealing important information. These students, despite their presumed prerequisite skills, did not do well in economics. Why not? Teachers of small classes may know of a personal situation that prevented particular students' good performance, but there may also be students in this group who fit Covington's theory (1989) of preserving self-worth through not trying very hard (see page 84). Or a sensitive test (oral or written) to determine which skills are really helpful may reveal that a student failed to learn certain essential concepts despite passing a course in geometry. The point is that the Classroom Researcher is in a good position to probe individual variations that traditional research has cast aside as error.

Now turn for a moment to the uses of these two types of research. The hypothetical results of the traditional design showed a strong probability that on average, students who had taken geometry recently would make higher grades in economics than those who had not. Such information might be used to make a policy decision, that is, to advise or require all students to take certain prior courses—albeit in full recognition that there will be some error in the predictions: some students who might have been successful will be excluded by the pretest; some students who are admitted to the class will do poorly. The information from this research design, however, will probably not change the way the teacher teaches; indeed, it may reinforce the teacher's tendency to conclude that certain students just should not be in the class and that teaching problems are most conveniently alleviated by selecting students who can benefit from the way the class is currently taught.[3]

Traditional research is most valuable when there is a large sample (not true in most classrooms), when the researcher possesses the technical skills for statistical analysis (not true of most college teachers), and when the action contemplated is an institutional or departmental policy decision rather than the improvement of teaching or learning.

Classroom Research, in contrast, is most useful to teachers who have a continuing relationship with their students and can observe them closely day in and day out (a method not available to most educational researchers), who know the sticking points of their own particular subject matter (not generally an option for educational researchers), and who can follow up on the questions raised in the process of the research (most educational researchers "quit" when the study is done). Classroom Research is designed to follow leads that improve a teacher's understanding of how individuals learn. It is likely to change teachers' behaviors in the classroom, and it is likely to lead to cascading research designs in which the findings from one study will suggest other studies.

Ideally, all research is cascading in the sense that it raises further questions for investigation. But the examples we have given here of a traditional design compared with a Classroom Research design also illustrate the difference between the next steps in the two models. The next step in the traditional design discussed here might be to administer a screening test for prerequisite skills, require all students to take the test, and then, on the basis of the scores, either advise students to take a prerequisite course or require them to do so. A good design would then do a follow-up study to see whether students self-selected themselves wisely on the basis of the advice or whether requiring a prerequisite course increased student success. Implementing the policy decision to eliminate students without the prerequisite skills, however, forecloses the further study of students who might have done well in economics had they been permitted to take the course. In summary, the typical pattern in applied educational research is to conclude the study, report the findings, make a decision about what to do, and finally do a follow-up evaluation.

In contrast, the logical next step for the Classroom Research design described here would be to follow up any interesting leads revealed in the interviews. For example, assume that the Classroom Research study just described reveals to the teacher that several students predicted to do poorly in economics because they lacked a recent course in geometry performed quite well because they had formed a study group that proved effective, or had taken some course other than geometry, or had found some study technique that worked for them. Perhaps they had found some useful technique, metaphor, or "trick" that had never even occurred to the teacher. The Classroom Researcher might then do any number of follow-ups—further interviews of these students (What did their study group do? How much time did they spend? Who or what were the resources?) or modifications in classroom procedures (perhaps assigning students to study groups, incorporating student-discovered techniques into the teaching, and so on). Teachers will want to evaluate the changes they make, but the point is that Classroom Research is exploratory and experimental; ideas can be tried and even modified midstream if they do not seem to be working.

Further Examples of Classroom Research. A major premise of Classroom Research is that expertise and experience in the subject matter of the course is an important qualification for conducting Classroom Research. The truly interesting questions for investigation will come from sensitive insights and observations of students in the process of learning that subject matter. We do not pretend to have those insights for the various disciplines. Therefore, for further research examples, we will suggest some questions that might cluster around the cognitive views underlying hypothesis 1, always with the caution, however, that the creative and challenging—and potentially most productive—questions for investigation come from the observations of classroom teachers who are experts in their disciplines.

For example, if a teacher is really curious about why a student who seems to be bright and conscientious has so much trouble learning a given concept, the teacher might sit down with that student and try to understand how he or she learns. An N of one is a perfectly acceptable N in Classroom Research—as long as the investigation has the potential for increasing understanding of learning. What is learned from an individual student may provide the basis for a whole series of cascading questions for Classroom Research.

Returning to the class as a whole, it might be interesting to ask if students who perform well on the first exam do progressively better on the subsequent exams while those who start off lacking background skills or knowledge score progressively worse? Do the "rich keep getting richer" in terms of exam performance? If indeed the findings suggest that students who start out poorly continue to do even worse, some intervention for poor performers on the first exam would be warranted in future semesters. The Classroom Research project would cascade if students who did poorly in the beginning of the semester were offered some sort of intervention, such as a review session. Then the teacher could compare the reviewers' performance on the second exam to that of students who also did poorly on the first exam but did not attend the review session.

A final suggestion for Classroom Research is that instructors build on the findings from Classroom Assessment activities. In the discussion of hypothesis 1, Concept Mapping (CAT 16, in Angelo and Cross, 1993, pp. 197–202) was suggested to discover students' understanding of relationships among concepts. The sophistication and accuracy of students' Concept Maps could be compared to their scores on exams to determine a relationship between the organization of students' schemata, or knowledge structures, and their performance in the course. A Classroom Research design that focuses heavily on the organization and hierarchical relationships among concepts in a course is ideally suited to faculty with discipline-specific knowledge.

INVESTIGATING HYPOTHESIS 2

Although Leslie Is Intelligent and Conscientious, Her Study Methods Are Not Productive

REVIEWING
THE LITERATURE

What Do We Know from Research and Theory About Metacognition and Learning Strategies?

Introduction. In the first hypothesis, we postulated that Leslie lacked adequate background knowledge and prerequisite math skills to succeed in economics. To get up to speed in the class, she needs to compensate for missing background knowledge at the same time that she attempts to understand new material—study tasks that require both effort and skill. Although Leslie has been studying diligently, she has not worked effectively in economics. Hypothesis 2 suggests a problem in Leslie's approach to studying economics.

Leslie has attended class and completed reading assignments faithfully, copying down notes all the while. The results of her efforts are pages upon pages of information from the lectures and right answers, which she does not understand, copied from the textbook. Leslie does not need to study longer or harder, she needs to study smarter.

The search for literature relevant to this hypothesis might well begin with the relatively recent work on metacognition and cognitive learning strategies. The concepts of metacognition and cognitive learning strategies refer to the self-awareness and learning skills that contribute to learners' successful understanding and retention of new material. More specifically, metacognition refers to the way students think about themselves as learners and the way they manage their own learning. Cognitive learning strategies are techniques that learners can use to improve their understanding, integration, and retention of new information. This review of the literature will provide background knowledge to inform our investigation of the kinds of smart studying that might help Leslie succeed in economics.

Metacognition: Knowledge and Control of Cognition. Metacognition has a two-part definition that covers both *knowledge* of cognition and *control* of cognition (see Brown, 1987; Brown, Bransford, Ferrara, and Campione, 1983; Flavell, 1987; Yussen, 1985; Wellman, 1985). The first part of metacognition is awareness of and reflection upon one's own learning processes, or thinking about thinking, if you will. Learning theory contends that the practice of observing oneself in the act of learning contributes to the ability to understand one's own learning process, and to the ability to manage and control it. Flavell (1970, 1976) first identified three main areas of knowledge about cognition that may help learners improve their learning process: knowledge about oneself, knowledge of the learning task, and knowledge of strategies available to complete that task. Leslie, for example, seems to have knowledge about herself, the first of these three areas of cognition. She exhibits metacognitive awareness when she concludes that her difficulties in the course are largely due to her lack of math skills. In addition, she is conscious of her tendency to get frustrated and to tune out whenever graphs are used to explain a concept. She also realizes that her current study approach is ineffective.

Although Leslie is relatively aware of characteristics of her own learning strengths and weaknesses, she is unclear about the other two cognitive requirements—the nature of the learning task and strategies for completing it. Her inexperience in the task of learning economics is apparent in her "stenographer" and "search and destroy" method of approaching the course objectives. Because she lacks knowledge of the task, she also has trouble devising and using effective learning strategies. Thus, she continues to plow through the text with her ineffective note-taking methods.

Leslie would probably benefit from reflecting on her approaches to studying economics. However, simply being aware of one's own learning strengths and weaknesses is not enough to improve learning. To improve understanding and retention, learners have to take conscious steps to control learning. Control of cognition, the second component of metacognition, refers to planning (goal setting, prequestioning, and analyzing a learning task, for example), monitoring (tracking one's attention and understanding), and regulating learning (self-testing, for example) (Brown, 1987; Pintrich, 1988a). Control of cognition also involves the appropriate application of learning strategies, which will be discussed later.

Much of the literature on metacognition comes from research on reading instruction that examined how students learn from text. Metacognitive strategies are critical to students' ability to comprehend and retain new information from text. Leslie's search and destroy method of finding right answers in the text book and copying them down—"in the eye and out the pen without a stop at the cerebrum"—is not uncommon, according to research on reading. Unskilled readers often plow through reading assignments reading the words but failing to comprehend the meaning; whereas more skilled readers attempt to construct their own meaning from a passage, using metacognitive strategies such as asking questions while reading, making connections with existing knowledge, and reacting to the text (Jacobowitz, 1990, p. 621). As Leslie approaches course objectives, she might benefit from organizing main points as she reads each chapter and by closing the book occasionally to ask herself questions to see if she really understands the material.

Fischer and Mandl (1984) conducted an experiment in which twenty-four university biology students were given a text and instructed to read it as if they were reading in preparation for a class discussion. To rule out the influence of prior knowledge, the biology students were assigned a social science text on a subject with which students were not expected to be familiar. While students were reading, the experimenters unobtrusively noted students' reading behaviors, including the time readers spent per page, and how they moved forward and backward through the text.

After reading, students took a multiple-choice recall test and were interviewed about their behaviors while reading. The interview included a free-recall segment on reading behaviors, more specific questions about what the researchers had observed while the students were reading, and additional questions about students' general study habits. Students were classified as good (top 25 percent), average (middle 50 percent), or poor (bottom 25 percent) readers based on their performance on the recall test and the reading time they needed. Interview data were analyzed to compare the good and poor readers.

Both groups engaged in metacognitive thinking but in different ways. The students classified as good readers spent time planning and scheduling their learning and exhibited adaptability in the face of challenges. Poor readers did less planning but spent more time introspectively questioning their ability as readers. The good readers confronted challenges to comprehension with new strategies. The poor readers, however, used self-monitoring information to confirm their doubts about their ability and, as a result, were more likely to give up. Thus, Fischer and Mandl (1984) suggest that self-awareness alone is not necessarily helpful to learners. Students need information about specific strategies they can use to improve their learning when self-monitoring makes them aware of poor performance.

Zimmerman and Martinez Pons (1986) conducted interview research with high school students. A comparison of eighty high-achieving sophomores with their lower-achieving peers revealed differences in students' use of self-regulatory strategies based on their achievement level. The interviewer, who was unaware of students' status as "high" or "low" achievers, asked students to describe the methods they used to participate in class, to complete assignments, to prepare for exams, and to engage in other academic tasks. Student responses were coded according to students' reported use of fourteen defined categories of possible strategies such as self-evaluation, goal setting and planning, seeking information, and keeping records and monitoring. For example, self-evaluation was defined as student statements indicating student-initiated assessment of the quality or progress of his or her work: for example, "I check over my work to make sure I did it right." The category of goal setting and planning referred to student statements indicating established goals for learning and plans for the sequence and timing of work related to those goals: for example, "First, I start studying two weeks before exams, and I pace myself" (p. 618).

The students in the high-achievement group reported greater use of thirteen of the fourteen categories investigated. This research confirms the importance of self-regulatory strategies to academic achievement. Indeed, 93 percent of the students could be correctly classified into the appropriate track group (high or low achieving) based on their reported use of strategies. (General implications for improving the performance of unsuccessful students through training in metacognition and learning strategies are discussed at the end of this review of the literature.)

Cognitive Learning Strategies. Cognitive learning strategies are methods learners use to focus attention, organize and rehearse new concepts, and build connections to existing knowledge structures, in order to facilitate later recall and use of new information. An assortment of learning strategies, categorized in numerous ways, exist in the literature. General cognitive learning strategies include rehearsal, elaboration, organization, comprehension monitoring, and resource management (McKeachie, Pintrich, Lin, and Smith, 1986; Weinstein, 1988; Weinstein and Meyer, 1991).

Rehearsal strategies include highlighting textbooks, using flash cards, or reciting material out loud for memorization. Leslie seemed to rely too heavily on this type of activity, which focuses the learner's attention but does not necessarily build connections to existing knowledge or ensure long-term retention. Although rehearsal is not a particularly sophisticated learning strategy, it does help the learner create a database of information to build on for later use and application.

Elaboration strategies help learners make meaningful connections with existing knowledge—the cognitive structures, or schemata, discussed in the review of the literature for hypothesis 1—to facilitate transfer of learning to long-term memory. Connecting new learning to existing cognitive structures is critical for understanding and retention. Students in a sociology course, for example, are using elaboration strategies when they paraphrase key points from a lecture presentation on urban poverty, relate what they hear in lecture with what they read in the text, or consider how their experiences as volunteers in a homeless shelter support or challenge the theories they learned in class. When learners use elaboration strategies to generate connections between new information and existing knowledge, they are engaging in what Wittrock (1974) describes as "generative learning" and what Ausubel (1963, 1968) describes as "meaningful learning."

Organization strategies help learners condense large amounts of new information and make sense of relationships among new concepts and existing knowledge. Organization strategies include outlining information such as book chapters or lecture concepts. Another form of organizing is creating diagrams, perhaps of a scientific process, a chain of events, or related course concepts. Clustering ideas into categories that indicate shared characteristics is another type of organization strategy. When studying economics, for example, it is easier to understand and retain the concepts of equilibrium or price elasticity when they are organized under the broader heading of supply and demand.

Comprehension monitoring includes such activities as pausing to focus one's attention and prevent mind wandering, and checking understanding through self-testing. Leslie could monitor her understanding in economics by answering the questions at the end of each textbook chapter or by following her teacher's suggestion of attempting to complete the course objectives without the book to see what she's really "mastered." Comprehension monitoring overlaps with the monitoring and self-regulating activities of metacognition mentioned earlier.

Finally, *resource management* strategies include practical study skills like setting up a homework schedule and creating a distraction-free study environment. Help-seeking behaviors, such as taking advantage of instructors' office hours or organizing study groups, also fall under the category of resource management. Another aspect of resource management is regulating affective factors such as mood and motivation though positive self-talk ("I can do this if I just keep at it") and study breaks and incentives (planning to meet a friend for coffee after finishing a problem set).

Can Metacognition and Learning Strategies Be Developed Through Instruction? Well-developed metacognitive skills enable students to determine how and when to apply cognitive learning strategies. Sternberg (1983), among others, has warned that it is not enough to teach students a new cognitive strategy, they should also be taught when to use it and how to monitor and evaluate its success. Recent research has investigated the possibility of improving metacognitive abilities and learning strategy use through instruction. Much of this research has focused on school-age children, with findings that suggest that training in learning strategy use does result in gains in metacognitive knowledge about appropriate strategy selection (Ghatala, 1986; Pressley, Borkowski, and O'Sullivan, 1985).

Research on college-age learners also suggests that metacognition and learning strategies can be taught. In a study by King (1992), underprepared college students were trained in two different study strategies: one group was trained in generating questions while the other was trained to write original summaries from lectures. A third group (control) received no training. The three groups attended a lecture and were tested on concepts immediately after the lecture and again a week later. Students in the two experimental groups who used the generative study strategies of self-questioning or summarizing demonstrated improved performance and long-term retention of lecture concepts when compared to the control group of untrained students, who simply reviewed their lecture notes.

There is general agreement today that college students can benefit from training in the area of metacognition and learning strategies. Claire Weinstein, a major contributor to research on learning strategies, teaches a semester-long course on learning at the University of Texas at Austin (Weinstein, 1988). The goal of the Texas course is to encourage students to take control of their own learning through learning strategies and an understanding of motivational and learning theory (Weinstein, 1988; Weinstein and Underwood, 1985). A variety of instructional techniques are used, with an emphasis on opportunities for students to practice and receive feedback on their acquisition of new learning skills. Evaluation of the Texas course showed self-reported gains in students' use of learning strategies, increased scores on a reading comprehension instrument, self-reported lower levels of anxiety, and improvement on other performance measures such as course assignment grades.

Fostering Metacognition and the Use of Learning Strategies in Large Classes. Research suggests that training can improve students' use of cognitive and metacognitive strategies, and the instructor in the Leslies case apparently understands that encouraging students to use such strategies may move them away from passive rote learning and toward deeper, more meaningful learning. At the beginning of the semester, the economics instructor promoted planning and monitoring strategies by advising students to "review [the objectives of the course] first to prepare your mind, read, then try to work toward them without the book to identify what you've really mastered." Leslie, however, and probably many others, missed his message amidst the confusion and information overload that usually characterizes the first day of classes.

Miles concluded that "ultimately, most students will become conscious masters of cognitive learning strategies only if teachers make this possible, appealing, and/or unavoidable" (1988, p. 335). What more can Leslie's instructor do to foster metacognition and encourage the use of learning strategies by future Leslies and other students? An introductory economics lecture class may enroll well over fifty students. Is it realistic to expect that instructors can be responsible for the use of active learning strategies by each one of their students?

Most of the research geared toward improving teaching in large college classes has been based on classroom observations of what *teachers* say and do. Less attention has been paid to what *students* say and do. This is not surprising, considering that there is not much to observe in a classroom where students, entrenched in a passive-receptive mode of learning after years of experience, sit silently and take notes. Goetz, Alexander, and Burns (1988), however, suggest that the important questions should focus not on what teachers do but rather on what students can do to improve the quality of their learning.

Faculty can encourage students to become active organizers, rather than passive recipients of knowledge. For example, instructors can break up a lecture to allow students to reflect on new material. Depending upon the size of class, students can be asked to work—either silently on paper or in pairs or small groups—to summarize, synthesize, and elaborate on main points from the lecture. Several Classroom Assessment Techniques, including the Punctuated Lecture and Diagnostic Learning Log described in the following section, encourage students to summarize, elaborate on, and monitor their learning of new material (Angelo and Cross, 1993).

The literature reviewed suggests that learning strategies and metacognition can be improved through instruction. As Weinstein and Underwood have pointed out, "Many effective teaching strategies are just the flipside of effective learning strategies" (1985, p. 255). In the section following the recommended readings, we suggest Classroom Assessment activities to aid teachers in the collection of information about students' metacognitive awareness and use of learning strategies. These Classroom Assessment Techniques can also serve as tools for teachers who wish to engage students in reflection on and organization of new learning.

RECOMMENDED
READING

Metacognition and Cognitive Learning Strategies

Brown, A. L. "Metacognition, Executive Control, Self-Regulation, and Other More Mysterious Mechanisms." In F. E. Weinert and R. H. Kluwe (eds.), *Metacognition, Motivation, and Understanding.* Hillsdale, N.J.: Erlbaum, 1987.

In this long and comprehensive chapter, Brown traces the historical roots of the concept of metacognition, reviews related research, and clarifies the connection of metacognition to related theories, including the concepts of self-regulated learning, executive control, and even the work of the developmental theorists. Brown ultimately questions the use of the term metacognition to encompass so many different concepts. This chapter, which overlaps a great deal with the review by Brown, Bransford, Ferrara, and

Campione described in the next item, is targeted toward the reader with some background in learning theory.

Brown, A. L., Bransford, J. D., Ferrara, R. A., and Campione, J. C. "Learning, Remembering, and Understanding." In J. H. Flavell and E. M. Markman (eds.), *Handbook of Child Psychology,* Vol. 3: *Cognitive Development.* New York: Wiley, 1983.

In a chapter frequently cited by others writing on metacognition, Brown and colleagues provide an overview of the concept of metacognition, its history, and related theories.

McKeachie, W. J., Pintrich, P. R., Lin, Y.-G., and Smith, D.A.F. *Teaching and Learning in the College Classroom: A Review of the Research Literature.* Ann Arbor: National Center for Research to Improve Postsecondary Teaching and Learning, University of Michigan, 1986.

In their discussion of learning strategies in Chapter Three, McKeachie and his colleagues provide an introduction and synthesis of the literature on learning strategies that is addressed to a higher education audience. Their typology of learning strategies includes cognitive, metacognitive, and resource management strategies. Suggestions for assessing and promoting students' use of learning strategies are provided.

Pintrich, P. R. "Student Learning and College Teaching." In R. E. Young and K. E. Eble (eds.), *College Teaching and Learning: Preparing for New Commitments.* New Directions for Teaching and Learning, no. 33. San Francisco: Jossey-Bass, 1988.

Metacognition and learning strategies are just two of the topics covered in this clear overview of cognitive theory directed toward a practitioner audience interested in instruction at the college level.

Weinstein, C. E. "Assessment and Training of Student Learning Strategies." In R. Schmeck (ed.), *Learning Strategies and Learning Styles.* New York: Plenum, 1988.

This chapter presents a categorization scheme for learning strategies, examples of research methods to assess learning strategies, and examples of efforts to train students in the use of learning strategies. The chapter includes an appendix highlighting topics from a course on learning at the University of Texas at Austin.

Weinstein, C. E., and Meyer, D. K. "Cognitive Learning Strategies and College Teaching." In R. J. Menges and M. D. Svinicki (eds.), *College Teaching: From Theory to Practice.* New Directions for Teaching and Learning, no. 45. San Francisco: Jossey-Bass, 1991.

In a chapter directed toward college-level classroom teachers,

Weinstein and Meyer introduce current views of cognitive psychology and cognitive learning strategies. They review types of student learning strategies as well as instructors' cognitive strategies for teaching and suggest the implications for teaching students how to learn. This would make an excellent introductory reading for a faculty seminar group.

Weinstein C. E., and Underwood, V. "Learning Strategies: The How of Learning." In J. W. Segal, S. F. Chipman, and R. Glaser (eds.), *Thinking and Learning Skills: Relating Instruction to Research*, Vol. 1. Hillsdale, N.J.: Erlbaum, 1985.

In a chapter with a heavier research focus than the Weinstein and Meyer (1991) chapter described earlier, Weinstein and Underwood summarize changing views on human learning and present an introduction to learning strategy research. They also summarize methods and instruments developed to assess learning strategies and discuss how to develop learning strategy programs.

CLASSROOM ASSESSMENT

Collecting Further Information

Introduction. Hypothesis 2 suggests that Leslie's study methods are ineffective, even though she shows some outward signs—pages of notes—of someone who has worked productively. Discovering more about the study methods and metacognition of Leslie and her classmates requires finding out what is going on in the minds of these learners. One way that instructors collect information on the cognitive engagement of the students in their classes is to look around the room and take a visual survey of students' attention. Students with their eyes closed or their newspapers open are clearly not engaged. Students who are awake, make eye contact with the teacher, and dutifully record what the teacher says may be engaged in the lecture or discussion—but not necessarily.

When Leslie's instructor poses a rhetorical question about how the equilibrium of a supply and demand diagram would change in the long run, it will be unclear to him whether a student seated in the front row is furrowing her brow over the equilibrium question or over finding a ride home from soccer practice. From the instructor's perspective, Leslie, who is constantly taking notes, probably looks like a student who is paying attention. However, Leslie has mentioned that when the instructor uses graphs to explain concepts in the economics lecture, all she sees are lines that have no meaning. It is likely that Leslie eventually tunes out and merely copies down diagrams without thinking about their meaning.

Although many college teachers think that they can get a good feel for how students are responding to a lecture, research by Milton, Pollio, and Eison (1986) suggests that some students have become quite proficient in appearing to be paying attention when, in fact, they are thinking about unrelated matters. Observers were trained to record student behaviors, coding them as "on-target" or "off-target" with respect to the lecture. On-target behaviors included attending to the lecture, taking notes, asking or answering questions, and so on. Off-target behaviors included talking to neighbors, reading a newspaper, looking at one's watch and so forth. The observed behavior was then compared with student self-reports of what they were attending to when a bell went off periodically during the lecture. An average of 49 percent of all behavior observed was coded as on-target, but 61 percent of the students' self-reports coded their attention as on-target.

When the researchers compared behavior observed just prior to the time of the self-report with the self-report, in an effort to get at the difference between what a student appeared to be doing and what he or she reported thinking about, they found that appearances agreed with self-reports only 67 percent of the time. Most surprising was the finding that students who scored high on motivation for making good grades as well as learning for its own sake were especially likely to exhibit large differences between what they were doing and what they were thinking. Thus, it appears that students that many teachers think of as the ideal—interested in learning as well as in making good grades—may have developed rather sophisticated methods of appearing to be paying attention. Classroom Assessment may help teachers—and students—to monitor students' actual involvement in learning.

Here we suggest Classroom Assessment Techniques to collect further information about what students are thinking and doing as they learn in and outside of class. These CATs were selected not only for the useful information they provide the instructor but also for their potential to encourage students to reflect on the effectiveness of their learning behaviors and to engage in more productive learning strategies.

Example 1: Punctuated Lecture. (See CAT 38 in Angelo and Cross, 1993, pp. 303–306.) The Punctuated Lecture technique is one way to improve on the looking-around-the-room approach to collecting data about student learning and attention in lecture classes. It is designed to provide on-the-spot feedback on how students are learning from a lecture or demonstration. Students are asked to pay attention to how well they are processing, or failing to process, the information being presented, and to consider how their behaviors and other factors are influencing their learning.

The Punctuated Lecture requires students and teachers to go

through five steps: *listen, stop, reflect, write,* and *give feedback.* Students begin by listening to a presentation by the instructor. After a section of the lesson has been completed, the instructor stops. Next, the students are asked to reflect on what they were doing while they were listening and how their behaviors may have helped or hindered their understanding of that information. They might also be asked to reflect on aspects of the presentation or the classroom environment that helped or hindered their learning. Students write down some of their reflections and, anonymously, provide this feedback to the instructor.

The Punctuated Lecture provides instructors with information about students' engagement in the class, and at the same time, it promotes active listening and self-monitoring on the part of students. Because the Punctuated Lecture takes just a few minutes to administer, students' comments are likely to be brief, and analysis of the feedback can be quick and easy. Thus, this technique is well suited for use in large classes like an introductory economics lecture.

The first time a Punctuated Lecture is used in a class, faculty may be disappointed with the quality of student responses. It is difficult for students to think about how they process information at the same time as they are trying to learn content. As the semester progresses, this CAT may be repeated a few more times to encourage students to continue to monitor their own learning and to demonstrate improvement in their ability to do so.

Susan Obler, director of the Teaching-Learning Center at Rio Hondo College in Whittier, California, notes that Rio Hondo teachers conducting Classroom Assessment Techniques use carbonless double response forms for students' responses. That way, both teacher and students can keep a copy of the written reflections from the Punctuated Lecture or other CATs, and students can refer back to the feedback they provided to the instructor as a record of the challenges they faced and the progress they made over the semester.

Example 2: Diagnostic Learning Logs. (See CAT 40 in Angelo and Cross, 1993, pp. 311–315.) Leslie was certain that her approach to mastering the economics course material was not working, but she was not sure why. Diagnostic Learning Logs, focused academic journals in which students keep records of their learning assignments and the successes and problems they encounter, could be useful for both Leslie and her instructor to diagnose her learning problems in this class.

In Diagnostic Learning Logs, students keep records of a series of class sessions or independent assignments. When responding to a class session, students write one list of the main points covered that they understood and a second list of points that were unclear. When responding to an out-of-class assignment, students record problems they encountered or errors made. In addition, they can record "correct" or exemplary responses to assignments and the learning strategies they found useful for understanding lectures or solving problems.

Diagnostic Learning Logs inform teachers and students about students' ability to identify their strengths and weaknesses as learners and about their ability to recognize, document, diagnose, and suggest strategies to address learning difficulties in specific classes. The learning log forces students to reflect on their understanding or confusion about each course topic. We know from this chapter's case study, for example, that Leslie tuned out the lecture whenever graphs were presented. If she had filled out a Diagnostic Learning Log early on in the semester, this pattern of confusion and disengagement during lectures would have been made apparent to Leslie and her instructor.

When the instructor provided Leslie with suggestions for more productively tackling the course objectives, he wondered why she did not remember the ideas that he had presented during his first-day-of-class instructions. The fact that Leslie missed this part of his first-day speech should not be surprising. In addition to the information overload students face on the first day of classes, Leslie did not have the prior experience with economics assignments that would have enabled her to understand the instructor's suggestions. Most people have attempted to assemble or operate a small appliance without reading the instructions. Only after familiarizing themselves with the pieces and encountering problems do they turn to the instruction manual. Similarly, on the first day of class, Leslie and her economics classmates were not yet ready to hear their professor's suggestions.

The learning log forces students to engage in course assignments and reflective thinking about them in an effort to determine where the potential challenges lie. Once students are aware of the learning activities required in a course, the instructor can work with a more receptive audience to identify strategies to address potential learning problems. He or she can use the information gained from the learning logs to improve instructional methods or to provide suggestions for appropriate learning strategies.

One drawback of Diagnostic Learning Logs is that they require time and effort for students to complete—and for teachers to analyze. To save students' time and to generate more useful feedback for the instructor, students should be provided with clear instructions, the topics they are to address in the log, and ideally, a sample log entry.

Exhibit 2.1.
Guidance for Students Using a Learning Log.

Diagnostic Learning Log for Economics 101 Homework

Instructions. You are being asked to complete this record of your learning and problem-solving processes during the reading and homework assignment for Chapter 4. This exercise is designed to help you diagnose your learning strengths and weaknesses and to help you strategize for successful learning and homework completion in the future. Please respond to the following items. Sample responses for last week's assignment are included to help you get started.

1. Briefly describe the assignment you just completed. What do you think was the purpose of this assignment?
2. Give an example of one or two of your most successful responses. Explain what you did that made them successful.
3. Provide an example of where you made an error or where your responses were less complete. Why were these items incorrect or less successful?
4. What can you do differently when preparing next week's assignment to improve your learning?

For example, if the economics instructor learned that students were having difficulty integrating lecture and text information while completing the homework assignments, he might ask them to complete a learning log along with the weekly homework assignment. He could prepare students for the Diagnostic Learning Log as shown in Exhibit 2.1.

The effort required from teachers and students to complete and review Learning Logs should be outweighed by the benefits of helping students identify strategies to address their learning problems. Exposure to learning logs may encourage students to practice self-assessment in other learning situations. In addition, Diagnostic Learning Logs offer teachers a rich source of data likely to stimulate ideas for ongoing Classroom Research projects. For an example of how learning logs are used in Classroom Research, see page 74.

Example 3: Building Bridges. Leslie was producing a great deal of information in her notes, but she seemed to be processing very little of it. One way that teachers can get feedback on how deeply students are processing new information using such learning strategies as organization and elaboration is a new CAT called Building Bridges, a modification of the Concept Mapping CAT (CAT 16 in Angelo and Cross, 1993, pp. 197–202). Using the Build-

Figure 2.3.
Sample Bridge Diagram.

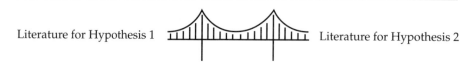

Literature for Hypothesis 1   Literature for Hypothesis 2

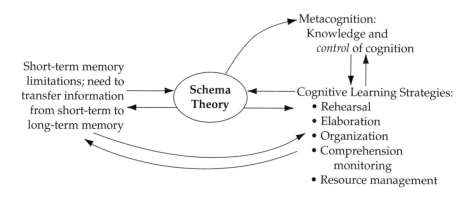

ing Bridges CAT, teachers can determine if students are successfully connecting today's lesson with the learning from the previous class sessions. If students are not already making those connections, this CAT will encourage them to relate today's lesson to previous ones.

Using diagrams similar to those used in the Concept Map described in hypothesis 1, students can sketch either a simple one-lane bridge that connects yesterday's topic to today's lesson, or a multilane, multispan bridge that relates today's information to learning from the entire semester and to other background knowledge.

The sample bridge diagram shown in Figure 2.3 connects the learning theory concepts from the literature reviews for hypothesis 1 and hypothesis 2.

The diagram in Figure 2.3 indicates that schema theory built upon the concept of short-term memory limitations and then bridged back to the concept of memory because existing knowledge structures (schemata) enhance learners' ability to transfer new information from short-term to long-term memory. The diagram also connects the literature review for hypothesis 2—the concepts of metacognition and learning strategies—to the schema literature introduced in hypothesis 1. The control function of metacognition is cognitive learning strategies, the tools learners use to make sense of new information and organize it for better storage in long-term memory, or a schema.

Feedback from Building Bridges will inform the instructor if students have successfully connected point A (previous lesson) to point B (today's lesson), or if they have missed point A altogether and some review is in order. The process of completing the Building Bridges CAT should encourage students to integrate course material into existing knowledge, rather than simply accumulating a semester's worth of discrete facts and principles. The data collected by teachers using this CAT may serve as a catalyst for considering different sequences for presenting course material, for investigating students' organization of new concepts, or for any number of discipline-specific Classroom Research projects.

CLASSROOM
RESEARCH

Explorations for Understanding

Introduction. Although we made a point in Chapter One of differentiating Classroom Research from traditional educational research, some college teachers, especially in the social sciences, are interested in using traditional methods to study questions of interest in their classrooms. Where traditional questions and designs seem relevant, we will present some ideas about them—as much, we admit, to further illustrate the difference between Classroom Research and traditional research as to assist teachers with traditional designs. Thus, the following section on Classroom Research includes further information about traditional research forms and a traditional question and design followed by a Classroom Research question and design.

In their helpful book on traditional research designs, Professors Light, Singer, and Willett (1990) describe three basic forms of traditional scientific inquiry: descriptive, relational, and experimental.

Descriptive Studies. Descriptive studies describe what is. They answer questions like these: How many students have taken a recent course in geometry? How do students rate this instructor? Surveys, a very popular form of inquiry, are usually descriptive. They tell what people think or do, but they do not tell why. A descriptive study to investigate hypothesis 2, concerning Leslie's use of learning strategies, might administer a learning strategies inventory and report the profiles of students in the class. Two such inventory instruments, the Learning and Study Strategies Inventory (LASSI) and the Motivated Strategies for Learning Questionnaire (MSLQ), are described on pages 76–79. Inventories such as these can inform both teacher and students about students' general level of sophistication in the use of learning strategies and, no doubt, just responding to the questions is a useful exercise for making students more aware of how they study. Studies of this type, however, describe the status quo; they do not offer explanations.

Relational Studies. Relational Studies, the second type of traditional research design, examine relationships between two or more things. Do women drop economics more often than men? Do students who have taken a recent course in geometry make higher grades in economics than those who have not? Do students scoring high on the LASSI time management scale make better grades in economics than those scoring low? Relational studies, although offering the potential for more understanding than simple descriptive studies, present a problem of causation versus correlation. In our earlier discussion of the use of a traditional design to investigate hypothesis 1, we showed how the researcher might determine whether students who have taken a recent course in geometry make higher grades in economics than students without such a background. A positive finding here, however, does not "prove" that a background in geometry is responsible for, or "caused," a higher grade in economics.

Some relationships appear so logical it is tempting to conclude a causal relationship. If, for example, a teacher using the LASSI in a traditional relational study discovers that people who score high on the time management scale do indeed make higher grades in economics, it would seem logical to conclude that better management of time results in better grades. Nevertheless, alternative explanations always exist in relational studies. Maybe smart people make good grades in economics and also score high on the LASSI time management scale. Thus, general intelligence rather than time management ability could be the causal factor in managing time well *and* in making good grades. The really important question for investigation here is, Knowing that time management is related to good grades, is it possible to teach students time management skills? For that, we need an experimental study.

Experimental Studies. Most teachers are really interested in knowing what *causes* students to perform better. To uncover that, they need to conduct an *experiment*, the third type of traditional research design. An experimental question for investigating hypothesis 2 could be, Can students be taught learning strategies over the course of the semester? Answering this question would involve comparing an experimental group (where the instructor attempted to teach learning strategies) to a control group (similar in all respects to the experimental group, except for the treatment) via criteria for determining whether learning strategies had improved (for example a rise in LASSI scores). This is really a form of evaluation research, and for most classroom teachers is of high interest and high difficulty. In the typical classroom, the numbers of students are small, control groups very difficult to establish, and criteria hard to test. Yet to date, many people purporting to do Classroom Research have tried to evaluate experimental classroom or teaching procedures—often with disappointing results. Or perhaps it would be more accurate to say that the failure to find statistically significant results is disappointing but often unconvincing.

In our view, the often negative findings from attempting traditional research in the classroom setting can do as much harm as good. Experienced teachers who "know" that the class responds well to an approach that the teacher is interested in evaluating, are often unable to prove it. Unfortunately, they then drop their innovative attitude as well as the particular classroom innovation with which they were experimenting. There is really no way, short of repeated replication and refinement of the research measures, to tell whether the research is not sufficiently sensitive to pick up the real merits of the innovation or whether the innovation is really not accomplishing what the teacher hopes—and perhaps believes—it is.

It is difficult to give sensible advice to classroom teachers about whether to trust the research or to trust their experience—especially when the research result is "no significant difference." Often, even when the results are disappointing, information collected in the research will reveal new insights and initiate a cascading series of experiments that will provide the teacher with new ideas about how to improve the innovation. At its best, Classroom Research continues to inform and deepen understandings about the learning process for both teachers and students. Rather than offering a final answer of "no significant differences," a Classroom Research experiment should raise questions. How can the innovation be made more effective? What are the research problems that may need more attention? How good were the measures and criteria used in the research? Are better measures available? What new data should be collected to make the results of the research clearer?

The three basic types of traditional research designs just described dominate the research literature on learning. Descriptive research designs are perhaps the most prevalent of all. Moreover, the descriptions frequently involve the use of unalterable variables— variables that educators can do nothing to change, such as race, gender, age, and the like (Bloom, 1980). These variables are often overused because they are easy to measure and they are useful in suggesting policy decisions. But they are not very helpful for teachers who must deal with individuals or classroom situations. Indeed, the results of such research may lead to stereotyping; that is, a given woman may be assumed to have a learning style that is characteristic of most women but that in fact is not characteristic of her.

Classroom Research Questions. The criterion for useful Classroom Research is that it help teachers and students *understand* the learning process. And of course, it should be do-able by discipline-oriented classroom teachers working with their students in their own classrooms. Because hypothesis 2 is heavily dependent on student attitudes and motivation, it might initiate a Classroom Research project that could involve students in carrying out the research, enabling both teacher and students to better understand the learning process.

For example, data from students' Diagnostic Learning Logs (see page 67) might be used in the following way (just once or twice a semester) in a Classroom Research design. A homework assignment that also called on students for self-analysis of the strategies they used in completing the assignment would be carefully prepared. The questions the self-analysis would ask are shown in Exhibit 2.1. The teacher would prepare a tabulation of the responses, and together teacher and students would analyze the data. How well was the purpose of the assignment understood? Where did misunderstandings occur? What did students consider successful responses and why? Are there some common themes in these successful responses? Where were errors made? Are they common errors? To the extent that the assignment is typical or recurring, students will be interested in knowing how others are responding to it, and the project itself is both a teaching technique and a descriptive study of the processes that are being used by students in the class.

Note that this design starts out fitting the definition of a traditional descriptive study; it tells how students responded to a questionnaire about a given assignment. But instead of stopping with the tabulation of data (for example, "42 percent of the students misunderstood question 3"), as traditional research typically would, the Classroom Research design goes beyond the basic results through its ability to explain and teach as well as to describe. It tells not only how many students had a particular kind of trouble, but it also gives both teacher and students an opportunity to discover why the teaching and learning problem occurred. In this way, the method is more like the currently popular focus groups often used in marketing studies to determine how (and why) people respond to a given product or candidate as they do.

Even though this type of design does not conform to many people's stereotypes about research, it meets the critically important requirements of Classroom Research. It involves and informs teachers and students about the learning that is relevant to that class and subject matter.

The question with respect to hypothesis 2 that is probably of most interest to classroom teachers is whether learning strategies can be taught. As mentioned earlier, cognitive psychologists McKeachie at Michigan and Weinstein at the University of Texas, among others, have taught freshman courses designed to help students develop more effective study skills. In general, the research indicates that such strategies can be taught effectively and that students' uses of cognitive strategies is related to academic achievement (Pintrich, 1988a; Weinstein, 1988). There is, however, some question about which strategies work best for which disciplines or for which goals.

Teachers who have hunches about learning strategies that work in their class or discipline might consider conducting a Classroom Research project that converts present knowledge about learning strategies into practice while also contributing to better understanding for both teacher and students of how learning strategies work. Dansereau (1988) describes several experiments in which students worked in pairs or dyads under different instructions. One experiment that is both practical and consistent with the high interest today in cooperative learning is designed to study the value of various learning strategies. In experiments of this general type, the class is typically divided into pairs that are then divided into two or three treatment groups plus a control group whose members simply study as they usually do. Members of one treatment group, consisting of any number of student pairs, might be told to study a given concept or reading with the idea that they would be expected to make an oral presentation. Another group might be told that they were to study with the expectation of answering a multiple-choice test. Still another group might serve as the control and be given no specific instructions for how to approach the task.

Clearly there are many variations on this theme, and any number of learning strategies can be taught and tested. In the pairs operating under the instructions to prepare for an oral report, for example, the expectation is that they will be practicing the learning strategy of elaboration, or putting into their own words their understanding of a concept, so that they can explain it to others. In contrast, the pairs working under instructions to prepare for an objective test might be expected to work quite differently, challenging one another with factual questions, memorization, the clustering of terms, and the like.

The criteria chosen to define effective learning are important in this type of Classroom Research, because the underlying assumption is that certain strategies work best for certain objectives. For the previous example, the criteria might be both an oral presentation and an objective test. The question for research is, Did instructions about study strategies make a difference in performance? Specifically, Were the strategies used specific to the task? However, instructors may find more than one-to-one correspondences. For example, it could be that the elaboration strategies called for in preparation for an oral report resulted in deeper understandings that also served students well in test performance.

Criteria will vary depending on the research question. They might include performance on various types of tests or parts of tests (for example essay versus definition questions). They might include student reactions to the helpfulness of various approaches, or long-term versus short-term retention (for example, how do students perform immediately after receiving some information compared to at the time of the final exam), or scores on a learning strategies inventory.

Although these experiments fall in the general category of traditional research, their exact classification depends on how they are carried out and what is done with the results. In traditional research, where the purpose is to advance knowledge and to publish the results, the researcher would have to be careful about the replicability of instructions and group assignments, control groups, significance of group difference, and criteria. In Classroom Research, where the purpose is to advance learning, students would have to be considered partners in the research, feedback and discussion of the results would be assumed, and publication (if it occurred at all) would be in a journal related to teaching rather than to the advancement of research in the academic discipline.

Finally because considerable research has been done recently on learning strategies, there are some good professionally developed learning inventories available, which ask students to report on the learning strategies they use, their motivation for study, test anxiety, and the like. Two of these instruments, the Learning and Study Strategies Inventory (LASSI) and the Motivated Strategies for Learning Questionnaire (MSLQ), have been used in research on college students.

The LASSI is a self-report instrument designed by Weinstein (1988) to measure students' use of learning strategies. It has ten scales: Anxiety, Attitude, Concentration, Information Processing, Motivation, Time Management, Selecting the Main Idea, Self-Testing, Study Aids, and Test Strategies. The Anxiety scale, for example, contains items about the degree to which worry about performance interferes with student learning. A sample item on the Anxiety scale is, "Even when I'm well prepared for the test, I feel very anxious." The LASSI Concentration scale contains items such as, "I often find I have been reading but don't know what it was all about." The Self-Testing scale addresses whether students monitor their learning as they go along: for example, "I seldom review except just before tests." The LASSI is designed for use by researchers and also college teachers, counselors, and others who work with college learners.

The Motivated Strategies for Learning Questionnaire (MSLQ) is another self-report instrument that practitioners can use to assess students' use of learning strategies. Developed at the National Center for Research to Improve Postsecondary Teaching and Learning (NCRIPTAL) by Pintrich, Smith, Garcia, and Mc-Keachie (1991), the MSLQ was tested over five years on students at a public university, a liberal arts college, and a community college.

The MSLQ is an instrument with two main sections, one on motivation and one on learning strategies. Within each of the two sections are a variety of scales that can be combined according to the needs of the researcher or teacher. The motivation section has scales that cover intrinsic goal orientation, extrinsic goal orientation, task value, control beliefs, self-efficacy, and test anxiety. The learning strategy section has scales that cover rehearsal strategies, elaboration strategies, organization strategies, critical thinking, metacognitive self-regulation, time and study management, effort management, and help-seeking behavior.

Items on the MSLQ ask students to rate the various descriptions of learning strategy behaviors on a seven-point Likert scale (an attitude scale in which each attitude is assigned a different number value for scoring purposes) ranging from "not at all true of me" to "very true of me." The scales in the learning strategy section include items such as, "I make simple charts, diagrams, or tables to help me organize course material" (organization); "When I study for this class, I practice saying the material to myself over and over" (rehearsal); and "I ask myself questions to make sure I understand the material I have been studying in this class" (metacognitive self-regulation).

Steadman (1994) administered the MSLQ as a pre- and posttest to several classes of community college students in an effort to measure change in students' use of learning strategies as a result of their teachers' use of Classroom Assessment. Although it was difficult to demonstrate statistically significant gains in learning strategy use with small samples (class sizes were around thirty students) over a short time period (three months), the instrument was useful for compiling a picture of the types of strategies used and not used by students in each class. Moreover, the students who took part in the research had their eyes opened to the variety of learning strategies available to them. Several students asked if they could keep the questionnaire to share with their friends.

Beyond allowing students to keep the questionnaire, the developers of the MSLQ recommend sharing with students feedback on their responses to the instrument. A sample individual feedback form is included in the MSLQ manual (Pintrich, Smith, Garcia, and McKeachie, 1991). The form includes a rating of the student's scores on each scale with instructions for interpreting the score. In addition, it defines each strategy type and suggests how students can improve strategy use in each area. For example, it explains that the rehearsal scale measures how often students use such strategies as rereading course notes and memorizing lists of key words and concepts, and it suggests ways they can improve their use of rehearsal strategies: for example, by listing important terms, organizing their lists into closely related items, and making up test items to measure their recall. In Steadman's research, following the posttest administration of the MSLQ, each student participant received a copy of the feedback form and attended a mini-workshop on learning strategies.

The MSLQ and other instruments of this type provide faculty and students alike with a categorization of learning skills and strategies that enhance learning. When they are part of a Classroom Research project, these instruments can be used by faculty as diagnostic tools (pretest only) to identify potential areas of weakness among students in the class. For example, if an instrument indicates a specific problem, say high levels of test anxiety, the teacher can use this information by taking steps at exam time to reduce student anxiety. If results indicate a general problem, say low use of metacognitive strategies among students in a class, the instructor might take some time in class to explain and model use of these strategies.

Some faculty may be interested in using these instruments to test a hypothesis about whether an experimental treatment reduces anxiety or increases the use of metacognitive strategies. In this type of research, judging results by self-reports may be suspect. Students in the classroom would (and should) know the purpose of the experiment and would no doubt try to cooperate by answering the questions in the "correct" way, that is, to say that the teacher who had tried to help them was successful. In this type of Classroom Research project, faculty need to be conservative in their interpretation of the results. Other teachers may find it interesting to seek out *relationships* between variables such as students' scores on learning strategy instruments and their final grades, for example. This type of Classroom Research project raises problems of confidentiality and unintentional bias. When instruments like the

LASSI or MSLQ are used in Classroom Research projects, we recommend that each student select a personal number and use that to identify his or her completed learning strategy instrument. That way, students can receive feedback on their scores and still remain anonymous.

In short, even though many learning strategy instruments were developed for use by traditional educational psychologists, the instruments described here are appropriate for Classroom Researchers as a starting point for investigating how their students learn.

Ordering Information for Learning Strategy Instruments. The LASSI (Learning and Study Strategies Inventory) may be ordered from H & H Publishing Company, 1231 Kapp Drive, Clearwater, FL 34525; telephone: 1–800–366–4079.

The MSLQ (Motivated Strategies for Learning Questionnaire) may be ordered from its author: Paul R. Pintrich, 1400 School of Education, University of Michigan, Ann Arbor, MI 48109.

INVESTIGATING HYPOTHESIS 3

Leslie Lacks Confidence in Her Ability to Do Well in Economics.

REVIEWING
THE LITERATURE

What Do We Know from Research and Theory About Student Confidence and Motivation?

Introduction. Our final hypothesis in this case is that Leslie *lacks self-confidence* in her ability to make sense of the quantitative aspects of economics and that she is therefore not motivated to persist in the class. Most teachers would find little on the surface of this case to suggest problems of motivation. After all, Leslie is working hard—perhaps even too hard—and she is conscientious about wanting to learn. Leslie is "intelligent and willing to work," but she still wants to drop economics. Nevertheless, the current work on motivation theory may shed some light on Leslie's decision to drop the course.

There are many theories of academic motivation, and most involve the premise that a lack of self-confidence leads to an unwillingness to try, that is, to a lack of motivation. Most cognitive theories of motivation hold that if people do not believe they can do something or learn something, they are unwilling to take the risk that trying and failing will pose to their self-esteem.

Three motivational theories appear relevant to this discussion of the Leslie case: self-efficacy theory, attribution theory, and self-worth theory. Although these theories cover common terrain, it is useful to touch on each one individually while covering the landscape of motivational literature.[4]

Self-Efficacy Theory. Self-efficacy models of motivation suggest that students' *beliefs* about their ability to succeed at a learning task are more important than their actual skill levels or the difficulty of the task (Bandura, 1977, 1982; Corno and Mandinach, 1983). Think, for example, of a child learning to ride a two-wheeler who may believe he can balance the bike only when his mother is holding on to the back of the seat. When she lets go of the bike without his knowledge, he pedals along perfectly, but whenever he realizes that she is no longer holding on, he loses his balance and falls over.

Self-efficacy models of motivation take on the puzzle of students who have adequate intelligence or skills but insufficient confidence in their ability to succeed at certain learning tasks.

Moreover, learners' beliefs about ability and expectations for performance may differ across situations (Corno and Mandinach, 1983; McKeachie, Pintrich, Lin, and Smith, 1986). For example, Leslie is confident of her ability to succeed in French but not in economics. Thus, she is likely to devote more productive effort to her French class. Self-efficacy models also posit that motivation will increase when learning tasks are interesting or important to the learner (Corno and Mandinach, 1983). Leslie's lower level of motivation in economics may exist because she perceives economics as less relevant to her interests and future goals than her other studies, and as less compatible with her language talents than her minor in French. Her motivation to pursue this course might be enhanced if the professor could succeed in helping her see the importance of economics in everyday life or in her understanding of international affairs, which would be valuable knowledge if she aspired to be, say, a United Nations translator.

Self-efficacy views of motivation make it clear that high ability and high motivation do not necessarily go hand in hand. Dweck and Bempechat (1983) suggest that individuals' implicit theories of intelligence, that is, whether they view intelligence as a characteristic that can be developed or as a permanent fixed trait, may account for their differing learning approaches, ranging from determination to dread, when confronted with cognitive challenges. Some students view intelligence as a stable you-either-have-it-or-you-don't trait that can be accurately judged by others. Dweck and Bempechat describe these students as having an "entity" theory of intelligence. Old notions of IQ (intelligence quotient) come from this view, which suggests that A students are those with high IQs but that those "born with" low IQs cannot do much to improve their grades. Students who believe that intelligence is a fixed entity are concerned about performing well on learning tasks and appearing "smart" to teachers and fellow students in order to be judged intelligent. These students often chose easy tasks that they are confident they can perform successfully.

Conversely, other learners believe that intelligence consists of an "ever expanding repertoire of skills and knowledge" that can be increased through effort (Dweck and Bempechat, 1983, p. 244). These students are said to have an "incremental" view of intelligence that motivates them to take on challenges to increase their skills and knowledge. They are characterized as having "mastery-oriented" patterns of motivation; they are learners who do not give up when the going gets tough (Dweck and Leggett, 1988), in contrast to the "entity" learners who are motivated toward "performance" goals, that is, toward performing well on easy tasks in order to avoid looking stupid. (Additional discussion of mastery and performance goals for learning is included in the review of the literature for hypothesis 2 of the Captive Audience case discussed in Chapter Three.)

Although motivational theorists tend to describe "people" or "personalities" with given motivational characteristics, motivation is usually situational. Leslie, for example, is not so much a failure-threatened person as she is a person who finds herself in a failure-threatening situation. Thus, in this situation (economics class), she plows through the assignments looking for performance-oriented "right" answers rather than for opportunities to improve her learning and increase her understanding.

Attribution Theory. Students' confidence in their ability to learn is also central to attribution models of motivation (Weiner, 1979, 1985, 1986). Attribution theory, as its name implies, suggests that students *attribute* success or failure to one or more things—ability, effort, luck, fatigue, an easy exam or a hard one, and the like. According to attribution theory, students' beliefs about their ability to succeed in a learning task are based on their perceptions of why they have succeeded in the past. Students who attribute success to factors that they feel they can depend on, such as their own ability, are likely to have more confidence in their future achievement than students who attribute success to unstable external conditions such as good luck or an easy test.

There are three important dimensions of attributions for success or failure: locus, stability, and controllability (Weiner, 1985). *Locus* refers to whether the cause for achievement or failure was internal or external to the learner. In Leslie's case, the locus is internal when she blames her failure in economics on her lack of ability in math rather than on external causes such as poor teaching by the professor or the difficulty of the exams. She explains to the teacher that "her Dad had always joked about the fact that math and she were not meant for each other," and that "her math SAT was not too hot."

Stability, the second dimension of attribution for success or failure, refers to whether the attributed cause is considered permanent or temporary. Ability, for example, is often perceived as stable, that is, not easily changed; whereas effort is easily modified and may vary from day to day. Indeed, students reflect this aspect of attribution theory when they say, for example, "I would have done better on the test if I had studied harder." As we shall show later, the assumed stability of personal ability—bright or not so bright—can be very threatening to self-concept and self confidence.

This brings up *controllability*, the third dimension of attribution, which refers to the power of the learner to influence success or failure. Effort, for example, is usually considered under the learner's control, whereas fatigue and task difficulty are not. In Leslie's case, she can control the amount of effort she puts into study for the economics class, but she cannot control the questions asked on the exams or the amount of math required. Thus, she feels powerless to deal competently with economics because her math ability (with an internal locus but not under her control—at least not until she decides to take steps to improve her math skills) is inadequate to give her a feeling of control over the perceived difficulty of the learning task.

Self-Worth Models. Self-worth models of motivation explain how students in competitive academic environments attempt to preserve their sense of self-worth, which is based in large part on self-perceived ability. Students who do well in the competition of the classroom feel good about themselves, whereas students who do poorly must question either their ability or their effort. And most students would rather question—and have others question—their effort than their ability. To be thought smart is a source of status and prestige to students; most students would rather be thought lazy than dumb (Brown and Weiner, 1984). In addition, Covington (1993) observes a conflict between teachers' and students' values. Teachers value and reward effort and success that is achieved through effort. However, it is risky for students to expend a great deal of effort when faced with low probability for success in an academic endeavor. This is because the implication of trying hard and failing is low ability.

The different ways students perceive failure result in different emotions. Failure attributed to lack of ability leads to feelings of shame, whereas failure attributed to lack of effort leads to feelings of guilt. Thus, effort may be a "double-edged sword" (Covington and Omelich, 1979). If students fail after putting forth the effort, they experience feelings of shame; if they fail because of lack of effort, they feel guilt.

Again, one way to avoid the shame that comes from failing due to lack of ability is to not try very hard or to procrastinate. If a student fails without trying, then he or she has a ready excuse, and failure is not necessarily attributed to low ability. And if a student manages to do well on learning task with little time or effort devoted to it, then he or she will appear to have high ability.

Another way to avoid failure is to select a very easy task. Despite the fact that a simple task may not be very interesting or rewarding, it does not carry the same risk of failure as other tasks and is therefore less threatening to a student's sense of self-worth. Heavy involvement in extracurricular activities is another, often acceptable, way of avoiding damage to self-worth by failure in the classroom (Covington, 1993). Very busy students may actually experience enhanced self-esteem through receiving recognition for participation in student activities while also possessing a ready excuse for failure to achieve academically.

The experience of failure is most damaging when it is attributed to low intelligence. In Leslie's case, she attributes failure in economics not to lack of intelligence but rather to lack of math ability, and her success in her other courses may help her maintain a positive self-concept even though she tried hard but did poorly in economics. But Leslie is still not prepared to deal with failure; she comments that she is dropping the class because she cannot take the chance of getting a D. This behavior makes sense based on Covington's view that "academic achievement is best understood in terms of students attempting to maintain a positive image of their own ability, especially when risking failure" (1989, p. 88).

In his studies of college students, Covington (1993) found four different typical patterns among students dealing with academic achievement and the threat of failure: success-oriented, overstriving, failure-avoiding, and failure-accepting. *Success-oriented* students enjoy learning for learning's sake—they want to perform well and usually do, and their perception of themselves as successful students with high ability remains intact even in the event of occasional failure. Because success-oriented students have succeeded at challenging assignments in the past, they are confident about their ability, and they can write off occasional failures as bad luck or the result of extremely difficult tasks. Success-oriented students study enough but not too much, and they usually do not experience anxiety associated with academic work.

Overstrivers, although they may have high GPAs, are never entirely confident in their ability to succeed. They strive for higher levels of achievement in order to prove their ability to themselves and others. Although overstrivers tend to have a repertoire of learning strategies that prepare them well for learning tasks, they spend a great deal of time studying, and they may experience high levels of anxiety that each new learning task will be the one that will expose them as being less able than they have appeared to date.

Failure-avoiders, like overstrivers, suffer anxiety as they struggle to avoid failure, but they are not always so successful. They may study, but without applying effective study skills. Failure-avoiders escape putting themselves to the test by avoiding challenges that pose a risk of failure. Thus, they end up missing out on many interesting opportunities. Overstrivers are trying to prove that they are the best, whereas failure-avoiders are just trying to prove they are not the worst.

Finally, *failure-accepting* students have given up trying, and are neither satisfied with success nor dissatisfied with failure. "These students appear to have given up on the pursuit of academic rewards and have resigned themselves to academic failure as a way of life. . . . They express little pride in their successes, but neither do they express much shame in the event of failure" (Covington, 1989, p. 93). Failure-accepting students rarely visit faculty during office hours, and they lack both the study skills and the motivation to apply themselves. In contrast, overstrivers huddle by the professor's door awaiting the posting of test grades and quibble over scoring increases when they already have earned an A. Failure-accepting students may not even bother to check the grade posting.

Leslie does not fit neatly into any single one of these four categories. Her copying "reams of notes" resembles overstriving, and her decision to drop economics might be perceived as failure avoiding, but her promise to work on her math skills and reenroll in economics suggests a success-oriented approach.

Conclusion. Having reviewed several major theories of motivation, can we summarize Leslie's situation? Academic motivation was described as being generally task specific, except when failure sweeps across the board and students eventually become failure accepting. Leslie appears to lack confidence primarily in the area of quantitative skills, but that does not affect her confidence in other areas. She is frank in her discussion with her professor about her problem in economics and does not attempt to make excuses for her lack of preparation in math. In fact, Leslie's lack of motivation to stick with the class may be quite realistic if she is lacking the math skills to understand the new material.

Leslie's professor recognizes the importance of students' beliefs in their ability to succeed if they work at it. He tries to boost Leslie's confidence by explaining that she can succeed in economics as she has done in her upper-level French courses because learning economics, like learning foreign languages, "just takes faith in yourself and practice." Leslie, however, still perceives math as harder to learn than French, even though her professor points out that math does not have as many exceptions and idioms. Perceived task difficulty, which influences students' expectations for success or failure, is an additional element of the motivational theories reviewed here.

One of the criticisms of current research on motivation is that it has been typically conducted in laboratories with volunteers participating in contrived activities rather than in schools with students engaging in compulsory learning tasks (see, for example, Brophy, 1987; Corno and Mandinach, 1983; Eccles, 1983; Pintrich, Cross, Kozma, and McKeachie, 1986). Classroom Research allows instructors to investigate the motivational issues faced by students like Leslie and to test the validity of current motivational models within the context of the college classroom.

RECOMMENDED READING

Motivational Theory

Corno, L., and Mandinach, E. B. "The Role of Cognitive Engagement in Classroom Learning and Motivation." *Educational Psychologist*, 1983, *18*(2), 88–108.

This article both reviews contemporary models of academic motivation and presents a model of cognitive engagement (referred to as self-regulated learning). The authors consider research and theories about motivation and self-regulated learning with explicit concern for the context of classroom, and they include a discussion of features of instruction that may positively or negatively influence learning. Although this article is written for an audience with background in educational psychology, teachers may appreciate its recommendations for instruction that fosters cognitive engagement.

Covington, M. V. "A Motivational Analysis of Academic Life in College." In J. C. Smart (ed.), *Higher Education: Handbook of Theory and Research.* Vol. 9. New York: Agathon Press, 1993.

In a readable style that should appeal to college teachers in all disciplines, Covington reviews past work on motivation with a focus on applications for college learners. Much of the chapter addresses his Self-Worth theory of motivation, including his research on college students. His findings are likely to hit home with college teachers, who will recognize the student motivational patterns he describes. The chapter concludes with explicit guidelines for fostering motivation, including the use of engaging tasks, sufficient reinforcers, and success-oriented assessment. For a classic article on research with college students, see also: Covington, M. V., and Omelich, C. L. "Effort: The Double-Edged Sword in School Achievement." *Journal of Educational Psychology,* 1979, 71(2), 169–182.

McKeachie, W. J., Pintrich, P. R., Lin, Y.-G., and Smith, D.A.F. *Teaching and Learning in the College Classroom: A Review of the Research Literature.* Ann Arbor: National Center for Research to Improve Postsecondary Teaching and Learning, University of Michigan, 1986.

In Chapter Four, McKeachie and his colleagues provide an introduction to the literature on motivation, organizing existing theory into a comprehensive model. They describe the seven components of an Expectancy-Value model (student goal orientation, expectancy for success, perceived task difficulty, and so forth), using existing literature from a variety of theoretical perspectives. This chapter, intended for a higher education audience with some psychology background, provides a good overview and an expansive bibliography for readers wishing to branch out into further literature.

McMillan, J. H., and Forsyth, D. R. "What Theories of Motivation Say About Why Learners Learn." In R. J. Menges and M. D. Svinicki (eds.), *College Teaching: From Theory to Practice.* New Directions for Teaching and Learning, no. 45. San Francisco: Jossey-Bass, 1991.

McMillan and Forsyth synthesize self-efficacy, attribution, self-worth, and need-based theories of motivation to form a useful heuristic model of students' motivation to learn in college. Their chapter is written for a practitioner audience, with references that will prove useful to faculty who wish to read in-depth original sources on particular motivational issues.

CLASSROOM
ASSESSMENT

Collecting Further Information

Introduction. The review of the literature on motivation shows that students' confidence in their ability to succeed in an academic task plays an important role in the effort and motivation they put forth. Therefore, Classroom Assessment might be used to gather information about students' past successful and not-so-successful learning experiences and about their self-confidence and beliefs about their ability in a particular academic domain.

Example 1: Course-Related Self-Confidence Surveys. (See CAT 32 in Angelo and Cross, 1993, pp. 275–279.) The Leslies case provides a good example of a student who has no basic problem with self-esteem. She does, however, lack self-confidence in her ability to perform well in quantitative subjects. A Course-Related Self-Confidence Survey may be constructed as a simple form asking students to rate their self-perceived confidence in specific topics related to the course. Rather than asking how students feel about their ability to deal with mathematical concepts in general, the goal here would be to develop a survey that specified certain mathematical operations important in economics. For example, the instructor might ask about levels of confidence in interpreting graphs, in constructing graphs, in solving algebraic equations, and the like. It is also helpful to illustrate each operation with an example. Five to ten skills categories might be described, along with several levels of confidence (for example, low, medium, and high).

Some students might show a pattern of low self-confidence across the board in math skills while others show high confidence in dealing with quantitative analyses. The most interesting data, however, will come from looking at specific skills checked by large numbers of students. These data have implications not only for the individual instructor but for the Department of Economics and perhaps for the Department of Mathematics as well. If, for example, large numbers of students lack confidence in their ability to construct graphs showing relationships between variables, then the question is, Where should they learn that skill?

Example 2: Focused Autobiographical Sketches. (See CAT 33 in Angelo and Cross, 1993, pp. 281–284.) To determine prospective students' motivations for attending a college, admissions officers frequently require them to submit an autobiographical sketch. It is assumed that students with good reasons for attending will have high motivation and will thus succeed at the college. The Focused Autobiographical Sketch is a shorter, more specific version of this rough measure of motivation.

Because research and theories about motivation show a strong relationship between past learning success and willingness to take the risk that learning something new always involves, it is relevant to try to understand students' past experiences with tasks or events important to the course. In the instance of Leslie's economics course, students might be asked to write about a math course in high school that they felt especially good or bad about. Or they might be asked to write about the experiences that entered into their decision about a college major—or why they chose the course of study they followed in high school. Clearly, this type of extended open-ended CAT works best with small classes; it is time consuming to write and to analyze.

Such student essays are inevitably revealing to teachers who may never have had difficulties learning their subject matter—or more likely, have forgotten how intimidating new concepts and a new vocabulary can be. Autobiographical sketches also give students an opportunity to reflect on their learning experiences and to gain in self-understanding.

Once again, however, we caution teachers to carefully explain the reason for the assignment, to assure anonymity, and to inform students how the sketches will be used. Some teachers, we have found, overestimate the level of trust between students and teacher and feel that anonymity is not a necessary condition for accurate and useful Classroom Assessment. Granted, in many cases, they are right. Many students are willing, even eager, to have a teacher show interest in their self-analyses. But it is also the case that most students have learned, over years of experience, to court a teacher's approval. Both the accuracy of the data and their analytic usefulness are compromised if students feel they are providing information that reveals their personal weaknesses in the academic arena.

Exhibit 2.2 contains an example of instructions for a Focused Autobiographical Sketch that might be used by a teacher in any course that requires some math background.

Exhibit 2.2.
Sample Instructions for Focused Autobiographical Sketch.

Autobiographical Sketch

Instructions to students. In one or two pages describe what stand out in your mind as significant positive and negative experiences in the way you learned math over the course of your schooling. Have your parents, friends, or teachers shaped your attitudes toward math in any way? How do you think your previous math education has prepared you for this course?

Here is a sample Focused Autobiographical Sketch from a student like Leslie.

My earliest memories of math are of first-grade workbooks in which it was possible to add and subtract apples and oranges. Math was all drill, not understanding, with worksheet upon worksheet to complete, and flash cards to practice each evening at home. Second grade was a turning point—I met and loved Roman Numerals! They were so much fun—like a foreign language or a secret code—and they were closer to letters than numbers! I was the best in my class in Roman Numerals, and got through all the worksheets a week before the rest of the class. My teacher provided me with some "advanced" Roman Numeral worksheets, but once I had completed them, she wasn't able to find anything else for me to do but return to regular math worksheets. Math was all downhill from there. I remember when I missed school with chicken pox or was visiting my grandparents, I had hundreds of make-up worksheets to do.

Because I moved in the eighth grade, I missed out on being selected for advanced math, although I was in advanced English, chemistry, and French. It was really different being in the "regular" math class, where the teacher's and the other kids' expectations weren't so high. Elementary school math had been so easy—I liked to be the first one finished with worksheets so I could go read on the beanbag chairs. When I got to high school, I did not have the patience for the long word problems and "solving for X" equations that came up in algebra. We only got three or four problems for homework, but it could take forever. I quickly figured out that Mr. Browning, our algebra teacher, modeled his homework after problems in the book, just changing letters and numbers here and there. I soon learned how to get the right answer without having to think too hard. Geometry the next year was the same way—as long as you memorized the proofs, you never really had to understand anything to do well on the quizzes and the mandatory state exam at the end of the year.

I almost took business math in the spring semester of my senior year because I was already accepted (early decision) to my first-choice college and I was taking four AP classes—in French, Spanish, English, and History. But Mrs. Arnold, the most interesting and fun math teacher I ever had, wouldn't let me wimp out. She encouraged me to enroll in pre-calculus with Miss Gelling, a brilliant and a little bit scary white-haired mathematician and scientist. The class was so hard, but she wouldn't let you flake out. When I got a D on the midterm, she suggested a peer tutor. Well, then I experienced the ultimate humiliation of having Drew Martin, the friendly but somewhat condescending future valedictorian, be my tutor. I had to sit with him and my pre-calc textbook in full view of the rest of the senior class in the cafeteria. It wasn't cool for girls at my high school to be too smart, and it also wasn't too cool to hang out with a tutor during free periods.

I survived pre-calc and placed out of math when I got here because upper-level math is not required for my major. The only math I do now is like adding up the phone bill with my roommates. My mom couldn't even figure out the tip on a bill, and my dad used to joke about the lack of a "math gene" in women. But it's not very funny, because I had a terrible time writing up my bio labs, and I had no clue about the statistical charts in the Psych. 101 book. I already bought the text for this class and am a little freaked out by all the graphs. It looks like Greek to me.

This sample autobiographical sketch brings to light several of the issues that Leslie's professor discussed with his colleague via e-mail. First, we learn that Leslie's past experiences in math class taught her that she could find the right answers without really understanding the material. Furthermore, her lack of solid math knowledge has caused her problems in other college classes. In addition, her autobiographical sketch confirms her professor's suspicion that she has been influenced by peer and parental attitudes toward women and math ability. Clearly, the data and insights from Focused Autobiographical Sketches may provide a rich starting point for Classroom Research projects.

CLASSROOM
RESEARCH

Explorations for Understanding

Classroom Research Designs. A promising opportunity for Classroom Research might consist of turning the Focused Autobiographical Sketch into a Classroom Research project. CATs like the Autobiographical Sketch exist on the narrow edge between Classroom Assessment and Classroom Research. One can learn a great deal by simply looking at the results of an autobiographical sketch and gaining an understanding of how students perceive themselves as learners in a defined situation. But a Classroom Researcher might wish to work with the data more extensively by coding the material in the autobiographical sketch to correspond to some hypothesis. For example, if the instructor in the Leslie case thought that gender played an important role in students' motivation to succeed in economics, he might wish to locate all references to gender in the autobiographical sketches (Leslie's father's perception of women as not suited for math, for example). If he were interested in other motivational factors, he might look for references to locus of control, threats to self-worth, or the value of the course to the student. CATs often raise questions for further investigation, and many can be pursued as Classroom Research by the refinement of the data collected in the CAT.

Yet another Classroom Research project, somewhat more difficult to implement but promising high returns, is to conduct an experimental study that builds on research already reported. For example, there is every reason in this case to hypothesize that Leslie's motivational problems are not pervasive in her personality but rather apply primarily to her performance in economics.

Research on the effectiveness of mastery learning and certain individualized, self-paced methods of instruction is now compelling. Over and over again, and over twenty years or more of research, traditional researchers have shown the superiority of certain individualized instructional approaches in enhancing subject matter learning over more traditional instructional formats such as lecture and recitation methods (Cross, 1976, chap. 4; Terenzini and Pascarella, 1994). The reasons these methods are superior are solidly based in both cognitive and motivational theory. Mastery learning emphasizes the importance of prerequisite knowledge; students are not permitted to go on to the next unit until they have mastered the prior one. And mastery learning implements motivational theory by permitting students to prove to themselves that they can learn through their own efforts (high control plus internal locus).

Thus, an important experimental study might involve offering a self-paced, individualized form of the course as an option to students who need to go at their own pace in mastering learning modules in sequence but who possess generally adequate academic self-confidence in other areas. Could the Leslies of the world succeed in this option? Past research suggests that it would be an option well worth the effort, and this type of experimental research would show whether it would succeed with students like Leslie. Although the research itself is not complicated; the design of an appropriate self-paced module calls for a high degree of analysis and experience. If for example, Leslie's problem is specific and confined to a lack of skill in interpreting and constructing graphs, would a self-paced module on graphs be of sufficient help to her and students like her to justify the creation of the module—taking into consideration that such a module could be of potential benefit to thousands of students in hundreds of economics courses throughout the nation?

By definition, a Classroom Research project must be of value to the students and teachers in a given classroom, but this type of experiment, although starting out as a Classroom Research project, could easily have nationwide implications for improvement in the teaching of economics. This is the type of research that needs the commitment and involvement of discipline-based teachers. Although educational researchers are increasingly likely to tackle learning issues—for example, in the teaching of science and languages—significant progress will be made when college teachers begin to address learning problems in their own areas of academic expertise.

In such research projects, teachers might want to plan continuing interviews with students electing the option of an experimental module, to see where the students run into problems (although teachers must be mindful that a teacher's attention in itself may account for success, which would then not be duplicated when the policy of offering the option was implemented on a wider scale). But monitoring the progress of students pursuing an individualized module would have high value for teachers, regardless of the outcome.

CHAPTER 3

"The Captive Audience"

Learning Issues: Learning Goals;
Deep and Surface Learning;
Student Ratings of Instruction

CASE STUDY

Professor Jean Hastings had found this a particularly tough year teaching her section of introductory physics lab. Of her twenty-four students, the six premeds had been the most negative about the lab activities all year. She thought, Thank God, they're sitting in the back corner of the laboratory so that most of the others don't notice them.

In lab this morning, Jean could see how exasperated one of the premeds, Dana, had become. She and her partner finally got their bulb to light after fumbling around with a battery and wires. The next instruction in the laboratory manual was something about inventing a circuit to keep a string of Christmas tree bulbs lit even if some of them burned out. Dana blurted out in a highly inflected voice: "Inventions? We're not electricians!" A few of the other students in the physics lab chuckled. Seth, who was sitting behind the two women, with folded arms, just leaned further back in his seat and smiled. He and his partners were letting Tim do the wiring at their table. They planned to copy Tim's diagrams into their lab notebooks later and sitting through the weekly labs was damn boring.

Jean dreaded the upcoming end-of-year student evaluations. Each year when the students completed their ratings, there were some who felt that laboratory work was a waste of time. Although

Note: Case study by Priscilla W. Laws, Dickinson College.

the student ratings were anonymous, Jean was certain that most of the dissatisfied students were juniors who were taking physics to gain admission to medical school. She was grateful that many of the underclassmen intending to major in physics and math actually enjoyed the lab work. These younger students were more flexible and creative in the laboratory.

Jean had discussed the typical premed hostility with one of her colleagues. She had told him: "Preparing physics laboratories is hard work. It would be so much easier to exempt the pre-health students from lab and have special lecture courses to prep them for their MCAT examinations." She knew that when course evaluation time came around, this year's crop of premedical students were really going to let her have it. Too bad, because Jean was being considered for promotion to full professor, and she dreaded the thought of the dean and members of the faculty personnel committee seeing the students' ratings.

As she wandered around the lab helping students with their inventions, Jean thought about how rotten the interpersonal chemistry in the lab was this year. Even though last year's lab been overcrowded, there had been excited students sitting in different sections of the room asking questions and stimulating collaboration in their groups. This year, by contrast, was flat. No one seemed very interested in the lab projects.

Dana and her partner sat at their table and tried to cope with their early morning lethargy by drinking coffee from a big thermos. This gave them enough energy to complain about the activities. Lynn would often mutter things like, "This is too hard," or, "I don't see what we're supposed to be getting out of this." Dana didn't just mutter, she often voiced her frustrations loudly, so that the whole class could hear. Jean felt simultaneously angry at Dana and sorry for her. Dana and the other premeds felt they had to have A's, but all of them except Dana seemed reasonably confident about their work. Jean hated to admit it to herself, but Dana seemed too dumb to make the grade in medicine. Dana must be desperate. Was getting into med school her idea or a trip her parents were laying on her? Dana and her partner were using up Jean's office hours every week getting help on problems and lab assignments. On one level, their interest in doing well in physics was encouraging, but it was frustrating working with them because they seemed more concerned about getting right answers than they were in learning the fundamentals that would allow them to grow intellectually. Dana's partner, Lynn, was no ball of fire, but she caught on to the lab activities more rapidly than Dana, who seemed ungrateful for the extra help she was receiving.

The premed men were another story. Jean always liked watching Tim work, he had a quiet competence and seemed to enjoy setting up the observations and discussing them with his partner. Tim's partner was passive, but he did help once in a while. However, Seth was incredibly aggravating. He seemed to be just as capable as Tim, but his open disdain for doing lab work ate at Jean during every lab period. Seth's lab partner just went along and acted bored too. Jean was not surprised after the invention activities to find that all four of the male premeds handed in very similar laboratory notebooks.

That Friday at the faculty club, Jean made a beeline for Sarah Saunders who was teaching the junior physical chemistry course. "I'm having a lot of trouble with your premeds." Sarah seemed interested. "What's the matter?" she asked. Jean unburdened herself. "Dana never thinks for herself. She gets all her answers from her partner, and they both bitch a lot. At least Dana tries to put the answer in her own words. Seth and his partner don't even do that. They let Tim do all the work. Tim's the only one I have any real respect for." "That's funny," said Sarah, "in p-chem, Seth does all the work while Tim and the others just sit around."

At the end of the year, Jean's premonition about the course evaluations was right on. For the most part, the junior premeds were hostile about the lab. She looked at a couple of the responses written in the space provided for "comments" on the course evaluations and tried to guess who wrote them. One of the juniors, whom she suspected was Dana, wrote: "It was discouraging to know that if I didn't like the lab requirement in this course and the format of the teaching of this lab that there was not another lab I could switch to. . . . There needs to be more lecturing. . . . [W]e don't need to do so such much experimenting to derive equations. . . . I need textbook questions with textbook equations to solve anything that's not intuitive. . . . I spent so much time doing out of class work that my other classes suffered and for that I am resentful."

Only one of the juniors was at all positive. Jean decided that it had to be Tim: "I found the lab to be extremely challenging and interesting. New techniques, especially on the computer, were valuable and applicable to other areas of study."

In her first teaching position at a large state college, Jean had complained about the standardized computer-scored rating sheets for faculty evaluation. She believed they were too generic to be relevant to her instruction in a physics laboratory. Besides, she was convinced that course evaluations were inherently biased. She believed that the students who got good grades rated her higher and that the students who did poorly rated her lower. Although she had little faith in the generic computer evaluations, the narrative comments encouraged at the selective small college where she now teaches are even more difficult to face.

Jean has a hard time emotionally when faced with criticism, and she found the ordeal with the premeds devastating. She and her colleagues had put countless hours into designing the new laboratory program. It seemed truly innovative to them. They had worked hard to get a National Science Foundation grant to outfit the laboratory with computers and had written a new curriculum to allow students to participate in a discovery-based approach to learning. Jean had spent hundreds of hours developing new software and hardware to turn the computers into interactive devices for the collection and instant display of data. Assessment of the program showed that most students completing it had a better grasp of fundamental concepts than the previous students. Nevertheless, every year there had been some recalcitrant juniors, and this year had been especially bad.

Jean could not resist talking about the trauma she felt to her colleagues at the summer meeting of the American Association of Physics Teachers. In responding to her, some of them seemed glib. They said things like, "Everybody has a different learning style. Maybe you should back off and let some of the students just do textbook exercises and standard lab projects. They might learn more."

One of her biology colleagues offered another perspective: "I've been teaching premeds for years. Physics is so different. They don't see how mastering it is going to help them be better doctors. Doctors have to make rapid diagnoses based on remembering a lot of well-accepted rules. Premedical students don't see why they should discover everything on their own and reason everything out. It's too tedious. Besides, they think they have to get A's to get into medical school. If your lab is too difficult, it could lower their grade in physics."

By midsummer, when Jean and her colleagues turned their attention to planning next year's lab sequence, she was still full of doubts. Should she have confronted the students at Tim's table about the similarities in their notebooks? Maybe she should have found an effective way to help Dana and her partner. Why hadn't she had the nerve to confront any of them and let them know how distressing their attitudes and behavior had been?

Thinking about how the premeds had behaved made her angry. Physics is not just about doing textbook exercises or following cut-and-dried procedures, she thought. It's about finding out how to approach an investigation. The basis of knowledge in physics is experimental. Why should I exempt students from the laboratory experience just because students dislike it, or because they feel it's not an effective way to learn and it's not tested on the MCAT examination, or because it might lower their grades? She sure hoped Dana wouldn't be following standard procedure mindlessly in the middle of a delicate surgical procedure where something has gone wrong and original thinking is required.

Jean wondered, How can we inspire next year's premeds to learn on our terms and not resent what my colleagues and I have to offer them?

CASE ANALYSIS

This case portrays the exasperation felt by Jean Hastings when her students do not seem to be rising to challenges set forth in a physics lab formatted for discovery learning. The task at hand is a systematic investigation into what has become a problem class for both Jean and her students.

Although this case singled out the premeds as students who are particularly grade conscious and intolerant of ambiguous learning tasks, most faculty have seen these traits in many students. The issues raised here will ring true to faculty who have experienced a less-than-enthusiastic response to their efforts to engage students in challenging assignments that require original thinking.

The resentment and frustration felt by both teacher and students created "rotten . . . interpersonal chemistry" in the classroom. Not only was Jean discouraged that students did not share her enthusiasm for physics in an experimental lab setting, she was concerned that students' negative attitudes would come back to haunt her in the form of poor teaching evaluations. She felt threatened that "this year's crop of premedical students were really going to let her have it." Most teachers have experienced classes that just did not "click," but negative evaluations are particularly distressing to Jean because they will be considered in her upcoming tenure review.

In general, this case presents a conflict between the students' and teacher's notions of what a physics lab should be. The premeds' intent to get through a required course with minimal effort and good grades goes against Jean's desire to offer a challenging, relatively unstructured physics lab.

Using information in the case that suggests plausible explanations for the problems in this class, we formulated three hypotheses for further study. As always, individual readers or faculty groups may generate and investigate additional hypotheses not developed here. Science faculty from other subject areas, for example, may wish to substitute their course for physics and investigate a discipline-specific hypothesis related to this case. The three preliminary hypotheses are as follows:

Hypothesis 1: Some students in this class, particularly the pre-meds, lack motivation for learning physics.

Hypothesis 2: Students are more concerned about getting good grades than about learning physics.

Hypothesis 3: Student ratings of instruction are threatening rather than helpful to Jean.

As in Chapter Two, these hypotheses lead to the next steps in our investigation: a review of relevant teaching and learning literature, the collection of further information via Classroom Assessment, and the development of Classroom Research projects.

INVESTIGATING HYPOTHESIS 1

Some Students in This Class, Particularly the Premeds, Lack Motivation for Learning Physics

REVIEWING
THE LITERATURE

What Do We Know from Research and Theory About Goals and Motivation for Learning?

Introduction. Premed majors are usually characterized as highly motivated students. Why is it that they stand out in Jean's class as insufficiently motivated to thrive in a discovery-learning physics lab? Premeds may lack motivation for learning physics because they do not perceive physics lab as relevant to their educational and career goals.

To expand the analysis of the issues in this hypothesis, the review of the literature will introduce relevant cognitive theories of motivation. The basic premise of cognitive theories of motivation is that motivation is increased when students believe they have the ability to complete an academic task successfully, that the task is worth doing, and that they will be appropriately rewarded if they are successful. (For additional literature on motivational theory, see the recommended reading for hypothesis 3 of the Leslies case, on page 79.)

Intrinsic and Extrinsic Motivation. Although the premed students in this case are portrayed as working hard to get good grades, this does not mean they are highly motivated to learn. Academic motivation means more than striving to get good grades. Students with high levels of academic motivation attempt to understand the material as opposed to learning just enough to "get by" or to make others think they know the material.

One way of addressing the difference between motivation to complete course requirements and motivation to truly understand new material is to distinguish between extrinsic and intrinsic motivation. Intrinsic motivation is what drives learning for the purposes of making meaning and using new information. Extrinsic motivation is what drives learning in order to fulfill requirements, gain rewards, or avoid punishments imposed by others.

McKeachie notes that "one of the major tasks in teaching is not how to scare students into doing their homework, but rather how to nurture their curiosity and to use curiosity as a motive for learning" (1994, p. 350). One purpose of lab courses is to capitalize on the natural curiosity of human beings by presenting experiments or problems to be solved. The discovery-based program that Jean and her colleagues have designed is consistent with the theory that curiosity drives an intrinsic motivation for learning.

Intrinsic motivation is present when a learning experience produces a positive psychological state. For example, some students in Jean's lab are intrinsically motivated by the assignment to design a circuit to light a string of bulbs. The challenge and accomplishment of the task makes them feel good. For other students, however, this task is wearisome and frustrating. Their efforts to design the circuit are driven by extrinsic motivation to get through the lab requirements. Still others will enjoy the lab tasks at the same time that they are striving to get an A. This is to say that intrinsic and extrinsic motivation are not mutually exclusive (Pintrich and Schunk, 1996).

Intrinsic motivation, however, is associated with more intense cognitive engagement in learning than extrinsic motivation supplies (Pintrich and Schunk, 1996). Students like Dana, who attempt to learn course material at only the most surface level, gain less knowledge and generally less enjoyment from the class.

If educators can tap into students' intrinsic motivation, students will become more deeply engaged in their learning. One way to foster students' intrinsic interest in college classes is to help them understand the relevance of the course material. Hodgson (1984) studied the role of relevance among students attending a lecture class. In one experiment, she met with students after class and played a short tape-recorded extract from the lecture. Subjects were to recall their thoughts and actions during the lecture at the time of the recorded extract and to explain why they thought they had responded as they had. Responses in the stimulated recall sessions were coded as reflecting either extrinsic or intrinsic experiences of relevance. Students who were thinking about whether or not the lecture information would be on the exam or how they might use it in an upcoming assignment were described as having an extrinsic experience because they were focusing on external demands. Students who related the lecture content to prior knowledge or experience were described as experiencing intrinsic relevance. Hodgson found that students taking courses they had elected, rather than required courses, were more likely to describe intrinsic experiences of relevance. Also, students with background knowledge in the subject matter experienced more intrinsic relevance. Another interesting feature of Hodgson's work is the concept of vicarious experience of relevance, which occurs when students become engaged in course material because the instructor uses examples and enthusiasm to bring concepts to life. Hodgson found that student comments portraying rich vicarious experiences were difficult to distinguish from comments expressing intrinsic experience of relevance:

Thus, when teachers capture students' attention using enthusiasm and examples, even in subjects that students do not initially find relevant, learners' intrinsic interest may continue to grow, leading to deeper engagement with course content.

Expectancy-Value Theories of Motivation. Expectancy-Value theories of motivation involve two basic factors: learners' beliefs about their ability to succeed at a learning task and the value learners place on the task and its anticipated outcomes. These factors, expectancy and value, interact to positively or negatively influence students' motivation for learning. This cognitive view of motivation, which has dominated the motivational literature since the 1960s provides a useful lens for examining the issues in this case (Atkinson, 1964; Eccles, 1983; Feather, 1982, 1988; Wigfield and Eccles, 1992).

Learners' perceptions of their ability to succeed depends on two factors—their perception of the difficulty of the task and their self-confidence in their own ability to achieve it. Physics courses at most colleges have reputations, deserved or not, of being quite difficult. Lynn's and Dana's lab complaints—"this is too hard"—seem to be uttered before they have even attempted the assigned tasks.

Learners' expectations for success differ across learning situations (Corno and Mandinach, 1983). Students can have generally high confidence in their academic abilities but still hold low expectations for success in certain circumstances. A premed like Dana, for example, might be quite confident in her ability to get high grades in a traditional lab class with textbook problems and solutions to memorize. She lacks confidence, however, in her ability to complete the tasks required in a problem-based physics lab.

Students who have not done well in school in the past have learned to expect failure when they tackle tasks where the outcome is uncertain. Thus, in order to reduce the threat of failure, they tend to be attracted to tasks that are either so easy that the students know they will be successful or so difficult that the students have a legitimate excuse for failure (Atkinson and Litwin, 1960; Atkinson and Feather, 1966; Covington and Omelich, 1991). In contrast, students with high levels of academic self-confidence have learned to expect success and are attracted to tasks with moderate levels of difficulty—tasks that are challenging but realistic.

The *expectancy* in Expectancy-Value theory refers not only to task difficulty and ability but also to expectations for outcomes. Some academic tasks leave students in doubt about their success as learners. Consider first-year premed students enrolled in a large introductory biology course, the type of course often described as "weeding out" less-qualified students from the premed major. Exams in these introductory courses are usually graded on a curve. Although students may study hard and feel confident in their understanding of exam concepts, they may have uncertain expectations for success because each student's grade depends on the performance of other students.

Even if a student expects to perform well, there has to be some *value* to the task (such as the enjoyment of challenging problems) or to the task outcome (such as a high exam grade) in order for the learner to be motivated. Feeling confident is important but not sufficient to engage a learner in a task that is not valued or does not result in a valued outcome. Thus, the value component of Expectancy-Value theory takes into account the relevance of the task and anticipated task outcomes to a learner's goals and values.

Task Value. Academic tasks may be valued for different reasons, including intrinsic value, attainment value, utility value, and cost (Eccles and Wigfield, 1985; Pintrich, 1988b; Wigfield, 1994).

The *intrinsic value* of a task refers to whether or not the activity is inherently interesting to the learner. Premeds who enroll in elective foreign language, political science, or art history courses presumably derive intrinsic value from study in these areas. In the required physics lab, some students may enjoy setting up and conducting the experiments but find writing up the results tedious. Not all learning tasks are inherently fun, but they may still hold worth for their attainment or utility value.

The *attainment value* of a task deals with its contribution to students' feelings of self-worth. Academic tasks that give students a chance to compete and succeed academically offer attainment value. An English major, for example, may not be intrinsically interested in the subject matter of a required physics class nor see any relevance of physics to her career goals. Nevertheless, successfully completing the course offers her attainment value by enhancing her feelings of academic competence and achievement.

Utility value, the third component of task value, arises when completing a task contributes to the achievement of other goals. Although many of the premed majors in this case are not intrinsically interested in the lab assignments, completing the course has utility value to them because physics is a required course for medical school admission. Moreover, the utility value of a learning task does not necessarily have to be academic. For example, students may gain utility value from a class because it gives them an opportunity to spend time with their friends.

The final issue in task value is the *cost* of completing the task. Students are unlikely to undertake a task that requires excessive effort, even if it offers utility and attainment value. If large opportunity costs, such as time taken away from other classes or extracurricular activities, are associated with a task, learners' motivation will also diminish. As one student put it, sometimes "the juice isn't worth the squeeze" (Ames, 1987, p. 143).

The Role of Goals. Students come to college with a variety of goals—career, educational, social, and so on—that in combination influence motivation. Research in the workplace suggests that workers with clearer goals are more motivated and more productive than individuals with vague goals or no goals at all (Locke and Latham, 1990; Locke, Shaw, Saari, and Latham, 1981). These findings can be applied to learners doing schoolwork as well.

Stark, Shaw, and Lowther (1989) present the following eight attributes of goals: specificity, clarity, difficulty (amount of work to achieve goal), temporality (short or long term), importance (relative to other goals), ownership (whether the individual set the goal or had it imposed by others), stability (over time) and commitment (the ability of the goal to motivate behavior).

Consider a premed's goal of admission to medical school in the context of these eight goal attributes. The goal of medical school admission is a reasonably *specific* and *clear* goal and also a *difficult* goal that requires effort and intelligence to achieve. Not all students come to college with the clearly defined career goals of premeds.

In terms of *temporality,* admission to medical school is a long-term goal, with many short-term goals (such as admission to college, passing a variety of courses, performing well on the MCAT, and so on) that must be achieved along the way. Research has shown that professionally oriented undergraduates are more likely to focus on long-range goals (Stark, Shaw, and Lowther, 1989).

The *ownership* of the goal of medical school admission was

highlighted in this case. A student who planned to be a doctor ever since she was a little girl performing elaborate operations on her dolls would rate the *importance* of medical school admission higher than a student who had this goal imposed on her by her parents. For the student who wanted to be a doctor for as long as she can remember, the goal of medical school admission is also very *stable*. The goal *commitment* of such a student will motivate her actions, such as studying rather than socializing before an important exam. As this example illustrates, the eight goal attributes are interrelated. For example, the levels of goal commitment and stability are likely to vary with goal ownership.

Implications for Instruction. Motivational theory raises several implications for instructional practice.

- *Identify student goals.* A first step for faculty in motivating students is to take into account students' goals, both long and short term. Stark, Shaw, and Lowther (1989) advocate assessing course-level goals, because much of the existing research on student goals has focused on the students' overarching goals for college. Students' long-term vocational and academic goals are interesting and important, but information about their short-term course-level goals may be more helpful to classroom teachers concerned with making instruction relevant to current groups of students.

Learning physics is a logical goal for a student to have in physics class, but that goal alone may not motivate behavior unless the student believes there is some value to learning physics other than meeting extrinsic demands of class requirements. Helping students see the connections between academic material and their goals is one way to enhance the relevance of required courses.

From an informal assessment of her students, Jean had a sense that Dana was overwhelmed by the long-term goal of medical school admission and uncertain of her progress toward this goal. Students like Dana can be encouraged to develop short-term, do-able subgoals and then be given frequent feedback on how well they are doing. Succeeding at short-term goals may lead to increased intrinsic interest and feelings of efficacy, which may subsequently result in increased motivation. This raises the issue of increasing expectations for success, a second implication of motivational theory for improving instruction.

- *Increase students' expectations for success.* The importance of task value and learners' beliefs about their ability to succeed was highlighted in the discussion of Expectancy-Value theories of motivation. In this case, Jean appears to have low expectations for Dana's ability to succeed in physics or in medicine. It is doubtful that Jean's low opinion of Dana goes unnoticed. If Dana senses her teacher's low expectations for her, her self-confidence in physics lab is unlikely to improve.

To increase students' expectations for success, faculty can "maximize optimism" and "minimize students' fear of failure" (Forsyth and McMillan, 1991, p. 57). Faculty should assign tasks with a moderate, but not threatening, level of challenge. In addition, faculty should communicate their own confidence in students' ability to complete the task.

A practical suggestion for promoting students' optimism for success is to provide opportunities for students to correct and revise their work. Teachers might also offer students choices in the types of assignments they will complete. When students perform well, their feelings of self-efficacy are further enhanced by positive feedback on their work.

Offering students a chance to succeed in one unit before moving to the next is another way to enhance intrinsic motivation. One of the reasons for the success of mastery learning strategies (Block, 1971; Bloom, 1971; Cross, 1976; Kulik, Kulik, and Bangert-Drowns, 1990) is that students attain a feeling of *mastery*—of doing something very well—before they proceed to a new unit of learning. Poor students, who are notoriously lacking in intrinsic motivation for academic work, rarely have an opportunity in school to demonstrate mastery to themselves and to others. Before they have done some academic task well enough to feel pride in their work, they are off to another learning task and to feeling, once again, all the old familiar feelings of doubt and anxiety about their performance as learners.

Ames's research (1987) on classroom environments in schools found that competition can negatively affect motivation. Classrooms that foster student anxiety about failure are damaging to self-efficacy and therefore to motivation. One strategy to minimize students' fear of failure is to deemphasize normative grading (grading that depends on the performance of others in the class). When students are graded on a curve, they know that no matter how hard they study, some of them have to be on the failing end of the curve. The competition fostered by normative grading is harmful because it focuses students' energy on outperforming others rather than on understanding and learning.

In Sheila Tobias's research on attrition of students from college science majors, she found many students were alienated by a "destructively competitive" culture that discouraged student cooperation and interaction (1990, p. 64). Jean is on the right track by allowing students to collaborate rather than compete on their lab assignments.

• *Tap into intrinsic motivation.* A third major implication of motivational theory for instructional practice is that intrinsic motivators are more effective than extrinsic motivators for involving students in learning. McMillan and Forsyth (1991) recommend that teachers avoid excessive use of extrinsic motivators such as grades or penalties because extrinsic motivators draw attention away from the substance of the learning task toward concerns about performance. Most faculty, except perhaps those at alternative colleges, cannot rule out grades altogether, but they can still emphasize intrinsic rewards over extrinsic ones.

Advising students to pay attention and study hard so they will get high grades does not help them discover the intrinsic value of new learning. Rather, faculty should focus students' attention on the importance of the information presented. Hodgson's research (1984) on learners' intrinsic and extrinsic experience of relevance suggested that even when subject matter is not directly related to students' interests, faculty can foster students' intrinsic interest by conveying enthusiasm and offering examples that students can connect to their existing knowledge.

Another way to add intrinsic value to academic tasks is to have students approach the subject matter by tackling a real problem, such as designing a circuit or explaining why a suspension bridge works. This approach differs from the usual order of teaching principles first and applying them later. An Australian study (Newble and Clark, 1985) compared students in an innovative problem-based medical school curriculum to students in a traditional medical school program. In the traditional program, students attended lectures and tutorials prior to any clinical experience, and they were assessed by end-of-year exams with objective questions. In the innovative program, students confronted clinical problems as soon as they entered the program, and used these problems to learn the basic material and clinical skills. A variety of assessment methods were used. Results of a self-report questionnaire revealed that the problem-based curriculum increased motivation and promoted deeper engagement in learning.

Problem-based learning is a promising way to tap into students' intrinsic motivation for learning (Ramsden, 1992). Jean's discovery-learning physics lab was designed to do just that. Although this lab format was effective for involving some students, it may have been anxiety provoking for those who lacked self-confidence. Classroom Assessment Techniques offer Jean a way to gather information about students' reactions to the course design and those aspects of the course students find particularly threatening or motivating.

RECOMMENDED
READING
Motivation and Goals for Learning

Ames, C. "The Enhancement of Student Motivation." In M. L. Maehr and D. A. Kleiber (eds.), *Advances in Motivation and Achievement: Enhancing Motivation.* Greenwich, Conn.: JAI Press, 1987.

Carole Ames's chapter overviews different views and theories of motivation and how they are interrelated and provides a comprehensive review of research on how competitive classroom climates affect student motivation. The chapter concludes with several research-based recommendations for structuring classrooms to optimize student motivation, such as eliminating social comparison and competition and providing opportunities for improvement and the correction of errors. In the same volume, see also "Socializing Students' Motivation to Learn," by Jere Brophy.

Covington, M. V. "A Motivational Analysis of Academic Life in College." In J. C. Smart (ed.), *Higher Education: Handbook of Theory and Research.* Vol. 9. New York: Agathon Press, 1993.

Covington's chapter uses examples to apply motivational theory to college learners and is ideal for groups or individuals who want a comprehensive review of the development of different motivational theories. The first half of the chapter is a thorough presentation of the self-worth theory of motivation and the four types of students in Covington's model: overstriving, success-oriented, failure-avoiding, and failure-accepting. Most faculty will recognize from their teaching experience the student motivational patterns that Covington describes. The second half of the chapter contains guidelines for helping students develop worthwhile educational objectives. Covington recommends that teachers offer engaging tasks, sufficient reinforcers, and success-oriented assessment.

Forsyth, D. R., and McMillan, J. H. "Practical Proposals for Motivating Students." In R. J. Menges and M. D. Svinicki (eds.), *College Teaching: From Theory to Practice.* New Directions for Teaching and Learning, no. 45. San Francisco: Jossey-Bass, 1991.

This chapter presents research-based proposals for classroom practices that can motivate students. For example, the authors suggest methods for helping students set goals and strategies for maximizing students' intrinsic motivation and expectations for success. These commonsense recommendations should appeal to classroom teachers. See the companion chapter in the same volume, titled "What Theories of Motivation Say About Why Learners Learn," by McMillan and Forsyth.

Pintrich, P. R., and Schunk, D. H. *Motivation in Education: Theory, Research, and Applications.* Upper Saddle River, N.J.: Prentice Hall, 1996.

This comprehensive text by Pintrich and Schunk provides an up-to-date overview of key theories and research findings on motivation. Each chapter describes the implications of theory and research for practice, including specific applications to classroom settings. Although most of the examples portray K–12 settings, the information is also applicable to higher education classrooms.

Tobias, S. *They're Not Dumb, They're Different: Stalking the Second Tier*. Tucson, Ariz.: Research Corporation, 1990.

In this provocative monograph, Sheila Tobias reports on the results of a study of intelligent, high-achieving nonscience majors (undergraduates, graduate students, and even a faculty member) who were paid to seriously audit undergraduate physics and chemistry courses. Readers learn firsthand how these "second tier" students experienced the distinctive culture of the science classrooms through student journal and interview excerpts combined with Tobias's astute analysis. This highly readable ninety-two-page publication is ideal for faculty—and student—discussion groups in any discipline.

CLASSROOM ASSESSMENT

Collecting Further Information

Introduction. The literature review suggested that a number of factors are involved in students' lack of motivation, primary among them are lack of self-confidence that they can do the work successfully and failure to see the relevance of the course work to their goals. We suggest two CATs that will help Jean target student perceptions of relevance, interests, and self-confidence.

Example 1: Interest/Knowledge/Skills Checklist. (See CAT 34 in Angelo and Cross, 1993, pp. 285–289.) Students are motivated to do those things that they know that they can do well and for which they will be rewarded. The Interest/Knowledge/Skills Checklist offers an easy way to determine not only what students are interested in—and therefore presumably motivated to learn—but also where their feelings of competence and incompetence lie.

Ideally, Jean would administer the Interest/Knowledge/Skills Checklist relatively early in the term, so that she can incorporate what she learns about student interests and competencies into her course plans and choice of lab exercises. Although this CAT is easy to administer and analyze, its construction requires careful thought. Jean needs to think not only about her goals for the lab but also of the possible interests of students. Exhibit 3.1 illustrates the type of instrument Jean might design.

Because the Interest/Knowledge/Skills Checklist should be

Exhibit 3.1.

Sample Interest/Knowledge/Skills Checklist.

Learning Interests and Background for Physics Lab 101

Part I: Interests

Directions: Please circle the number after each item below that best represents your level of *interest.*

Scoring:
0 = Not interested
1 = Somewhat interested
2 = Quite interested
3 = Very interested

Interests:

1. Doing the experiments	0	1	2	3
2. Seeing examples of the applications of physics to medicine	0	1	2	3
3. Working with other students	0	1	2	3
4. "Hands-on" learning	0	1	2	3
5. Figuring out how to solve a problem	0	1	2	3
6. Other _____	0	1	2	3

Part II: Self-Assessment of Skills and Knowledge

Directions: Please circle the letter after each item below that best represents your level of *skill or knowledge* about that topic.

Scoring:
N = No skills; no knowledge
B = Basic skills and knowledge
F = Functionally adequate skills and knowledge
A = Advanced level of skills and knowledge

Skill or Knowledge:

1. Using lab equipment	N	B	F	A
2. Using computers	N	B	F	A
3. Conducting experiments	N	B	F	A
4. Writing up lab reports	N	B	F	A
5. Algebra	N	B	F	A
6. Calculus	N	B	F	A
7. Wiring circuits	N	B	F	A

---

designed to meet the needs of a particular class, items can be as narrow or broad as seems useful. An equally good alternative to asking students to indicate their *skills and knowledge* is to ask students to indicate their *level of confidence* that they can accomplish various lab activities. An interesting follow-up on this CAT is to administer the same instrument at the end of the course to see if students have gained confidence in their ability to handle various learning tasks. (This option is discussed further in the section on Classroom Research.)

Example 2: Assignment Assessments. (See CAT 49 in Angelo and Cross, 1993, pp. 356–358.) One of the most troubling aspects of this class for Jean is some students' "open disdain for doing lab work." Thus, a question that should arise is why? Are the lab experiments really boring? Irrelevant? Too hard? The Assignment Assessments CAT helps faculty answer this question by seeing their assignments through student eyes.

This is a simple CAT that takes very little class time and can even be assigned as homework. The instructor just asks students to evaluate a given assignment. For example, Jean might select a particular lab exercise and ask students in what ways it was effective or ineffective as a learning exercise. It is generally more productive to ask students to think about themselves as learners rather than to ask whether they "liked" an assignment or even what they "liked" or "disliked" about it. Jean might also ask for specific suggestions about how to make the assignment a better learning experience (this method is also used in the Group Instructional Feedback Technique [GIFT] described later in this chapter).

A variation on the theme of evaluating individual assignments is ask students to evaluate the lab experiments over the longer period of the term or semester. Jean's assumption is that some students see the physics lab generally as irrelevant to their career interests. But it may be that some experiments are perceived by students as more relevant and interesting than others. If that is so, it does not mean that students should do only those experiments that interest them, but if only a few lab exercises are responsible for setting the stage for negative reactions, it may be that Jean can find substitutes or make modifications just for those few.

To perform the longer-term evaluation, Jean might first make a list of the major experiments done during the term, asking students to rank or rate the value of each experiment to them as learners. Depending on how many experiments there are, Jean might list either all of them or just five or six that are major assignments or that she has questions about. It is well to annotate each experiment briefly, to remind students of each experiment's content. Jean might ask students to respond to the questions in Exhibit 3.2.

An alternative to open-ended questions is illustrated in the Interest/Skills/Knowledge Checklist in Exhibit 3.1. Jean might ask students to rate each experiment on a scale of one to three, for example, from "of little interest" to "very interesting."

Exhibit 3.2.

Sample Questions About Assignment Value.

---

1. Which experiments did you find most interesting?
2. Which did you find most relevant?
3. From which experiments did you learn the most?
4. Which were most confusing?

If, as Jean suspects, the premed students are hostile because they fail to see the relevance of the lab experiments to their careers, she might use the feedback from this CAT to open a discussion on the relevance of physics principles to medicine. The caution we offer here is avoid being defensive. This is not the time to pound into students' heads that an understanding of the principles of physics *is* relevant to the practice of medicine. One of the most important rules of Classroom Assessment is, If you don't want to know or you are not going to do anything with the information that students provide, don't ask.

CLASSROOM
RESEARCH

Explorations for Understanding

Example 1: A Study of Competence and Confidence. Expectancy-Value theories of motivation stress the importance of self-confidence to motivation. Students who lack confidence that they can accomplish a task are reluctant to put themselves to the test. Most teachers hope that students will become both more confident and more competent in the skills and knowledge of their subject matter. Theory as well as personal experience suggests that the two variables move together. As students become more competent at performing certain tasks, they also become more self-confident. And the reverse order is also familiar; as students grow in confidence, they are willing to take the risks that learning something new always involves, and they grow in competence.

The Interest/Knowledge/Skills Checklist described earlier offers an interesting opportunity to study the simultaneous—or sometimes uneven—growth of confidence and competence. In part 2 of the checklist (Exhibit 3.1), students are asked to indicate their levels of skill and knowledge in performing various laboratory tasks. We also suggested that an interesting variation might be to ask students to state their level of self-confidence in performing each of the skills listed. If students were asked to indicate levels of both confidence and skill at the same time—say in the beginning of the year—instructors would expect a very high degree of overlap.

That is, students would feel most confident in performing tasks for which they judged they had the prerequisite skills and knowledge. It would then be interesting to investigate how students' self-perceptions changed on the tasks from the first week to the last week of class. This Classroom Research project might consist of a cluster of investigations involving the following questions.

1. On which lab tasks did students feel they made the most gain in *competence?* If the Interest/Knowledge/Skills Checklist was administered in the first week of classes, the papers might be coded[1] and saved by the teacher and the answers then compared with students' self-perceptions of competence in the last week. Clearly, Jean might hope for positive change on all tasks, but some items are likely to show more growth in self-perceived skills and knowledge than others. If, on the one hand, wiring circuits was done in only one lab exercise and also was fairly unpopular, students might feel they had gained little knowledge about electricity or skill in wiring circuits. If, on the other hand, Jean's computer programs are as interesting and challenging as she hopes they are, students should show considerable growth in their estimates of their own competence in using computers.

2. On which lab tasks did students feel they made the most growth in *self-confidence?* This investigation is very similar to the first one, and instructors would expect similar patterns to be revealed. Students should gain in their self-confidence in conducting laboratory experiments, but they may make greater gains in some areas than in others. An interesting question for investigation is, Are gains in self-confidence more likely to be related to *amount of time* devoted to the task or to perceived *relevance* to the student's interests?

3. On which lab tasks are there discrepancies between self-estimates of competence and confidence? It is possible for students to feel that they gained in knowledge and skills during the term but still to feel less than confident about their ability to perform particular tasks. It is also possible for students to gain in self-confidence but not in competence. Jean might also look for reports of loss of self-confidence in performing certain lab tasks over the term. Some students might expect that they could use lab equipment well but then find out that the tasks were more difficult than they thought.

4. How do student self-perceptions of competence and confidence compare with external judgments? Sometimes, students think that they know more—or less—than they do. Therefore, Jean might compare student levels of self-rated confidence and competence with external criteria of competence. Such external criteria

might consist of (1) Jean's judgments about student competence on each of the lab tasks, (2) a colleague's judgments, say, about the quality of the lab reports at the beginning of the term and at the end,[2] (3) students' assessments of the work of their lab partners or of the competence of a work sample such as a lab report, or (4) performance measures or tests of competence.

There are many questions of interest within this Classroom Research option: How accurate are students in estimating their own competence when judged against some external criterion? How does self-confidence relate to external judgments of competence? Are students able to judge their competence on some tasks more accurately than on others? What is the student pattern of competence across tasks: are some students competent at everything while others show distinct patterns of variation? Over a time period of several semesters, are there differences in the tone and energy of classes in which many students expressed high levels of self-confidence compared to classes where self-confidence seemed to be low?

The worth and success of this Classroom Research project is heavily dependent on the care with which the lab tasks are identified and defined. The murkier the definition of the task, the harder it will be for students—or anyone else—to determine how well they do it.

The literature review on motivation for learning illustrated that researchers link confidence and competence together. And teachers want and expect students to gain in both confidence and competence. But some of the most interesting insights into learning problems arise when discrepancies show up between these two critically important variables.

Example 2: An *N* of One. To test the hypothesis that some students in a class lack motivation for learning, we suggest a second project that capitalizes on the particular strengths of Classroom Research. It is easy for most classroom teachers to do and is likely to result in more understanding than are the many statistical studies that often have more credibility as "real" research. We call this classroom research project An *N* of One because it departs deliberately from the traditional educational research emphasis on the size and representativeness of the research sample. Instead, it focuses attention on the learning of one student—in our example, we use Dana, the premed who illustrates some learning problems related to hypothesis 1.

A great deal of attention is given to the size and appropriateness of the sample in traditional research. The rationale is that a large sample permits the researcher to generalize the findings to a larger population. If, for example, 65 percent of a sample of one thousand students at a particular university say they have cheated on an exam within the past year, then one may conclude with a reasonable degree of confidence that cheating is common among students at that school. One cannot draw the same conclusion from sampling only twenty students. Thus, traditional researchers have an obsession with the size and appropriateness of the sample because the very purpose of their work is to draw some general conclusions about the larger population.

But the purpose of Classroom Research is to *understand.* For such purposes, an *N* of one may be far more revealing and useful than an *N* of one thousand. For instance, all the example of the cheating survey reveals is that 65 percent of the students *said* they cheated *within the past year.* It is not said why they cheated, whether they also cheated in high school, whether particular pressures at the university—or lax enforcement—were responsible, or how students felt about their cheating—was it "wrong" or "necessary" or "okay because everyone was doing it?" Because the goal of Classroom Researchers is to understand, an *N* of one presents an opportunity to understand how students approach learning tasks.

In this case, Jean wonders, almost as a footnote, whether "she should have found an effective way to help Dana and her partner." Jean's reluctant hypothesis is that Dana "seemed too dumb to make the grade in medicine." But what does Jean know about Dana and her motivation? Suppose Jean were to take advantage of some of the office hours that Dana and her partner were "using up . . . every week" to find out more about Dana? Is medical school her ambition—or that of her parents? What was her experience in science courses in high school? What does she like about college? What are her frustrations? These are questions that can be worked into a general conversation and that might have the double advantage of helping Jean learn something about Dana's motivation while also showing Jean's interest in Dana, which might, in itself, improve Dana's attitude.

Research on motivation for learning has so many interesting pathways that merit exploration that Jean might elect to pursue the ideas of some particular theorist or realm of work of particular interest to her. For example, an initial conversation with Dana might reveal that she is under enormous pressure from home to succeed as a doctor and also that she is afraid she will not make it and will disappoint her parents.

There are two roles that Jean might play in this latter case. First, she might take the role of counselor and convince Dana that she should talk frankly with her parents about her lack of interest in a career in medicine. That may be a helpful and legitimate role, but we are concerned here with Jean's role as Classroom Researcher. What can she learn about students who are under pressure to succeed and who are afraid of failing? Dana already reveals one symptom of students motivated by a fear of failure. She wants the reassurance of "right" answers; she does not want to take the risks that discovery-based learning requires. Discovery-based learning capitalizes on the natural curiosity of self-confident, adventuresome, achievement-oriented students. And that is a reasonable and worthy learning approach for most college students. However, the literature is silent, for the most part, on how students who find themselves in a failure-threatening situation will respond to the challenge of trying to discover their own answers. If Jean can shed some light on this, it will be a contribution to her own teaching as well as to the literature of discovery-based learning.

The related research questions for Jean might include the following: What are the acceptable risks for Dana in discovery-based learning? Can her curiosity be aroused at some level without her fear of failure taking over? Where does she feel competent? Are there tasks in the lab where she has a reasonable expectation of success? These questions are related to Expectancy-Value theories of motivation. The more instructors know about research and theory in this realm, the richer will be their hypotheses for investigation, and there is also a good chance that they will gain some insights in their research with an N of one that will merit further exploration by traditional as well as Classroom Researchers.

INVESTIGATING HYPOTHESIS 2

Students Are More Concerned About Getting Good Grades Than About Learning Physics.

REVIEWING
THE LITERATURE

What Do We Know from Research and Theory About Grades and Their Effect on Student Learning?

Grades: More Than a Simple Fact of College Life. As background for our investigation of this hypothesis, we will look at recent research on the purpose and impact of grades in higher education, then consider differences in student approaches to grades, studying, and learning. Although grades and grading systems frequently fuel controversy, the practice of grading students is generally viewed as a fact of life (or a necessary evil) in higher education. Milton, Pollio, and Eison, in their book *Making Sense of College Grades* (1986), argue that grades, rather than being just a fact of life for college students, play a central role in educating students, because grades "determine very explicitly how and what students will learn" (p. xiii). Grades are significant motivators, "the basic currency of the college classroom—the reward promised to students for good performance and the punishment threatened for failure" (McMillan and Forsyth, 1991, p. 55).

Most teachers are eager for students to share their enthusiasm for their subject areas and cannot help but feel disdain for students whose concern about grades overshadows their interest in learning. Yet students' fixation on grades is not unreasonable. College transcripts are used in decision making by graduate schools and employers. As Bornholdt explains, "Grades can and do open or close gates of opportunity in American higher education and thereby determine entry to the most prized careers" (1986, p. x).

Grades serve a variety of purposes, but the gatekeeping function highlighted by Bornholt is recognized by a variety of higher education constituents and may have a particular impact on student learning and attitudes. As part of the National Grade Survey conducted by Milton, Pollio, and Eison (1986), faculty, parents, business people, and over four thousand undergraduates were asked to rate several different purposes for grades on a scale of importance ranging from "major" to "none." The possible purposes of a grade, generated from interviews with a pilot sample, are as follows (pp. 230–231):

> Communicates to the student how much learning was achieved.
>
> Provides reward (or warning) for outstanding or unsatisfactory performance.
>
> Provides student with information for making educational or vocational decisions.
>
> Provides other educational institutions, such as graduate or professional schools, with information for making decisions about the student.
>
> Provides potential employers with information for making decisions about the student.
>
> Provides the instructor with information about teaching effectiveness.
>
> Reflects academic standards of a department, college, or university.
>
> Helps maintain academic standards.
>
> Provides historical record of a student's educational experiences and achievement.
>
> Helps prepare students for the competitive nature of adult life.
>
> Helps remind students that school is really work, not fun.
>
> Provides a way of pleasing parents and meeting their demands.
>
> Affords an accounting to society of how well the university or college is educating its students.

The purpose of grades rated as most important by all respondent groups (faculty, parents, students, and businesspeople) was "providing other educational institutions, such as graduate or professional schools, with information for making decisions about the student" (Milton, Pollio, and Eison, 1986, p. 60). The researchers interpreted this finding as "verification of the fact that colleges and universities serve as personnel selection agencies for society" (p. 61). Many students see grades as the keys to unlock future educational and career opportunities and are understandably concerned about their academic standing. Milton, Pollio, and Eison explained that their research led them to become more sympathetic toward grade-conscious students "in a society that demands at least a modicum of success in higher education as a prerequisite for any sort of reasonable occupation" (p. 140).

Another reason for students' anxiety about grades is the relationship between academic performance and students' feelings about themselves. According to self-worth theories of motivation, "the search for self-acceptance is the highest priority among humans," and in academic settings, "self-acceptance typically becomes equated with the ability to achieve competitively" (Covington, 1993, p. 58).

Competitive classroom practices such as grading on a curve or publicly posting exam scores signify to students that grades are indicators of ability. To demonstrate academic ability and preserve feelings of self-worth, students seek good grades and avoid bad ones. Some students seek good grades by working hard at their studies. Others select courses or assignments based on the potential for good performance. For example, 47 percent of student respondents in the National Grade Survey reported that they had dropped or audited a course because they were afraid of getting a poor grade (Milton, Pollio, and Eison, 1986, p. 97).

Students also attempt to preserve self-worth by using strategies that remove them from the competition, such as procrastinating, avoiding effort altogether, or choosing impossibly difficult tasks so that their ability will not be questioned if they fail (Covington and Omelich, 1979). Feelings of self-worth are particularly threatened when students do put forth a great deal of effort but still perform poorly. The most annoying grade grubbers may be students who lack confidence in their ability and are therefore especially anxious about their academic performance.

Understanding the broader implications of grades for students' self-worth and future educational and professional opportunities may help teachers become more tolerant of students' grade-conscious behaviors. Yet of more immediate concern to Jean is the impact grades have on student learning. The anxious search for "right" answers on the physics lab assignments may be interfering with the learning and creativity of some students. In the following sections, we look at theories that characterize the potential tension between the pursuit of grades and meaningful learning.

Introduction to Students' Approaches to Learning. Educational researchers have been very interested in exploring variations in students' behaviors and attitudes around academic tasks. Several have developed theories that *type* students by their approaches to learning. What these theories have in common is the notion that some students approach learning by attempting to understand new information, whereas others approach learning by attempting to get through the task with the least effort and the best performance possible.

We will look at three theories that categorize students according to their approaches to learning: being learning oriented versus being grade oriented, having mastery goals versus having performance goals, and taking a deep versus taking a surface approach. In each theory, one approach (learning-oriented, mastery-oriented, or deep) is preferable to the other (grade-oriented, performance-oriented, or surface). However, a single student may demonstrate a combination of approaches to learning, even within a single academic task. This occurrence is similar to the situation described in the literature review for hypothesis 1, that a student can be both intrinsically and extrinsically motivated during a single learning task.

Orientation Toward Grades and Learning. Are some students interested mainly in learning and its intrinsic rewards whereas others must be motivated by the external rewards of grades? Throughout the research on the role of grades in motivating learning, there lurks the question of whether there is such a thing as a grade-oriented personality or whether grade grubbing is largely a product of excessively competitive learning environments. Are Jean's irritating premeds grade-oriented people or are they only grade oriented in this particular required course, because of the pressure to keep up their GPA in order to qualify for admission to medical school? Is it personality or the situation?

When Milton, Pollio, and Eison started their studies in 1976, they attempted to develop an instrument that would differentiate learning-oriented (LO) students from grade-oriented (GO) students, describing the two types of students in these words: "Learning-oriented . . . students view the college classroom as a context in which they expect to encounter new information and ideas that will be both personally and professionally significant. Grade-oriented students view the college experience as a crucible in which they are tested and graded and which is endured as a necessary evil on the way to getting a degree or becoming certified in a profession" (1986, p. 126). They developed a questionnaire, based on this impressionistic description, to assess students' attitudes and beliefs about grades. They called their instrument LOGO and found—when they compared LOGO profiles with a variety of other measures of personality, anxiety, study habits, and the like—that students who scored high in the LO area seemed to have what would be considered more favorable characteristics on the other instruments. Compared to GO students, they were more emotionally stable, relaxed, had better study methods and lower levels of debilitating test anxiety, and were more collaborative and less likely to be avoidant and competitive (Milton, Pollio, and Eison, 1986, pp. 127–128).

Despite these early findings showing differences between these two types of students, the researchers were dissatisfied with LOGO because they recognized that some students were both learning oriented and grade oriented. So, they developed LOGO II, which identified four different types of students (pp. 130–131): high learning orientation/high grade orientation (High LO/High GO), high learning orientation/low grade orientation (High LO/Low GO), low learning orientation/high grade orientation (Low LO/High GO), and low learning orientation/low grade orientation (Low LO/Low GO).

Of particular interest to Jean might be their initial hypothesis that preprofessional students (premed and prelaw) might best be described by the first type, High LO/High GO, students "presumably . . . motivated both to learn and to achieve high grades, the former perhaps out of personal interest and avocation, the latter out of necessity" (p. 131). What they found, however, was rather different. The portrait that emerged for the High LO/High GO profile was "not one of a learning-oriented student burdened with excessive concern over grades but one of an extroverted but relatively less able student seeking concrete information (grades) concerning how well he or she is doing" (p. 136). Furthermore, they did not find a LOGO pattern that was characteristic of preprofessional students; thus, they concluded that their initial hypothesis was wrong—preprofessional students are "probably not to be found among students in the H-H [High LO/High GO] group" (Eison, Pollio, and Milton, 1986, p. 66).

Most of the research of the LOGO group suggests that undergraduates are more grade-oriented than learning-oriented, but the researchers plead for faculty understanding of grade-oriented students. "We feel that a student may be grade-oriented not because he or she necessarily wants to be, but because such an orientation is a plausible and situationally effective way of dealing with the traditional classroom environment as well as with early post-college endeavors. In many instances, an instructor's classroom policies and procedures make such an orientation seem both logical and reasonable for the student" (Milton, Pollio, and Eison, 1986, p. 142).

A valuable contribution of Eison and colleagues' research on orientation to grades and learning is their investigation of faculty attitudes. An instrument called LOGO F was administered to over thirteen hundred faculty at a variety of institutions (Eison, Janzow, and Pollio, 1989). Like the LOGO II questionnaire for students, the LOGO F instrument took into account both faculty attitudes and behaviors. For example, a LOGO F item representing a learning-oriented *attitude* is, "Students' concern about grades often interferes with learning in my classroom." A learning-oriented *behavior* is indicated by the item, "I encourage students to raise questions in class that are topic-related but go beyond the scope of the tests that I prepare." A LOGO F item representing faculty grade-oriented *attitude* is, "I wish my colleagues across the campus were tougher graders." One representing faculty grade-oriented *behavior* is, "I encourage students to focus primarily on their studies and to limit their participation in extracurricular activities that might jeopardize their GPA" (Janzow and Eison, 1990, p. 98).

Some 20 to 30 percent of the faculty respondents to LOGO F said that they emphasized the importance of good grades in conversations with students, and 60 to 65 percent agreed with this statement: "I think it useful to use grades as incentives to increase student performance." Faculty are often critical of students' preoccupation with grades, but this research suggests that faculty have a role in fueling students' concerns. We know from this chapter's case study that Jean is clearly aware that grades influence her students' attitudes toward learning. Her teaching goals appear to include using discovery and interactive learning methods to teach students the fundamentals of physics. However, she needs to ask whether her testing and grading practices reflect her goals.

Existing research suggests frequent inconsistencies exist between faculty members' goals for teaching and their actual teaching and assessment practice. Milton, Pollio, and Eison (1986) cite research by Semb and Spencer (1976) in which University of Kansas faculty from a variety of disciplines reported that their tests required students to use complex problem-solving skills. However, when their exams were evaluated by independent judges, "only 8.5 percent required complex skills; the remainder were of the recall or recognition variety" (p. 21). If Jean were to examine how students are assessed and how grades are distributed in her class, she might find that her assessment measures such as lab reports or exams are inhibiting rather than enhancing students' creativity and risk-taking behaviors in this lab with a discovery-learning format. Grades based on a curve are often used in large introductory and prerequisite courses as a way to weed out poor students. However, if Jean is grading on a curve, taking a norm-referenced approach, that practice may be adding to the anxiety about grades for premeds and other students facing competitive graduate school admissions.

To increase student motivation and to reduce anxiety-producing competition, Ames (1987) recommends that teachers use criterion-based grading systems, in which students' grades are based upon their successful completion of assigned tasks. Under this system, all students in a class, if they demonstrate mastery of course material, could earn A grades. Criterion-referenced grading, however, may not be compatible with some institutional grading policies.

McKeachie observes that many students see grades as a "fearsome, mysterious dragon." One way to reduce the threat of the dragon is to allow students to help "determine the system by which they are devoured (or rewarded)" (1994, p. 107). At the very least, instructors can reduce student anxiety by presenting clear and explicit grading procedures and criteria.

Jean may assign lab problems that enable her to assess students on their use of high-level thinking skills. If this is the case, then students who rely on low-level learning strategies from high school or perhaps other college classes (such as memorizing assigned content or hunting through textbook chapters for answers to problems) will find Jean's course difficult. Janzow and Eison (1990) recommend offering a variety of assignments and evaluation methods, to meet the needs of both grade-oriented and learning-oriented students and sustain the motivation of both groups. Better yet, Jean might work with grade-oriented students using unsuccessful learning strategies to help them develop the learning-oriented strategies more appropriate to her class.

Mastery and Performance Goals. Goal orientation theories are a second set of explanations developed by educational psychologists to describe student achievement behavior in a school setting. Goal orientation theories explain the *reasons* behind a student's academic goal. Rather than defining a student's goal (for example, "getting an A in physics"), goal orientation theories attempt to explain *why* the student wants an A: to demonstrate ability, to outperform others, to understand new information well, and so on. Some researchers describe certain students as having "learning goals" (Dweck and Leggett, 1988) or "mastery goals" (Ames, 1992) for academic tasks. They are motivated to undertake academic assignments out of intellectual interest and the challenge of making sense of new material. Students with mastery-oriented patterns of motivation for academic tasks are willing to take on difficult activities, and they believe that their efforts will lead to eventual success (Dweck and Bempechat, 1983). Mastery-oriented students can be compared to the learning-oriented students described previously.

Other students are characterized as having "performance goals" for learning. They are more concerned about doing well on academic tasks so that they appear smart to themselves, teachers, and fellow students (Dweck and Leggett, 1988). Students' desire to appear smart is consistent with self-worth theory (described in the literature review for hypothesis 1 of this case and hypothesis 3 of the Leslies case), which holds that people avoid failure in an effort to preserve positive feelings about their ability. Individuals who focus on performance goals are concerned about whether or not they can perform the assigned task and how their performance compares with that of other students. In the event of failure, such students may conclude that their ability is inadequate and adopt patterns of helplessness when undertaking future challenges (Dweck and Leggett, 1988).

Students with performance goals for learning can be compared to the grade-oriented students described in the previous section. Academic outcomes such as test scores or grades provide performance-oriented students with the feedback they need to assess their ability. Performance goals for learning have also been associated with students who are "work avoidant," getting by with the least amount of work possible (Pintrich and Schunk, 1996, p. 236).

An experiment illustrates some of the differences between mastery- and performance-oriented learners. In research with fifth- and sixth-graders (Diener and Dweck, 1978, 1980), children were trained to use particular problem-solving procedures and then given twelve problems to solve. The problems were designed so that all the children could successfully solve the first eight, but the final four were too difficult for children their age. The children were asked to talk out loud as they attempted to solve the difficult problems. When confronted with the difficult problems, the mastery-oriented children increased their effort by using a variety of strategies, maintained positive feelings about their ability, and remained optimistic that they could solve the problems. The other students, characterized as having helpless responses to difficult learning tasks, blamed their difficulty on their own inadequacy. Their appropriate use of strategies declined, and they gave up hope of successfully solving the problems (cited in Dweck and Leggett, 1988).

Students with performance goals for learning shy away from

difficult learning tasks where the possibility of failure is high (Dweck and Leggett, 1988). Dweck and Bempechat cite a study (by Elliott and Dweck, 1981) in which students were given a choice between two different boxes of tasks they would undertake. One box contained performance tasks and the other learning tasks; however, the subjects were not told this. The performance-task box was presented to the students with this introduction: "In this box we have problems of different levels [of difficulty]. Some are hard, some are easier. If you pick this box, although you won't learn new things, it will really show me what kids can do." For the learning-task box, the students were told: "If you pick the task in this box you'll probably learn a lot of new things. But you'll probably make a bunch of mistakes, get a little confused, maybe feel a little dumb at times, but eventually you'll learn useful things" (Dweck and Bempechat, 1983, p. 249).

Students who were concerned about evaluation "sacrificed altogether the opportunity for new learning that involved a display of effort or confusion" (Dweck and Bempechat, 1983). Thus, the premeds' preference for traditional textbook problems and procedures over a challenging problem-based physics lab is consistent with the patterns of students with performance goals for academic tasks. In addition to their concerns about medical school admission, they may be attempting to guarantee positive portrayals of their ability with good grades, even at the expense of new learning.

Is the pursuit of a high grade point average incompatible with meaningful learning in college? One classic study has suggested that students' emphasis on their grade point averages interfered with interest in learning. As one student in this study said, "if you try to really learn something, it would handicap you as far as getting a grade goes" (Becker, Geer, and Hughes, 1968, p. 59).

Deep and Surface Approaches. Much of the research in the United States contrasts learning-oriented behaviors with grade- or performance-oriented behaviors. However, scholars in the United Kingdom have been studying the concept of deep and surface approaches to learning (Biggs, 1989; Gibbs, 1983; Ramsden, 1984, 1992). A surface approach to learning describes learners' attempts to reproduce information provided by others (often with the least effort possible), whereas a deep approach to learning describes learners' attempts to understand and apply new information.

Students with deep approaches to learning undertake academic tasks with a serious intention to understand new information and problems with which they are presented. They have an "internal emphasis" on learning because they are more concerned about satisfying their own curiosity than meeting the demands of others

(Ramsden, 1992, p. 46). Like the performance- or grade-oriented students described earlier, students who adopt a surface approach to learning are more concerned about such external factors as grades and course requirements than the actual information to be learned. Their interest in academic material is generally limited to completing an assigned task with minimal mental exertion.

Students' descriptions of their own learning illustrate the difference between surface approaches ("an intention to memorize") and deep approaches ("an intention to understand") (Gibbs, 1983, p. 86). First, consider these statements, which characterize a surface approach:

> I just concentrate on trying to remember everything.
> It's just a matter of getting it all down and regurgitating it in the exam.

In contrast, the following statements reveal students with a deep approach:

> It was what the point of the lecture was about.
> I was just thinking about how it related to my own experience.

The process of completing a learning assignment differs between these two types of learners. When presented with new information, students who use a deep approach will attempt to connect it to what they already know or to what they are learning in other classes. When reading, students who use a deep approach can usually identify arguments presented in the text.

Students who use a surface approach often miss the point of new information because they focus on discrete elements of a reading, lesson, or problem rather than on the big picture. When studying for an exam, they are likely to spend their time memorizing disjointed pieces of information rather than organizing and making sense of the information as a whole (Ramsden, 1992).

Students' beliefs about what it means to learn are related to their approaches to learning. Some students have a conception of learning as "reproducing a body of knowledge," whereas others view learning as "constructing their own understanding" by interpreting new information they receive from teachers or texts (Saljo, 1982, p. 23). In one study (Van Rossum and Schenk, 1984), researchers administered a questionnaire to identify students' conceptions of learning, then gave the students a reading task and asked them how they went about completing it. Conceptions of learning that involved memorization, an increase of knowledge, or an acquisition of facts were found to be associated with surface approaches to learning. Conceptions of learning as an abstraction of meaning or an attempt to understand reality, however, were associated with deep approaches to learning (Van Rossum and Schenk, 1984).

Early research on deep and surface learning, like the study just described, focused on how students learn from text. Several studies found that students with a surface approach focused on the *signs*—the words and sentences—in the text, rather than on what was *signified*, that is, the overall meaning of the text (Ramsden, 1992). One experiment required college students to read an article and then answer questions about what it said (Marton and Saljo, 1984). Subsequent interviews with the students revealed that individuals had processed the text in different ways. Students with a surface approach to learning reported that they were concentrating and trying to memorize as much as possible. They concentrated on text itself, attempting to memorize names, figures, and pages. Further, they expressed anxiety about the demands of the task. The students described as using a deep approach reported that their activities while reading included figuring out the point of the article and determining whether or not it made sense. They made an effort to understand the intended message of the text but did not try to memorize any text. However, even though these students were not trying to memorize the article, the results indicated that "they remembered it very well" (Marton and Saljo, 1984, p. 41).

Research on approaches to learning has also investigated other types of learning tasks, such as problem solving and writing, and students' overall study habits. For example, college students, interviewed in an investigation of how they approached problem solving in science and engineering courses, made these contrasting comments (Laurillard, 1984, p. 133):

> You can't really go wrong, it's all done on the diagrams for you, you can go through without thinking at all.
>
> What I'm trying to do is picture what's going on and see the model they're using.

Students who approach problem-solving tasks in a surface manner, as depicted in the first student's comment, are "content to treat the elements of a task in a purely mechanical way" (Laurillard, 1984, p. 123). The second student's comment, however, describes an attempt to visualize and understand the problem.

Now, consider these two additional excerpts from Laurillard's interviews concerning approaches to problem solving in an engineering assignment (pp. 134–135):

> I knew how I'd do it from looking at it; it practically tells you what equations to use. You just have to bash the numbers out. . . . It's really just a case of knowing what's in the notes and choosing which block of notes to use.

> You have to think about it and understand it first. I used my knowledge of [Operations Research] design of starting with one point, testing it and judging the next move. I try to work through logically. Putting in diagrams helps you think clearly and follow through step by step.

The first comment represents a surface approach, and the second comment portrays a deeper approach. What is interesting about these two comments is that they come from an interview with a single student who was describing how he or she went about two different learning tasks. The implication of this result, according to Ramsden, is that "one cannot be a deep or surface learner; one can only learn the content in a deep or surface way" (1992, p. 49). Although the terms deep learner and surface learner, or mastery-oriented student and performance-oriented student, are often used for convenience to describe students' general approaches to academic tasks, it is important to remember that individuals may use different approaches to learning in different situations.

Although deep approaches to learning are generally associated with more successful learners, Saljo suggests that the deep-surface distinction does not apply to all learning situations. A deep approach would be more effective, for example, when reading "a text which presents arguments, scientific principles and constructs, and/or is intended to provide a coherent way of explaining or analyzing a phenomenon" (1984, p. 86). However, surface approaches are entirely appropriate for learning tasks that require nothing more than memorization. Memorizing grammar forms in a foreign language class is an example of a learning task for which surface approaches are effective (Saljo, 1984). Students may also consider surface approaches to be a logical tactic in classes where assessment methods reward memorization over comprehension. Even in classes where faculty have designed tasks to engage students more deeply in their learning, a number of classroom conditions can discourage students from deeper learning. Testing methods, deadline pressures, and excessive work loads may prevent students from taking the time to use deeper approaches to learning. Even some textbook designs may discourage deep approaches by "present[ing] knowledge in such a neatly parceled way that there is scope for little beyond mere memorizing" (Saljo, 1984, p. 88).

Students' perceptions of the demands of a task will influence their approach to problem solving. Even a task that a teacher characterizes as requiring problem solving may not necessarily demand deep approaches to learning (Laurillard, 1984). Word problems in algebra are an example of problem-solving assignments that do not always require deep approaches to learning. Once students recognize that the word problems follow typical patterns, they are likely to accumulate a set of cues (consisting of certain phrasings, for example, "If a train leaves the station . . .") that identify various problem types. In many cases students can reproduce the required formula and "bash the numbers out" without thinking about the underlying principles of the problem. Many students are skilled at reproducing equations or formulas to successfully complete assignments with little serious thought. They may get good grades without ever really understanding the material. However, if these students are confronted with problems that require them to use their knowledge in nonformulaic ways, they will experience great difficulty.

Deep or mastery-oriented approaches to learning may be inhibited by classroom environments in which students feel anxious as a result of competition, criticism, or threats to their self-esteem. One experiment investigated how conditions of intrinsic and extrinsic motivation influence college students' approaches to learning in a reading task (Fransson, 1977). Eighty-one college students were divided into four experimental groups: high intrinsic motivation/high anxiety, low intrinsic motivation/high anxiety, high intrinsic motivation/low anxiety, and low intrinsic motivation/low anxiety. Students in the high intrinsic motivation groups were assigned a relevant reading task about examination methods in their department. The students in the low intrinsic motivation groups were assigned the same reading, but because they were from a different academic department they were not expected to find the reading relevant to their interests. The students were also divided according to the presence of an extrinsic motivator in the task condition. Some of the students were told that they could be asked to give an oral report about the article and that their presentation would be taped. Other students were given an extrinsic motivator that was intended to be more relaxing. They would simply have to write down what they could remember after reading the article. After the students from all experimental groups finished reading, they were simply asked to write what they remembered. In reality, none were asked to do an oral report.

As expected, students who were intrinsically interested in the article were more likely to use a deep approach to reading. Also, students who felt anxious about the task were more likely to use a surface approach when reading the article. What was interesting, though, was that among the students in the learning situation designed to be more threatening (those who thought they might have to give a taped presentation), not all found that situation terribly stressful. Moreover, some of students in the supposedly more relaxed learning condition were quite anxious. Thus, it was not the learning situation in and of itself but how students felt about it that affected student approaches to learning (Frannson, 1977).

These results suggest that deeper approaches to learning are associated with conditions of intrinsic motivation and the absence of negative extrinsic motivators. This presents a challenge for a faculty member like Jean, who is faced with low levels of intrinsic motivation among students who enrolled in the class only to fulfill a requirement. Furthermore, Jean should be aware that students may feel threatened by the perceived difficulty, work load, and competition (the weed-out function) in introductory science courses.

Implications for Promoting Deeper Approaches to Learning. Scholars in England, Scotland, and Australia have made significant progress in research on deep and surface approaches to learning and have also attempted to translate their findings into concrete recommendations for classroom practice. A published effort to provide practical suggestions for course designs that promote deeper approaches to learning is the brochure "Improving Student Learning," by the Oxford Centre for Staff Development[3] (1992; reprinted in "Deep Learning, Surface Learning," 1993).

To set the stage for offering strategies for improved course designs, the brochure authors highlight research findings about conditions that influence students' approaches to learning. On the one hand, the following course conditions have been shown to foster a surface approach in learners: "a heavy workload; an excessive amount of course material; little opportunity to pursue subjects in depth; little choice over topics or methods of study; and an anxiety-provoking assessment system that rewards or tolerates regurgitation of factual information" ("Deep Learning, Surface Learning," 1993, p. 10). Courses that promote deeper approaches to learning, on the other hand, involve the following four elements: a motivational context that encourages students' interest in the subject, active learning, opportunities for students to interact with others, and new information presented in a logical, integrated format to establish a well-structured knowledge base.

The Oxford Centre for Staff Development offers nine strategies for improving student learning. These strategies are intended to create classroom environments that incorporate the four elements known to foster deeper approaches to learning.

1. *Encourage independent learning.* Independent learning involves giving students greater control over choice of subject matter, learning methods, pace of study, and assessment of learning outcomes. Methods associated with this strategy include the use of learning contracts and self- and peer-assessment.
2. *Support personal development.* This strategy emphasizes student motivation and involvement of feelings as well as intellect in learning. The method most commonly associated with this strategy is intensive group work.

3. *Present problems.* Problem-based learning involves learning through tackling relevant problems. This is distinct from learning how to solve problems (problem solving) and applying previously acquired knowledge to problems (project work). Its main features are the use of "real world" problems out of which learning and action arise, the integration of knowledge from different disciplines, and interaction.

4. *Encourage reflection.* Reflection on learning is crucial for a deep approach. Methods which encourage reflection include the use of learning diaries, reflective journals, and . . . video and observers when learning skills.

5. *Use independent group work.* This strategy focuses mainly on interaction. Methods which emphasize independent group work include group-based project work and peer tutoring, in which students teach each other.

6. *Learn by doing.* Experiential learning emphasizes learning activity. Methods associated with learning by doing include the use of games, simulations and role plays, visits, and work experience.

7. *Develop learning skills.* The development of learning skills requires students to have a real sense of purpose and an awareness of task demands and flexibility. The development of study skills in a narrow technical sense is not successful in moving students from a surface to a deep approach.

8. *Set projects.* Project work is perhaps the most common strategy used in higher education for the purpose of fostering a deep approach. It involves the application of knowledge to new situations and demands a high level of motivation whether done individually or in groups.

9. *Fine-tune.* The above eight strategies might seem to imply that radical alternatives to conventionally taught courses are necessary to support a deep approach to learning. However, it is possible to have a marked impact through modifications to conventional teaching methods and without abandoning existing course structures, for example, through the introduction of active learning tasks and peer-group discussion into otherwise passive lecture classes.

Whatever strategy is used, students will be powerfully influenced by the assessment system they work within. Assessment strategy modifications that can influence students' approach include involving students in the design of assessment tasks and negotiating criteria and marking, through the use of contracts and self- and peer-assessment, for example (Oxford Centre for Staff Development, 1992, reprinted in "Deep Learning, Surface Learning," 1993).

As part of the Oxford Centre's Improving Student Learning

project, eleven instructors representing ten courses (one was cotaught) were selected from one hundred applicants. They convened in Oxford over a period of two and one-half years to diagnose course issues, prepare alternative course designs, and develop methods to evaluate change. With support from the Oxford Centre, the instructors implemented course changes, based on the nine strategies to foster a deep approach to learning, and collected information from students through interviews and other methods. These data, developed into ten case studies, were used by the Oxford Centre to generate several conclusions about the project (Gibbs, 1992).

First, the nine strategies for course design did result in significant improvements in student learning. However, the Oxford Centre Staff warns that even when effective course design strategies are carefully implemented, assessment methods continue to have a large influence on students' approaches to learning. If testing methods reward the reproduction of knowledge, then students will adopt a surface approach to learning.

The Oxford Centre's final conclusion is that "students' conservatism and deep-rooted habits of reproductive learning can obstruct change" ("Deep Learning, Surface Learning," 1993, p. 13). This returns us to the case study with which this chapter opened. If Jean's students are concerned about getting good grades, they may prefer course designs and grading systems that require merely reproduction of knowledge. Those students who are confident in their memorization skills and are more concerned about grades than learning will probably be most comfortable in courses where they are only expected to remember facts or plug in formulas.

Overall, this synthesis of what is known about the impact of grades on deeper learning has been consistent with Jean's diagnosis. Her students appear to be largely extrinsically motivated by the threat of a low grade, whereas Jean would like them to see the value of the kinds of learning that her physics lab is designed to promote. The lab is already doing many of the things suggested in the research on how to encourage deeper learning: students are actively involved; they are interacting with others; they are working on projects and engaged in problem solving. In these respects, the format of the lab incorporates some principles that are harder to adhere to in a classroom—especially in a lecture setting. Instructors like Jean have devoted their efforts to providing challenging discovery format classes to engage students more deeply in their learning. Yet even in the most carefully designed and exciting classes, teachers will be faced with students' anxiety over grades and preferences for reproductive learning.

So what might Jean do to learn more about how students are

interpreting the learning task and to develop less anxiety, more intrinsic motivation, and deeper learning? We will address these questions through Classroom Assessment and Classroom Research.

RECOMMENDED
READING

Grades and Approaches to Learning

Gibbs, G. "Changing Students' Approaches to Study Through Classroom Exercises." In R. M. Smith (ed.), *Helping Adults Learn How to Learn.* New Directions for Continuing Education, no. 19. San Francisco: Jossey-Bass, 1983.

Gibbs's chapter is concerned with "helping people learn how to learn" and is "most emphatically not concerned with teaching study skills" (p. 83). It briefly overviews students' deep or surface approaches to learning and the issue of students' awareness or lack of awareness of academic task demands. At the heart of the chapter are three strategies that Gibbs has used to help students develop a conception of learning and to move away from surface approaches toward deep approaches. These strategies (teaching students to learn through direct explanation, clarifying learning task demands, and training in specific study techniques) are clearly illustrated so that faculty can adopt them in their own classrooms.

Janzow, F., and Eison, J. "Grades: Their Influence on Students and Faculty." In M. D. Svinicki (ed.), *The Changing Face of College Teaching,* New Directions for Teaching and Learning, no. 42. San Francisco: Jossey-Bass, 1990.

Janzow and Eison survey the impact of students' views about grades and learning in this concise yet thorough chapter. They summarize the research about the instrument LOGO II, which measures students' relative orientation to grades versus learning, and supply the added bonus of a description of a newer instrument, LOGO F, that measures faculty attitudes and behaviors related to grading and considers the interactions between faculty members' and students' orientations to grades and learning. The chapter concludes with recommendations for practice.

Milton, O., Pollio, H. R., and Eison, J. A. *Making Sense of College Grades: Why the Grading System Does Not Work and What Can Be Done About It.* San Francisco: Jossey-Bass, 1986.

This book begins with a thoughtful analysis of the purposes and impact of grades in higher education. The authors highlight the role of grades as a sorting device for the allocation of advanced education and desirable careers. Chapters Three through Five outline the development, administration, and findings of a national survey on grades among students, parents, and businesspeople.

The second half of the book introduces the concept of learning- and grade-oriented students. (The 1990 Janzow and Eison chapter described in the recommended reading offers a brief review of related research and concepts and might be a more practical, that is, shorter, reading assignment for a faculty group. However, this complete book offers in-depth analysis in a style that engages a broad higher education audience.)

Ramsden, P., *Learning to Teach in Higher Education.* New York: Routledge, 1992.

Australian scholar Paul Ramsden's book is at the top of a recommended reading list for any faculty development or graduate seminar on teaching and learning. The concepts of deep and surface approaches to learning provide the underlying theory that supports most of the recommendations in this book. Ramsden's review of the literature on learning and motivation is useful for educational researchers but also written to appeal to both new and experienced faculty who may not have any background in learning theory. The research cited includes numerous excerpts from student interviews that bring the theories to life in the context of the college classroom. Ramsden includes strategies for designing courses, assessing student learning, and evaluating the quality of higher education.

CLASSROOM
ASSESSMENT

Collecting Further Information

Introduction. Although Classroom Assessment is often used to reveal students' *reactions* to their learning experiences, it can also be used to uncover students' approaches to learning and other student characteristics. Over the years and especially within the last decade, there has been considerable research interest in studying students' orientation to learning. The literature review, for instance, presented information about grade- and learning-oriented students and about deep and surface learners. Thus, Jean might do a Classroom Assessment project by using one of the questionnaires that she has read about or heard about, to see how her students compare with the research sample. This form of hypothesis testing is discussed later in this chapter as a Classroom Assessment project and also as a Classroom Research proposal.

Yet another use of Classroom Assessment is the use of student responses to a particular learning situation as a point of departure for discussion about learning. To illustrate this purpose we have chosen a modified version of Classroom Assessment's simplest and most famous CAT, the Minute Paper. Most CATs have pedagogical as well as diagnostic functions. In this case, Jean might like to emphasize the pedagogical merits of Classroom Assessment to see if she can motivate students to deeper learning.

Example 1: Use of Existing Questionnaires. At the time of this writing, a group of educators, primarily from England and Australia, were engaging in a spirited discussion on the Internet (isl@mailbox.ac.uk) about the use of the Approaches to Studying Inventory (ASI) by teachers and researchers. The original ASI is a sixty-four-item inventory designed by Entwistle, Hanley, and Housell (1979), subsequently modified to thirty items (Entwistle, 1981), and then further modified to an eighteen-item Approaches to Studying Questionnaire (ASQ) (Gibbs, Habeshaw, and Habeshaw, 1988). The latter purports to categorize study methods into *meaning orientations* (deep approach) and *reproducing orientations* (surface approach). Examples of typical items indicating a deep approach are, "In trying to understand new ideas, I often try to relate them to real-life situations to which they might apply," and, "When I am tackling a new topic, I often ask myself questions about it which the new information should answer." Typical items indicating a surface approach are, "I find I have to concentrate on memorising a good deal of what we have to learn," and, "I usually don't have time to think about the implications of what I have read" (Ramsden, 1992, p. 52).

The debate on the Internet featured research experts, some of whom debunked the psychometric quality of the eighteen-item ASQ, and teachers who found the short ASQ form useful for opening up discussions with students about the nature of their learning. The two uses, however, are quite different. Psychometric analyses (see Richardson, 1994) document some technical problems with the ASQ when employed in rigorous quantitative research designs. But there are also problems with the more psychometrically satisfactory sixty-four-item ASI for teachers wishing to engage students in learning more about their own approaches to studying. In the first place, the long version probably requires more time than classroom teachers wish to give it, and it also probably tells both students and teacher more than they want or need to know.

The message to teachers wishing to use existing instruments, which are often interesting conceptually, is that teachers should be quite clear about the purpose of their Classroom Assessment or Classroom Research. If the purpose is to engage in positivistic scientific approaches to the search for "truth," "universal consistencies," or whatever else one believes to be "out there" awaiting discovery, then one needs to observe the rules and conventions of the scientific community. If, however, the purpose is to make teachers and students more reflective and thoughtful about learning, then it should be recognized that "good" instruments for promoting discussion may differ from "good" instruments for research.

The use of various questionnaires—from professionally developed to self-developed—is quite legitimate in Classroom Assessment, where the goal is to improve the understanding of the learning process for both teachers and students. Three examples of possible instruments to use for exploration are

> Approaches to Study Questionnaire (ASI). This is the eighteen-item questionnaire just described. It has been used primarily in England and Australia to study differences between deep and surface approaches to learning (Gibbs, Habeshaw, and Habeshaw, 1988).

> Learning-Orientation/Grade-Orientation (LOGO II). This thirty-two-item instrument has been used primarily in the United States to study differences in attitudes and behaviors of grade-oriented and learning-oriented students' approaches to learning (Milton, Pollio, and Eison, 1986, pp. 132–133). The use of LOGO is discussed in the section on Classroom Research.

> Learning Styles Inventory (LSI). This instrument, developed by David Kolb (1981), has generated a great deal of interest in recent years. It is a self-descriptive inventory depicting four types of learning preferences aligned along two dimensions—from concrete to abstract learning and from active to reflective learning. This instrument is also discussed in the following Classroom Research section.

Example 2: Minute Papers. (See CAT 6 in Angelo and Cross, 1993, pp. 148–153.) One of the reasons for the great popularity of the Minute Paper is its simplicity. It consists of asking students to take a few minutes at the end of the class period to write answers to these two questions: What is the most important thing you learned today? What questions remain unanswered as you leave class today? Richard Light, director of the Harvard Assessment Seminars, comments that "this extraordinarily simple idea is catching on throughout Harvard. Some experienced professors comment that it is the best example of high payoff for a tiny investment they have ever seen" (1990, p. 36). The payoff of the reflection required of students is often as great as the payoff of information provided for the instructor.

In an adaptation and extension of the Minute Paper—one that will require considerably more time than a minute—Jean might select a lab experiment, preferably one that has some strong implications for deeper learning, and inform students that the assignment for this experiment is to write a brief paper on what they *learned* by doing the experiment. (Given the extrinsic motivation of some students, it is probably well to *substitute* this assignment for the standard lab report rather than *add* something that will likely be seen as extra work.)

Students should be carefully oriented to the purpose of the assignment. Jean should make it clear that she is not looking for such obvious answers as, "I learned that lights wired in series will all go out if a burned-out bulb breaks the circuit." Rather, she is looking for what students learned about themselves as learners. Their papers should address questions such as these: What did you learn from doing this experiment about your own skills and learning preferences? About working with a lab partner (who did most of the work and why)? What questions did the experiment raise for you about your own skills? About how you learn best? About your own motivation? Were you curious about the outcome, or did you know the answer and were just going through the motions?

Given that Jean's primary purpose is to get students to reflect on their learning and that honest responses may be threatening to grade-conscious students, student anonymity must be preserved. Jean should make sure that everyone hands in a paper, but ask that students not identify themselves. After reading the papers carefully, picking out common themes or especially interesting or insightful comments, Jean will be prepared to give feedback to students at the next class period and to open a discussion of what students should be learning from this lab experience. The insights and comments of their peers are of high interest to students, and after students have reflected on their own learning, they will be want to hear how their classmates responded. If Jean can encourage an open discussion, students may be exposed to some new ideas about how they might make their learning time more productive.

Explorations for Understanding

Example 1: Using Grades to Promote Learning. Even though Jean is obviously irritated with the grade-grubbing attitude of the premeds, researchers working in this area of study (Milton, Pollio, and Eison, 1986, p. 142), remind us that grade-oriented students are being quite realistic, given that grades play such an important role in their futures.

Despite the pleas of many—and the efforts of some—to deemphasize or even abolish letter grades, there are no signs that grades are likely to become less important in the future in either academe or society at large. For better or for worse, grades and grading are probably going to continue to play important roles in the lives and careers of both Jean and her students for the foreseeable future. And Jean does show the usual faculty conflicts about grading. She wants students to be motivated by interest in the subject matter, but she knows that grades are effective—and for some faculty, necessary—motivators. She wants students to work collaboratively, but she also wants some independent measures of their work. Apparently, she has tried to define where collaboration ends and cheating begins, but students are not clear on the issue—or at least pretend not to understand her distinctions.

One question that Jean might investigate is, How can she use students' natural interest in grades to motivate learning? Instructors know from both research and experience that grades are powerful motivators and that students will learn whatever they think they will be graded on. So well known is this fact of academic life that specialists in testing joke that a motto for their profession is "What you test is what you get" (WYTIWYG, pronounced "witti-wig").

Jean might devise a quiz or test that is heavily dependent on actually doing a lab experiment. Her Classroom Research project might be to construct a test in which high test scores correlate with high participation in conducting the experiment. To the maximum extent possible, students would have to have done the experiment in order to respond correctly, and the test would also favor those who had thought through and written the lab reports. Granted, making good tests—defined as tests that measure accurately what instructors want students to learn—is not an easy task. But thinking through the issues involved is salutary for both teachers and students. Jean would have to think about the purpose of her course, the reason for requiring it of premeds, the contribution of each lab experiment to students' learning, the rationale for conducting the experiment, and so on.

This case study gives us an opportunity to illustrate a Classroom Research project that is somewhat different from most peoples' conception of research and is also different from most of the Classroom Research projects described in this book. For many graduate students and other inexperienced researchers, the excitement and major activity of research consists of collecting and analyzing the data. Most experienced researchers, however, put their major efforts into planning and carefully—even painstakingly—designing the measures that will collect the data. So important is this emphasis on the planning that must take place before any data are collected that three professors who teach graduate courses in research methods at the Harvard Graduate School of Education titled their textbook on such methods *By Design*, noting in the preface that "you can't fix by analysis what you bungled by design" (Light, Singer, and Willett, 1990, p. v). A poor test is a poor test, and nothing coming after the fact can fix that. The emphasis in this Classroom Research project is on the *design* of an instrument (test) that will define what students need to learn and accurately measure what they have accomplished.

Tests are rarely popular with either teachers or students, yet there is no question that they serve powerful and important purposes in education. They help teachers evaluate students. They motivate students and help them direct their academic efforts. They help teachers evaluate how successfully they are teaching. And they reinforce learning by helping students diagnose where they need additional work (Davis, 1993, p. 239; Jacobs and Chase, 1992, p. 2).

In this case, evaluating student work as it is presented in the lab notebooks appears not to be serving any of these functions very well. Thus Jean's Classroom Research project might consist of designing a modest informal experiment to see if she can devise a test or quiz that will make the lab work a true learning experience for students while it also addresses the issue of the similarities in notebooks (cheating?) by giving Jean—and her students—a separate measure of whether students are learning what she expects them to learn from actually *doing* the lab experiments.

This is not the place for a short course in test construction. Fortunately, there are many excellent materials written in practical nontechnical language for teachers from all disciplines who wish to improve their own classroom tests. The following references are especially helpful: Davis (1993), Fuhrman and Grasha (1983), Jacobs and Chase (1992), McKeachie (1994), McMillan (1988), and Milton, Pollio, and Eison (1986). The single most important thing for Jean to do in starting this Classroom Research project is to make a list for herself—and ideally to share with students—of specifically what she expects students to learn from doing and writing up the lab experiments.

Jean's hard work on developing a new discovery-based course and her annoyance with students who want to follow "cut-and-dried procedures" suggest that she is interested in helping students develop higher-order thinking skills. Fifty years ago, Benjamin Bloom and his colleagues developed the well-known hierarchy of six cognitive levels, ranging from simple to complex in their intellectual demands (Bloom and others, 1956). Some helpful charts that define these cognitive levels and illustrate types of test questions that evoke each level appear in several of the references on testing cited earlier (see Davis, 1993, pp. 241–242; Fuhrman and Grasha, 1983, p. 170; or Jacobs and Chase, 1992, pp. 17–22). The following list of cognitive skills, from low to high, is taken from Davis (pp. 241–242) and may prove useful to Jean in thinking about what kinds of questions she might ask on a quiz specifically designed to show what students are learning from conducting a given experiment.

> To measure *knowledge* (common terms, facts, principles, procedures), ask questions that use verbs such as these: *define, describe, identify, label, list, match, name, outline, reproduce, select, state.* Example: "List the steps involved in titration."

> To measure *comprehension* (understanding of facts and principles, interpretation of material), ask questions that use verbs such as these: *convert, defend, distinguish, estimate, explain, extend, generalize, give examples, infer, predict, summarize.* Example: "Summarize the basic tenets of deconstructionism."

> To measure *application* (solving problems, applying concepts and principles to new situations), ask questions that use verbs such as these: *demonstrate, modify, operate, prepare, produce, relate, show, solve, use.* Example: "Calculate the deflection of a beam under uniform loading."

> To measure *analysis* (recognition of unstated assumptions or logical fallacies, ability to distinguish between facts and inferences), ask questions that use verbs such as these: *diagram, differentiate, distinguish, illustrate, infer, point out, relate, select, separate, subdivide.* Example: "In the president's State of the Union address, which statements are based on facts, and which are based on assumptions?"

> To measure *synthesis* (integrate learning from different areas or solve problems by creative thinking), ask questions that use verbs such as these: *categorize, combine, compile, devise, design, explain, generate, organize, plan, rearrange, reconstruct, revise, tell.* Example: "How would you restructure the school day to reflect children's developmental needs?"

> To measure *evaluation* (judging and assessing), ask questions that use verbs such as these: *appraise, compare, conclude, contrast, criticize, describe, discriminate, explain, justify, interpret, support.* Example: "Why is Bach's Mass in B Minor acknowledged as a classic?"

In most lab courses, the learning emphasis moves away from lower-level cognitive skills such as the memorization and explanation prevalent in many lecture courses toward requiring students to use the higher-level skills of application, analysis, and evaluation. Thus, Jean's quizzes should frame questions that call for demonstration, illustration, comparisons, and conclusions and other questions requiring students to think deeply and analytically about the purposes and messages of the lab exercises. If Jean wants to get students actively involved in doing the experiments instead of watching or copying, then her quizzes should be designed to reward the behavior she is trying to reinforce.

Jean's quiz might be as simple as two or three questions pertaining to the purposes and outcomes of the experiments or as complex as ten or twelve questions concerning application and evaluation. The important thing is that she test what she thinks it is important for students to learn from doing the experiment.

The advantage of this Classroom Research project is that it experiments with the use of tests to motivate and direct learning; the disadvantage is that an overemphasis on testing or the use of poorly designed tests may drive grade-oriented students to be even more competitive and grade conscious. Although competition among students in this class does not seem to be a problem, the point of the research project is to see what happens if Jean exerts more direction over the learning situation by using testing and grading in the service of learning.

Example 2: Using Existing Instruments. There are literally thousands of instruments available today, attempting to measure everything from self-esteem to the extent to which respondents "lie" on self-report forms—to themselves, possibly, as well as to others. Some researchers, noting the continual duplication and reinvention of the wheel in developing measuring instruments have performed a service by publishing directories where people can get information about some of the better-known instruments. Robinson and Shaver, for example, first published their *Measures of Social Attitudes* in 1973, to direct researchers to published instruments measuring self-esteem, sociopolitical attitudes, values, and the like. For their recent update of that work (*Measures of Personality and Social Psychology Attitudes,* Robinson, Shaver, and Wrightsman, 1991), they invited expert scholars to select, review, and critique the instruments most frequently cited in the literature, discuss some of the key issues in the research, and make recommendations for instrument use. Often instruments that are not copyrighted or otherwise restricted are displayed in full, along with directions for scoring. Information is also given regarding definition of the variables, frequency of citations, reliability, and validity, and Robinson, Shaver, and Wrightsman supply addresses for further information, plus a bibliography of research. There are also directories on specific topics such as women's issues and even a directory on previously unpublished questionnaires that have appeared in the literature (Goldman and Osborne, 1985). A research library usually has such directories among their reference materials.

Perhaps one of the best sources of information about existing instruments is Pascarella and Terenzini's massive volume of research *How College Affects Students* (1991). Sprinkled throughout the nine hundred pages are references to hundreds of tests, questionnaires, and inventories that have been used with college students. This work has the further advantage of summarizing past findings in chapters covering specific topics of high interest to those studying college students (some chapter titles, for example, are "Cognitive Skills and Intellectual Growth," "Attitudes and Values," and "Moral Development").

The use of existing questionnaires and inventories is attractive to Classroom Researchers for a number of reasons. In the first place, professionally developed instruments usually (but not always) have met the basic psychometric requirements of good measurement, such as reliability, validity, independence of scales, and the like. Second, many existing instruments have histories of use that provide comparative norms and research results from the work of people who have used the instruments in a variety of studies. Furthermore, some of the best-known instruments are based in theory, and their widespread use with independent samples contributes to shaping and refining the theory, as bits and pieces of research support, refute, or modify it. Finally, the use of common measures ties researchers together in a network of colleagues with shared interests.

The downside for Classroom Researchers in using existing instruments is that too often the availability of the instrument dictates the question for study rather than vice versa. Instructors may use a questionnaire because it is there, without thinking about what they would do differently if they knew how their students scored on a given test or inventory. Most existing inventories provide scores that indicate a "profile" or a "type" of person. They group students on the basis of common scores or dimensions, and this can result in sorting students into simple bipolar types, such as introverts and extroverts. Other instruments develop more elaborate typologies. There are, for example, the learning-oriented and grade-oriented students (or four-way combinations thereof) categorized by LOGO II (Milton, Pollio, and Eison, 1986). Biggs and Collis (1982) use the Structure of the Observed Learning Outcome (SOLO) taxonomy to group students by their orientation to deep and surface learning. Covington and Berry (1976) construct a four-way typology, describing students' approach to academic achievement. Again, the underlying assumption of such groupings is that they represent types of people that share common characteristics on the measuring dimensions.

One of the most popular typing schemes currently in use lies in grouping students on demographic variables such as gender, race, and age. This sort of typing is popular in part because of its simplicity and presumed objectivity; the variable is usually ascertainable through a single instrument item, which is then related to a great variety of other characteristics or attitudes. Researchers have demonstrated, for example, that women have different "ways of knowing" than men (Belenky, Clinchy, Goldberger, and Tarule, 1986; Miller, Finley, and McKinley, 1990) or that older people show a different kind of intelligence than younger people (Cattell, 1963) or have different approaches to studying (Gibbs, 1994, p. 81).

The dangers in interpreting and applying this sort of research are fairly obvious. Stereotyping any particular woman as if she were typical of women in general is a profound misinterpretation of the research. In any given typology, there may be almost as many people who do not fit the type as who do, or as in most bipolar typologies, people may fall at any point along the continuum from one type to the other. The research raises questions not only about the purity of the type but also of the meaning of the research itself. What are we to conclude from such research about the learning characteristics of an elderly African American woman, for example? It makes no sense to try to understand her by adding together what is known from the research about women, blacks, and the elderly. Nor does it make sense to try to construct a narrow and distinctive profile for elderly African American women. Then we might be faced with trying to determine further the differences between the well-educated versus the poorly educated or those who grew up in the South versus those who grew up in the North. The combinations are endless. The legitimate—and important—message from all of the research purporting to show differences among various populations is that *people differ.* Teachers, then, are well advised to gain an understanding of the variety of motivations, learning styles, and preferences that exist in today's very diverse student populations and to use variety in their teaching methods. Despite such caveats about the practical implications of any typology, there are interesting Classroom Research projects that can be carried out with existing instruments.

Classroom Research is sometimes used to scratch the itch aroused by an observed paradox or curiosity. In this case study, for example, we are told that Seth and Tim behave quite differently in Sarah's p-chem class and in Jean's physics lab. Why is it that Tim seems so constructive and Seth so aggravating in Jean's class, whereas they seem to take opposite roles in Sarah's class? Curiosity about this observation takes Classroom Researchers back to the old question that educational researchers, in their need to simplify, do not often address. Is it the *personality* or the *situation* that makes for surface learners who do just barely enough work to get an acceptable grade? Even though most researchers generally favor combination or situational explanations over student type explanations, they continue to try to develop measures that are consistent over time and place (reliable), and they continue to refer to grade-oriented and learning-oriented *students* rather than to grade-oriented and learning-oriented *situations.*

Jean and Sarah might investigate this paradox with a joint project in which each administers a carefully modified[4] LOGO in her class, instructing students to respond to the questionnaire as it applies to that particular classroom. If social security numbers or student IDs are used to identify the instruments in both Jean's and Sarah's classes, comparisons can be made for individuals such as Tim, who exhibit different profiles in the two situations, without identifying those individuals to the instructors by name. (However, in the case of LOGO, observe that there are some very sensitive questions that probably cannot be asked in individual classrooms even when anonymity is guaranteed: for example, "I am tempted to cheat on exams when I'm confident I won't get caught.")

The question for investigation then is why do these individuals differ across classes? Possible hypotheses are that p-chem is more relevant to the students' goals, developed skills, sense of self-efficacy, or other factors that are related to grade- versus learning-orientations. This experiment might lead to a subsequent Classroom Research project, which is to see how the types revealed on LOGO relate to a Goals Ranking instrument (see CAT 35 in Angelo and Cross, 1993), a measure of self-efficacy, or other measure assumed relevant to the grade versus learning orientation of students. For example, what are the goals of students who are typed by LOGO as having a high interest in learning for the sake of knowledge combined with a low interest in grades? This is a good example of the cascading nature of Classroom Research. Research findings often lead to more questions and further investigation rather than to a final answer.

INVESTIGATING HYPOTHESIS 3 _____

Student Ratings of Instruction Are Threatening Rather Than Helpful to Jean

REVIEWING
THE LITERATURE

What Do We Know from Research and Theory About Student Evaluation of College Teaching?

"The pressure of my department for good evaluations has put enough pressure on me that I often find myself thinking of my students as the enemy and these forms as the weapons they use in a thoughtless way to damage me. The last time I handed them out I nearly got sick to my stomach before class" (anonymous teaching assistant, Hoffmann and Oseroff-Varnell, 1989, p. 6).

Jean is not alone in dreading end-of-term student evaluations. Her reaction is a mixture of embarrassment (colleagues will see the written comments), a feeling of being threatened (poor ratings may affect tenure and promotion), and a difficulty in dealing with criticism. In today's world of increasing use of student ratings to evaluate teachers, her fears are not unrealistic. In liberal arts colleges such as Jean's, 90 percent of the faculty agree that student evaluations of courses are important (45 percent say very important; 45 percent fairly important) in granting tenure in their department. In fact, more liberal arts college faculty assign more importance in tenure decisions to student evaluations than to any other type of evaluation, including observation of teaching by colleagues (69 percent), recommendations by scholars inside and outside the institution (79 percent and 42 percent respectively), and research grants received (38 percent) (Carnegie Foundation for the Advancement of Teaching, 1990). The fact is that student ratings of instruction are important to the careers of college teachers, especially young, untenured teachers such as Jean. The increasing use and rising importance of student ratings is attributed to two broad trends in higher education: concern about the quality of education and the accompanying emphasis on assessment and evaluation, and generally positive findings from research on the reliability and validity of student ratings.

There is no lack of research on student ratings of instruction. One conscientious tabulator reported over thirteen hundred studies, making it the single most common form of research on the evaluation of college teaching (Cashin, 1990) and leading researcher Peter Cohen to complain that "student ratings have been studied to death" (1990, p. 123). We quite agree! When the senior author started out to do a "brief and simple monograph" on the subject of student feedback to classroom instructors, she ended up with sixty-nine citations of relevant research (Cross, 1988a). Yet, despite this huge volume of research, faculty misperceptions persist.

Theall and Franklin (1990, p. 22) relate their firsthand experience with a faculty member who proposed that the ratings of A and B students should be weighted more heavily than the ratings of D and F students. He would no doubt be surprised to learn that in one study analyzing student ratings in more than two thousand courses, 70 percent of the "worst" ratings on overall instruction came from A and B students, and D and F students provided only 11 percent of such ratings. Moreover, one of the consistent findings of the research is that there is no evidence that students who do poorly in a course attempt to punish their instructors with low ratings (Marsh, Overall, and Kesler, 1980; Cross, 1988a; Cohen, 1990). Although Jean expresses some feeling that the premedical students are "really going to let her have it" when it comes time for course evaluations, she may recognize, at some deeper level, that the low ratings are more an expression of genuine dissatisfaction with the course than vindictive punishment of the instructor.

The hope of those who do research on student ratings is that the dissemination of the findings will reduce negative attitudes. But as Cohen points out, "Negative attitudes toward student ratings are especially resistant to change, and it seems that faculty and administrators support their belief in student-ratings myths with personal and anecdotal evidence, which outweighs empirically based research evidence" (1990, pp. 124–125)

One of the advantages of the overkill in research on student ratings, however, is that researchers have been forced to synthesize what they do know, producing brief synopses combating the "myths" of faculty misperceptions (Cohen, 1981, 1990; Marsh, Overall, and Kesler, 1980; Cross, 1988a; Centra, 1993). Drawing from the reviews of the research since the 1970s, which Centra (p. 50) labels the "golden age" of research on student ratings, we offer the following succinct list of general findings. There are, of course, always exceptions, but the exceptions are far less prevalent than many faculty assume.

> Student ratings are reasonably valid indicators of learning. Students tend to rate highly those courses from which they learn the most. "Easy" classes may be elected more often than "difficult" ones, but there is no evidence that they are rated higher.
>
> The reliability of student rating scales is good. That is, students are in general agreement about courses, and they are consistent over time in their ratings.
>
> Alumni do not tend to change their opinion about a course after they have been out of school for a while. There is little merit to the argument that maturity and reflection will make a hero of an instructor who was not appreciated by undergraduates.
>
> Student ratings are not unduly influenced by the grades they receive or expect to receive.
>
> Student ratings are not greatly affected by external factors such as gender, race, and other characteristics of students, teachers, or courses (see Centra, 1993, pp. 47–79, for exceptions).

Most of these research findings are from large-scale studies of machine-scorable rating scales such as those constructed by institutional researchers or commercial agencies. And most build on past research by making sure that the instrument contains items dealing with the major dimensions shown to be related to teaching effectiveness. Those dimensions, usually derived by factor analysis or some comparable statistical analysis, are listed by Centra (1993, p. 57) as follows:

1. Organization, planning or structure
2. Teacher-student interaction or rapport
3. Clarity, communication skill
4. Work load, course difficulty
5. Grading and examinations, assignments
6. Student learning, student self-ratings of accomplishments

Thus, the conclusion from the research is that rating scales do use what is known about effective teaching and students are one good source of information about teaching. We emphasize *one source.* There is high agreement in the literature that student ratings should always be used in combination with other sources of information, especially in making decisions about promotion and tenure.

Most of the controversy over student ratings arises over the use of the ratings. Ratings of teaching may be used for summative or formative purposes. *Summative* evaluations are used to judge teaching effectiveness, usually with the intention of making decisions about promotion and tenure. *Formative* evaluations are used to help the teacher improve. Unfortunately, there is no agreement in the literature about whether the same student ratings can be used for both summative and formative purposes. There are those who state flatly that "to be effective, formative and summative activities must be separated" (Weimer, 1990, p. 57), and those who contend that with proper precautions, "a single faculty evaluation system can be made to serve both formative and summative purposes" (Arreola and Aleamoni, 1990, p. 37). Most of those who endorse combined functions for student ratings, go on to offer a complex set of precise instructions about how to serve both summative and formative purposes with the same collection of data.

We come down heavily in favor of separating formative and summative functions. This book is based on our conviction that the information that will have the greatest impact on teaching improvement is that generated by faculty for their own use. Items, instruments, and techniques that are designed by the faculty member to be specifically relevant to a particular class are likely to be taken more seriously by the students and the teacher than are generic rating scales that must necessarily apply to a great variety of class sizes, formats, subject matters, and purposes. Scales that ask students to evaluate the clarity of lectures, for example, do not hold high credibility in a laboratory or small class where lectures are not used.

Now that there is general agreement among researchers that student ratings are reliable and valid and can serve as one very important source of information about the quality of teaching, attention has turned to whether the ratings improve instruction. Do faculty change their teaching in response to student ratings? Centra contends that at least four conditions must be present for student evaluations to lead to improved teaching. "First, teachers must learn something new from them. Second, they must value the new information. Third, they must understand how to make improvements. And finally, teachers must be motivated to make the improvements, either intrinsically or extrinsically" (1993, p. 81).

There is plenty of common sense as well as solid research support behind Centra's four necessary conditions for improvement. New teachers, for instance, or teachers who have never seen student evaluations of their courses, have a greater potential for learning something new from them than teachers who have seen many student ratings and stand to learn nothing new from more of the same. Thus, new knowledge is important. And some teachers are surprised by the perceptions of students. Interestingly, feedback from students appears most effective for those who need it most—those who think they are doing a better job of teaching than students think they are doing. Teachers who received what they interpret as criticism in the form of low ratings do make changes, and in some cases, they do so in as little as six weeks. The changes that are most likely to occur are in such specific behaviors as preparation for class, summarization of major points in lectures or discussions, openness to other viewpoints, and making helpful comments on papers or exams (Centra, 1973a; Murray, 1985). Faculty must also value students' opinions and believe that students are valid judges of the impact of teaching upon their learning. Certainly those faculty of Eble's acquaintance, who "fulminate against student evaluations, with little or no examination of the large body of research" (1983, p. 65), stand to gain little from use of student ratings.

Centra's third condition, that faculty must know how to make improvements is critical, and is related both to the formulation of the rating items and to how the information is fed back to teachers. An item that gives students a chance to say that they cannot read the writing of the instructor or cannot hear him or her is specific enough to carry its own recommendation for improvement. In contrast, a teacher who receives low ratings on an item that asks about effectiveness as a discussion leader, for example, may already be distressed by lackluster discussions but have no idea how to go about improving them.

Most authorities on teaching improvement suggest that instructors who review student ratings with a consultant who is knowledgeable about teaching and learning will make more changes than those who review ratings alone (Cohen, 1980; Lewis, 1991). Cohen examined twenty-two research studies on the impact of student ratings on change and found that teachers who received feedback at midterm received higher end-of-term global ratings in twenty of the twenty-two studies than faculty who received no midterm feedback. The improvement was sufficient to place the typical instructor in a feedback group at the 65th percentile in the judgment of the students, compared with the 50th percentile for instructors in the control group. But even more interesting is Cohen's finding that "augmented" feedback, which included consultation with a knowledgeable consultant, resulted in an average increase which placed the teacher at the 74th percentile by the end of the term.

Finally, a great deal of attention has been given recently to the reward of good teaching in the hope that appropriate rewards will motivate faculty to work conscientiously on improving their teaching. Most people seem to be concentrating on institutional policies regarding promotion, tenure, and other extrinsic rewards. There is some indication, however, that we should be working just as hard to implement the intrinsic rewards for good teaching. Most faculty members want to teach as well as they can, and in an article provocatively titled "Financial Rewards Are Ineffective for Faculty," McKeachie (1979) argues that faculty, most of whom are highly achievement-motivated people, are more responsive to intrinsic than to extrinsic rewards. Unfortunately, Jean is sufficiently threatened by external motivators, namely the possible damage that poor student ratings can do to her chances for promotion and tenure, that she is giving very little attention to the formative uses of the ratings. She is pretty sure the premeds will be critical in their ratings, and accepting criticism is hard enough, but she believes that the poor ratings will also affect her reputation with her colleagues and her career advancement and that makes ratings a source of considerable strain.

Many faculty today report experiencing personal strain from their jobs, with almost half of the faculty across all kinds of institutions, from community colleges to research universities, agreeing "strongly" or "with reservations" with the Carnegie survey item, "My job is the source of considerable personal strain" (The Carnegie Foundation for the Advancement of Teaching, 1990).

Moreover, it appears that much of the strain is due to teachers' uncertainty about the criteria used to evaluate teaching (Gmelch, Lovrich, and Wilke, 1984). Whatever her institution's policy regarding student ratings, Jean would be well advised to conduct her own student evaluations. If the ratings required by the college are to be used summatively to judge her teaching performance, she may as well find out what needs to be corrected before those end-of-term evaluations are due. Moreover, at the pragmatic level, there is some indication that a teacher's concern about the quality of her teaching when shared with students tends to raise ratings (Steadman, 1994). More fundamentally, if Jean understands and accepts the research finding that students are not out to get her but are instead responding to their serious concerns about whether the class is meeting their needs, she needs to know what those concerns are and where the dissatisfactions lie. Many people have made suggestions about how to construct teacher rating scales and other forms of feedback that are useful in formative evaluation, and those suggestions will be incorporated into our examples of Classroom Assessment and Classroom Research.

RECOMMENDED
READING

Faculty Evaluation

Centra, J. A. *Reflective Faculty Evaluation: Enhancing Teaching and Determining Faculty Effectiveness.* San Francisco: Jossey-Bass, 1993.

John Centra, professor and chair of the Higher Education Program at Syracuse University, is one of the foremost researchers on faculty evaluation. He has been doing research in this area for some twenty years, and this book, his most recent, is a treasure of good information about what faculty members, administrators, and faculty development specialists can do to evaluate and improve teaching. Chapter Three, "Student Evaluations of Teaching: What Research Tells Us," offers an up-to-date synthesis of the voluminous research on student evaluations of teaching: its history, the reliability and validity of student rating scales, possible biases, and the types of instruments available. An appendix lists sample instruments and tells where to get them.

Light, R. J., Singer, J. D., and Willett, J. B. *By Design.* Cambridge, Mass.: Harvard University Press, 1990.

Richard Light and his colleagues Judith Singer and John Willett are themselves excellent teachers of research methods at the Harvard Graduate School of Education. It would be hard to find a book that is as clearly written and interesting for the nontechnical Classroom Researcher as this recent paperback is. Classroom Researchers who want authoritative information about traditional research design and analysis would do well to have a copy of this useful book on their reference shelves. Chapter Seven, "How Can You Improve Your Measures?" offers thoughtful advice about designing and improving measurement, and fortunately, many of the examples used and issues raised in this chapter concern the evaluation of teaching. The authors discuss issues of reliability and measurement error and describe six strategies for improving measurement quality: selecting and revising items, increasing the number of items, lengthening item scales, administering the instrument systematically, using appropriate timing for data collection, and using multiple raters or scorers.

Theall, M., and Franklin, J. (eds.). *Student Ratings of Instruction: Issues for Improving Practice.* New Directions for Teaching and Learning, no. 43. San Francisco: Jossey-Bass, 1990.

This monograph concerns improving the decisions made about use of student ratings in evaluating teaching. Its nine fairly brief chapters, written by researchers and practitioners, address some of the major issues in the uses of student ratings: the complexity of the system in which evaluation takes place, the ethics of faculty evaluation, the use of personnel decisions, and how to use the research in practice. Written in nontechnical language, this volume is most useful in providing an overview of how student ratings are used, and more importantly, should be used.

Weimer, M. *Improving College Teaching: Strategies for Developing Instructional Effectiveness.* San Francisco: Jossey-Bass, 1990.

Maryellen Weimer is director of instructional development at Pennsylvania State University. With experience in research, teaching, and faculty development, she straddles the worlds of practice and research comfortably, offering practical advice about how to work with faculty to encourage teaching excellence. The book employs realistic examples from her extensive work with faculty and department chairs. Chapter Four, "Ongoing Assessment and Feedback," is especially relevant to the Captive Audience case because it reviews the literature on how faculty might obtain continuing feedback from students and use it constructively to improve their teaching.

CLASSROOM ASSESSMENT

Collecting Further Information

Introduction. There are a number of good ways to find out what students are thinking about a course or an instructor before the more threatening and less helpful summative student ratings come due at the end of the term. Ten such Classroom Assessment Techniques are described in some detail in Chapter Nine ("Techniques for Assessing Learner Reactions to Instruction") of Angelo and Cross's *Classroom Assessment Techniques* (1993). We have selected two of these CATs for illustration and application to Jean's case.

We chose Group Instructional Feedback Technique because it is especially recommended for problem classes of twenty-five to one hundred students. Jean's lab of twenty-four students is a little small for application of this rather formal structure, but the lab has become a problem class for both teacher and students, and it may be worth some formal effort to identify the problems. Our second choice for an assessment technique for Jean is Electronic Mail Feedback. Because one of Jean's goals for the class is to improve students' skills in using computers, she might reinforce that goal by asking students to use e-mail to respond to some very specific questions about a given lab experience.

Example 1: Group Instructional Feedback Technique. (See CAT 44 in Angelo and Cross, 1993, pp. 334–338.) The Group Instructional Feedback Technique (GIFT) is similar to the Small Group Instructional Diagnosis (SGID) discussed in Weimer (1990, pp. 107–108). Under any name, its basic purpose is to provide information about student consensus on issues affecting the class. GIFT works like this: in the last twenty minutes or so of the lab session, Jean explains to students that she is interested in making learning in her physics lab as useful as possible, and she explains the role of GIFT in her analysis. Next, Jean introduces a teaching colleague who has agreed to assist in the evaluation, and then Jean leaves the room. The colleague asks students to take three or four minutes to write their answers to two or three specific questions that usually represent some formulation of, What works in this class? What doesn't? What can be done to improve it? In Jean's case, she might request the colleague to obtain the answers to some questions along these lines: Give one or two specific examples of things about this class that are helpful to you in learning. Give one or two specific examples of things that happen in this class that hinder your learning. Suggest one or two specific, practical changes that the instructor might make that would help you improve your learning in this class. After students have had a chance to write out brief responses, they are asked to meet with three or four students near them to compare their responses and report on the consensus.

This group collaboration has the triple advantage of weeding out idiosyncratic responses, of quickly summarizing for the instructor the dominant themes, and of giving students a chance to compare their reactions with others. A skillful colleague can get a picture of the scene pretty quickly and convey, through the lens of a sympathetic outsider, both positive and negative reactions to the class. For example, Jean assumes that it is largely the six premeds who are dissatisfied. Is that an accurate diagnosis or are the premeds just more aggressive in showing their dissatisfaction?

Weimer (1990, p. 108) does point out that care should be taken in selecting the facilitator. She relates the sad tale of a faculty member who, while serving as facilitator for a colleague, got into a major argument with the students and lectured them over their grade-grubbing attitude. Jean and her collaborator need to have a clear understanding of the purpose of this kind of assessment. The other caution that needs attention when using GIFT is the time required. Angelo and Cross (1993, p. 336) suggest allowing fifteen or twenty minutes; Weimer (1990, p. 108) notes that a thirty-minute time frame was "too tight." Even so, she found that some instructors declined to use the technique because they could not give up thirty minutes of class time. Instructors need to weigh for themselves the best use of time. Is using the thirty minutes as the Seths and Danas in Jean's class are currently using them more productive than using the time to diagnose the problems and address them?

Whatever the answer to that question, the unhappy compromise would be to do a hurry-up job of the Classroom Assessment. Rushing students through the exercise without adequate preparation or time to reflect in order to take a serious and constructive attitude toward the assessment is probably worse than useless. If Jean wants to "save" this problem class, she needs to get at the problems early—before they are so serious that students use the GIFT time to gripe—and she needs to allow enough time for planning with her collaborator, for students to think seriously about what kind of work they would assign in the class, for a debriefing with her collaborator, and for her own exploration of how she can use the students' suggestions.

Example 2: Electronic Mail Feedback. (See CAT 42 in Angelo and Cross, 1993, pp. 327–329.) On campuses where e-mail exists, the Electronic Mail Feedback CAT has three major advantages: it reinforces students' perceptions of computers as tools for communication; it saves class time by permitting communication between faculty and students outside of class; it establishes a pattern of communication between teacher and students that reinforces the constant research finding that the frequency of faculty-student contact is an important predictor of student motivation and achievement. The big disadvantage to it is that if only a few students respond, their comments may represent a host of unknown biases. Are the respondents those who are most comfortable with e-mail? Those who have an ax to grind? Those who have easy access to a computer? If Jean is using this CAT to get an early clue about how her student ratings are going to look at the end of the semester, she will have to be aware of the potential for a possibly small and biased response.

Nevertheless, if Jean is interested in building up a partnership with students of shared responsibility for the quality of learning in the lab, e-mail offers a quick and easy way to maintain communication. This CAT will probably work best if Jean sets up an expectation that she will be communicating via e-mail about a variety of things—from assignments, to tips for homework, to reactions to the lab experiences. She might occasionally introduce some humor into her messages, or pose a provocative question that some students would find hard to resist, or find other ways of attracting students to read and respond. In this kind of continuing communication, there would be nothing unusual about Jean's asking for an evaluation of how well a particular lab session met students' expectations and needs or for ideas about changes in the lab procedures and assignments. In order to establish a cooperative spirit, the evaluation aspect of the e-mail should probably be the occasional rather than the primary purpose of the e-mail.

CLASSROOM RESEARCH

Explorations for Understanding

Example 1: Designing and Administering a Midterm Course Evaluation. How student observations[5] can be used to improve instruction is a research question of high interest and high relevance to classroom teachers. It is, perhaps, the question that dominates traditional research on student ratings today, now that the surge of research regarding the fairness of using student ratings summatively has been nearly exhausted. As the literature review of student ratings illustrated, research on the validity and reliability of student ratings is sufficiently positive that student perceptions can be used, albeit with certain precautions (see Centra, 1993, chaps. 3 and 4), as *one* responsible source of information for decisions based on teaching performance.

Traditional researchers have also devoted considerable attention to the use of student perceptions in the improvement of teaching. The value of student ratings to individual teachers depends basically on two things: how useful the information is, and how receptive the teacher is. Given that Classroom Research is a voluntary activity undertaken by those who are curious about the effectiveness of their own teaching, we assume here that faculty motivation is not an issue in Classroom Research and turn our attention to suggestions for Classroom Research projects that improve the diagnostic measures and methods for collecting student perceptions and that demonstrate how and whether change is taking place.

Improving measures and methods. Through the extensive experience of traditional researchers in collecting student reactions to teaching, much has been learned about how to construct instruments that are reliable, valid, and helpful. Although there are many ways to collect information about learning from students—fifty are described in *Classroom Assessment Techniques* (Angelo and Cross, 1993)—we are concerned here with exploring student ratings in relation to hypothesis 3, that is, with ways that Jean, rather than feeling threatened by student ratings, can use them to improve the learning in her physics lab.

Many colleges today use a "cafeteria-style" rating form divided into three sections. The first section might contain global comparative questions that appear on rating forms that go to all instructors (for example, How does this instructor/course compare with others at this college?). The second section differs by department and consists of a set of items developed by each department and assumed relevant to that department's discipline and style of teaching. The third section might offer a pool of items from which individual instructors can choose those most interesting or relevant to their particular style of teaching. This is a well-meant effort to combine summative and formative purposes into a single survey administration, but if scoring is done centrally (which is a presumed advantage of cafeteria-style forms), individuals, and sometimes even departments, are going to select items that make them look good, rather than items that may show weaknesses that need attention.

Guidelines. In Jean's case, it would be highly desirable for her to construct her own instrument to collect student reactions to her lab. The following discussion pulls from the literature some general guidelines for constructing good diagnostic student rating instruments. (See also Chapter Seven of Light, Singer, and Willett, 1990, described in the recommended reading for faculty evaluation.)

1. Students should be oriented to the project and the purposes of the assessment made clear to them. They should be brought on board as "members of the team," responsible, along with the teacher, for the quality of their learning in the class.

2. The instrument should contain a balance of positive and negative items. Even for a problem class, an overdose of negative feedback can be demoralizing and decrease students' motivation rather than improve it. Moreover, as Weimer reminds us, "Teaching can be improved in two ways: Weaknesses can be eliminated, and strengths can be improved" (1990, p. 62).

3. To the greatest extent possible, specific behaviors that the

instructor is willing and able to change should be emphasized. Research shows that the changes most likely to occur as a result of student evaluations will be in specific behaviors such as preparing for class, using class time, summarizing major points in lectures or discussion, exhibiting openness to other viewpoints, and writing helpful comments on papers or exams (Centra, 1973b; Murray, 1985).

4. The questionnaire should be administered early enough in the term that the teacher has time to put suggested changes into effect or to practice new skills. Research suggests that evaluations of teaching are generally quite stable after the first few weeks of class; thus, there is little reason for waiting until the end of the term to gather reactions to teaching (Costin, 1968; Kohlan, 1973).

5. Student respondents should be an adequate sample of the class, both in number and representativeness. If only six students respond, for example, they may be students with an ax to grind (Jean's premeds?) or a desire to be flattering or reassuring. Either way, the assessment of class perceptions will be inaccurate. Centra suggests that "generally, if two-thirds or more of the students in a class respond, the results are fairly representative" (1993, p. 60). The best way to ensure adequate class representation is to provide adequate class time for students to complete their responses, rather than assigning the task as homework or trying in other ways to minimize the amount of class time taken for the exercise.

6. The instructor should consult with someone knowledgeable in the area about both the formulation of the questionnaire and the interpretation of the results. Analyzing student input by oneself can lead to misinterpretation as one's own biases and interests take over.

7. In most cases, if not all, assessment results should be shared with students, both to clarify any contradictions in the data and to emphasize that the quality of learning is a joint responsibility of teacher and students. In Jean's case, where she perceives a serious threat in the end-of-term evaluations, there is also a very practical reason for letting students know that she is seriously interested in improving her teaching. Weimer puts it bluntly: "That [show of interest] has got to be to an instructor's advantage when students complete the end-of-course evaluations" (1990, p. 63).

Designing the instrument. Although Classroom Researchers need not be experts in instrument design, they should be clear about their purposes, and they should give attention to selecting a format likely to be practical and useful in their classroom situation. Weimer (1990, pp. 65–81) presents a good discussion of four types of instruments that can be devised for formative feedback, their pros and cons, and some helpful advice about how to use each type. Briefly, the types are as follows.

Closed-question instruments consist of a fixed set of items with responses scored on a set three-, five-, or seven-point scale (for example, "always," "sometimes," "never"). The chief advantages of closed-question instruments are that they offer anonymity to students (no handwriting) and efficient scoring (especially for large classes). The chief disadvantage is that the teacher may be unaware of or insensitive to some student reactions and fail to ask about them in the instrument.

Open-ended instruments encourage free responses from students, but it is still important to give careful attention to question formulation. Open-ended instruments require more work from students, who may be inclined to give superficial and brief responses unless they are oriented to the task and the questions encourage reflection and thought. For example, in the simplest and most frequently used question in instruments of this type, it is usually more constructive to ask how the class is effective or ineffective in promoting students' learning than it is to ask what they liked or disliked. The latter question is likely to bring forth an easy answer, such as the class hour or location. Sometimes, however, even the easy answer ("Jiggling the change in his pocket drives me nuts") reveals teacher behavior that is easily corrected.

The chief advantage of the open-ended instrument is that it may turn up things that never occurred to the instructor. The chief disadvantages are that students may feel a lack of anonymity, especially in a small class (Jean, for example, tried to figure out who wrote certain comments), and the instrument is difficult to score. When teachers use this instrument for their own purposes, however, a quick read through of the responses can give an amazingly revealing picture—and of course, there is really no need to "score," or quantify, the data.

Checklists and inventories are most often distributed by people interested in informing or reminding college teachers about the characteristic practices of good teaching. The Faculty Inventory derived from "Seven Principles for Good Practice in Undergraduate Education" (Chickering and Gamson, 1987) is a good example of this genre. It lists ten items for each principle of good practice. For example, under principle 4, "gives prompt feedback," it includes these practices: "I give students detailed evaluations of their work early in the term," and "I ask students to keep logs or records of their progress." Checklists and inventories are not especially likely to be constructed by individual teachers doing Classroom Assessment or Classroom Research, but they may be useful as a reminder of the classroom behaviors that the teacher wants to exhibit.

Focused topic instruments may be of any design—open-ended, closed-question, or checklist. Their chief distinction is that they zero in on a particular problem—almost any student perception on which the teacher needs more information: the fairness of exams, the helpfulness of teacher comments on written work, the usefulness of the textbook or assigned readings, the productivity of small group sessions, and the like.

These four major categories of instruments used in formative feedback make different demands on the instructor, and our point is that teachers should be aware of the variety in student response forms and should select and develop the type that best suits their needs. In Jean's case, it seems desirable for her to use a mostly open-ended instrument for two reasons: first, she does not have a clear idea of what is bothering these students, and they may be able to provide some insights that have not occurred to her, and second, she has no real need for an easy-scoring instrument or to quantify the data or determine trends in her small class of twenty-four. She can get a very good idea of student reactions by reading the comments on a brief open-ended instrument. Exhibit 3.3 illustrates how Jean's midterm evaluation instrument, prepared according to the guidelines listed previously, might look.

Exhibit 3.3.
Jean's Midterm Evaluation Instrument.

Midterm Course Evaluation
Physics Laboratory 101, Spring Semester 1996

The purpose of this midterm course evaluation is to help us make this laboratory the best possible learning experience for you. I will appreciate your frank and thoughtful answers.

1. What is your major or planned major?
2. Why are you taking this course?
3. What learning activities do you find most helpful in this laboratory?
4. What learning activities do you find hinder or impede your learning—or are just not very helpful?
5. What specific suggestions do you have for making this laboratory more relevant to your learning needs?
6. [Here, Jean might add a few of the most relevant items from the end-of-term evaluation form used by her college.]

Rationale for the items included in Jean's evaluation. The rationale for including items 1 and 2 is that they are highly related to Jean's hypothesis that it is the premeds who are dissatisfied. She needs to check the accuracy of her perception. At the same time, she needs to keep her instrument brief and focused on the value of the learning experience for students. Many people designing questionnaires have an urge to collect easily obtainable information about such student characteristics as age, full time or part time, ethnic background, and the like. However, Classroom Researchers should collect no more personal information than is needed to answer the research questions. The ultimate test of the usefulness of an evaluation item is, What would the instructor do differently if he or she knew the answer to that question? In addition, Jean's class is small enough that she must be very careful not to compromise the anonymity of students by asking about personal information that could identify them. It might also be nice to know, in this particular case, what grades students expect to receive in the lab, but that is a sensitive issue and might imperil student trust and the answers to other questions.

Items 3 and 4 are worded to keep students' attention focused on the value of the *learning* rather than on their "likes" or "dislikes" or the "strengths" or "weaknesses" of the instructor.

Many students will leave item 5 blank because it is hard work to think constructively, that is, about solutions rather than problems. But the question is still worth asking, both because a few students will have helpful suggestions and because students who are complaining should at least be confronted with the task of thinking what they would do differently. Students should be oriented to the importance of thinking seriously about this question *prior* to administration of the instrument.

Item 6 and subsequent items might be included because of Jean's concern about the impact of the end-of-term evaluations on her career. These additional items should be limited to addressing issues that she thinks she can do something about in the time remaining in the course.

Example 2: Measuring Change. Measuring change is probably the most common—and most complex—research question in education. People usually want to know how to change something for the better. In Jean's case, there are a number of things that she might like to change. They range from the narrowly expedient to the broadly educational.

At the expedient end of the scale, we know that Jean would like to improve her end-of-term student ratings. She also worries about the effect of the premeds' complaints on the other students. "Thank God, they're sitting in the back corner of the laboratory so that most of the others don't notice them," is her practical thought. Ideally, however, Jean would like these students to see the relevance of the lab work to their college and career goals. She would like them to revamp their motivation, changing from grade-grubbing students concerned about their eligibility for med school to learners appreciative of the relevance of physics to their lives and careers. Jean and her colleagues have worked hard to implement a discovery-based approach to learning, and she has program assessment data to show that "most students . . . had a better grasp of fundamental concepts" as a result of the innovative curriculum. What might Jean do to demonstrate to her students—and to herself—that this approach is valuable and relevant to student goals?

Jean first needs to formulate one or more specific research questions to guide her design. She probably has at least these four questions about change: Can she improve her end-of-term student ratings? Can she improve students' attitudes? Can she improve her own teaching? Can she improve students' learning? These questions are, of course, interrelated. Improving her teaching so that students see the relevance of the lab exercises to their goals would change students' attitudes, which would change their motivation for learning, which would improve their learning, which would change their ratings. Ultimately, the question is students' learning, but immediately, for Jean, the question is students' ratings, so we will start there.

1. *Can Jean improve her ratings?* The easiest way for Jean to conduct an experiment to see whether she can improve her student ratings is for her to administer the college student ratings instrument at midterm, to work on the things that need improvement, and then to administer the same instrument at the end of the term.

One problem with this design is that students, like teachers, are prone to reward people who show that they are sincerely trying to improve. As we have mentioned, there is evidence that when teachers show their interest in making their teaching relevant and interesting to students, through discussion, Classroom Assessment, or any other method of seeking student input, students tend to reward them with higher ratings (Angelo, 1991; Cross, 1988a; Steadman, 1994). However, setting out to improve ratings without necessarily improving teaching can backfire. Just as the strategies of grade-grubbing students backfire when teachers perceive they are more interested in grades than in learning, so the strategies of rating-grubbing teachers can backfire when teachers fail to implement students' suggestions for improvement. Nevertheless, just as grade-grubbing students often work hard at learning, so teachers interested in improving their ratings often work hard at teaching.

Before Jean decides to conduct an experiment to see if she can raise her ratings from midterm to end of term using her college's standard instrument to evaluate faculty, she should first determine whether that instrument has items that are truly helpful in formative evaluations. How many items are there on the instrument that have implications for Jean? How many items concern practices that

Jean can and would change if she knew how students were responding to them? If the college instrument has been designed for formative as well as summative purposes, and she decides to administer it at midterm to see if she can improve her ratings, then in her comparison of the midterm and end-of-term results, she should look at the items that show change. Are they the items she deliberately worked on or is the change broad and general across all items? The latter finding raises the question whether students were simply responding favorably to her solicitation of their advice. And although the former finding does not "prove" that Jean has improved on the items she worked on, giving heightened attention to areas targeted for improvement has some merit in and of itself.

2. *Can Jean improve students' attitudes?* Conducting traditional research on attitude change is complex and not very satisfactory. It is extremely difficult to show such change as a result of some educational intervention, and even if change is shown on an attitude inventory, there may be no corresponding change in behavior. In this case, however, no grand research design is needed. In the same way that Jean discovered poor student attitudes and "rotten . . . interpersonal chemistry" by observing them, she can observe whether student attitudes are improving and whether this change results in new behaviors toward physics lab learning.

Jean's working hypothesis with respect to students' attitudes is that the premeds do not see the relevance of the lab exercises to their futures as health care workers. If she does not know how to make her physics lab work more relevant, then her Classroom Assessment projects may prove useful. But beyond that, her Classroom Research project might consist of working with some local practitioners or academics in the field of medicine to devise some class exercises and assignments that *are* relevant to careers in medicine.

This brings up an important point regarding the use of colleagues in Classroom Research. The apparent hostility of the premeds may not be Jean's fault, especially if such attitudes continue from year to year. Perhaps the faculty responsible for the physics lab requirement should be challenged to be explicit about expected learning outcomes. If the requirement is deemed useful for premeds, but students do not understand the relevance, then the faculty might help students see the value of the requirements. For example, they might design one or two optional evening programs for the premeds, inviting local medical practitioners to talk about what premeds should learn in college. Maybe Jean or a colleague from the physics department should be a member of a panel articulating the rationale for the relevance of the experimental, investigatory nature of physics to the practice of medicine. Or the director of admissions of a medical college might be invited to talk with all premeds—not just the students in Jean's lab—about the criteria for admission to medical schools. Telling students why they should be interested in learning physics will not necessarily change attitudes, but sometimes correcting misinformation or pointing out unseen relevancies will help. Ultimately, attitudes and motivation for learning will change when—and probably only when—students see the relevance of the learning to their values and needs.

Again, Classroom Research need not be a "study" involving the collection of quantifiable data. It might very well be a modest experiment or a series of experiments to see what works. Changing student attitudes from open hostility to cooperation and involvement does not call for an instrument with rigorous criteria to determine whether change has occurred. Jean will be able to see a change in student behaviors, just as she is able to see the present hostility.

3. *Can Jean change her teaching?* One way for Jean to study change in herself or her course is to construct her own midterm evaluation, targeted to areas that are of high interest to her *and* that she knows how to change. This option has been discussed fully in the previous Classroom Research project. It would be desirable for Jean to continue to revise and improve her instrument and to administer it to several different classes to gauge her improvement as a teacher. Although having a problem class is apparently somewhat unusual for Jean, every experienced teacher has a class now and then that just does not work. That does not mean that Jean can ignore the problem and hope that it does not happen again. Instead, she can use some kind of continuous monitoring to keep informed about underlying dissatisfactions.

4. *Can Jean improve students' learning?* This question is the ultimate question. Jean has program assessment data that indicate that the discovery-based approach she and her colleagues have worked so hard on is successful in the sense that "most students had a better grasp of fundamentals." The choice of criteria is one of the most difficult and important decisions any researcher has to make. In this case, Jean might use performance on her final examination as the criterion for student learning, she might use an instrument specifically designed to test those aspects of student learning that the discovery-based approach is designed to enhance, or she might use the departmentally designed instrument that tests students' "grasp of fundamental concepts" of physics. What is it that students should learn in Jean's physics lab? Jean and her students should know the answer to that question, and any test that she uses as a measure must reflect that understanding.

There are literally hundreds of professionally designed instruments to test all manner of learning outcomes, and Jean might be tempted to use an instrument for testing changes in critical thinking, or postformal reasoning, or any of the other complex concepts of intellectual development. We are tempted to advise against Classroom Research projects that involve the measurement of complex intellectual skills. Despite the easy availability of adequately designed instruments and despite the importance of higher-level cognitive skills as the ultimate aim of all educators, such research is best left to professional researchers. In the first place, evidence of broad intellectual growth is quite unlikely to show up in any single classroom, limited to a short period of time and a specific subject matter. Furthermore, most such research requires answering too many psychometric and technical design questions, given the time, interest, training, and resources of the average classroom teacher. Pascarella and Terenzini (1991) have reviewed thousands of studies on the impact of college on student learning conducted over the past twenty years. Their findings are reported in a volume of nearly 900 pages, replete with more than 150 pages of references!

In conclusion, there are many assessment and research projects Jean can do to get useful and productive indications of change. There is no particular reason for her to quantify change or to engage in rigorous experiments involving control groups. The kind of change Jean is dealing with here is a common one, and any teacher dedicated to making an accurate diagnosis and implementing a series of small changes designed to address the problems should be able to observe the resulting changes in his or her continuing relationship with the students.

CHAPTER 4

"But Is It Working?"

Learning Issues: Peer Learning;
Intellectual Development
and Critical Thinking

CASE STUDY _____

Sam Marston and Susan Green have been team teaching History
and Its Methods at City College for three years now. They have tin-
kered with the course in various ways, and developed an extensive
set of course materials that has changed a bit each semester, but
they have been happy with their general focus on historical thinking and have continued it this semester. Susan likes to explain the
course through the metaphor of the blind man and the elephant:
"History," she tells students at the beginning of each semester, "is
like the elephant. What it looks like depends a lot on where you're
standing."

This orientation is reflected in the syllabus as well, a nine-
page document that lists and explains six goals related to understanding and evaluating various explanations of the past.

It is now seven weeks into the semester, and students have
been reading about and discussing various modes of historical

Note: Case study by Pat Hutchings, director, American Association for Higher Education's Teaching Initiative. This case study is excerpted from a longer, four-part
case that Hutchings wrote in 1991 as part of a national project on cases as prompts
for faculty conversation about teaching and learning. It has been revised for inclusion here in order to raise questions related to Classroom Research. We join Pat
Hutchings in gratefully acknowledging the assistance of Valerie French, professor of
history at The American University, who contributed to the design of the case in
numerous ways.

analysis—studying the ways historians "make" history depending on their points of view and purposes. Students have also had a chance to experience the process of "making" history by working on personal family histories.

For the most part, Susan and Sam have been happy with the course thus far. The students are good natured and pleasant; they seem attentive and responsive during lectures, and a good number of them chip in during class discussions, keeping things lively. But with the midterm ten days off, both instructors were surprised when a student made a distinctly disturbing comment.

Brian's Complaint

Susan was lecturing that week on "analytical and narrative approaches to history"—a focus of the upcoming midterm. On Wednesday, almost before she got started with her comments, Brian Durbin, an older student and an obviously bright one (he had gotten an A- on the first exam), interrupted her.

"I thought this was supposed to be a history course," Brian called out from the back of the room, where he and several other older students typically sat. When Susan asked him to say more about what he meant, Brian said, "I guess I thought this class would deal more with *real* history rather than just methods and analysis. I mean, I see what we're doing, but it seems that in this class we seem to be just walking around the edges of history. We don't ever talk about events."

Surprised, but too experienced to be really shaken, Susan referred the class back to the syllabus. "Remember the story of the blind man and the elephant," she said. "This is not a course about facts; it's about how we make sense of facts, how we understand them, how history is *made*." But as she confessed to Sam after class, she was troubled by the Brian's question. "Most of the class did pretty well on the first exam," she mused, "but maybe they're not getting the big picture. Maybe they're not really learning what it means to think like an historian. If Brian is confused, what about the other forty-six students?"

An Antidote

Susan and Sam meet for coffee in order to strategize before each class. Today's class, Susan and Sam hope, will be an antidote to the problem raised by Brian's question. As in several past class sessions, students will work together in groups, today's task being to analyze a short account of an historical event (the student protests on the Kiev University campus at the turn of the century) in terms of its "mode of thought."

"I think it may help," Susan suggests to Sam as they walk together into room 302, "that our example is actually about students. University students. Surely that will help Brian feel more connected to the subject."

"Well, yeah," Sam agrees, "and the small groups should be helpful too. The groups seem to force students to be involved."

Small-group discussion is, in fact, a new addition to the course this year, one Sam and Susan have agreed to try. Some of their colleagues have become strong advocates of the method, and it seems to both Susan and Sam not only a good way to keep students interested and involved—not an easy task, as Sam frequently points out, in a room full of nonmajors eager to get the course behind them—but also a way to encourage students to be more independent thinkers. Feeling good about the day's plan, Susan and Sam smile at each other as they enter the classroom.

Small Groups

"Okay, now, listen up," Sam shouts out across the noise as the students unzip backpacks, open notebooks, borrow pencils, cough, and shuffle papers. "We're going to have you work in small groups today, as you did a couple of weeks ago—this time on a topic we've been talking about for the last week: modes of historical thinking and writing. Be sure you've got one of the blue handouts that Dr. Green is passing out. It will tell you what to do in your group." (See Exhibit 4.1 for the class handout.)

Exhibit 4.1.
Case Study Handout for Small-Group Work.

History 230: History and Its Methods, Spring Semester

Instructions. We have been discussing narrative and analytical modes of thought. Read the following paragraph carefully. Critically evaluate the explanation it provides of student demonstrations in Russia. Then come to consensus in your group about the mode of historical thought employed and be prepared to explain why you think so.

The penalty of conscript service for taking part in student demonstrations was bitterly resented. Resentment had not died down when the universities opened again in the autumn. All through the following year there were small threatening incidents. Towards the end of 1900 passions flared up again in Kiev University, where a protest meeting was broken up by troops and police and some five hundred students were arrested. About half the number were drafted into the army. Immediately there were sympathetic student disorders in Kharkov, Moscow, and St. Petersburg" [quoted from Richard Charques, *The Twilight of Imperial Russia* (New York: Oxford University Press, 1958), p. 68].

"So, is everybody clear about what he or she needs to do?" Susan asks, waving the handout in the air. "You have the directions in front of you: decide whether the short account of the student revolts in Kiev is narrative or analytical. And be prepared to explain why." She glances at Sam.

"Okay," Sam says. "Is everybody clear about the two modes of thought we're working with here? Jerome? Marcy? Melissa? Anybody? Can somebody summarize what the reading assignment instructions mean by 'narrative and analytical modes of historical thought'?" Sam glances at Susan, then picks up the *City College Daily* from Melissa Anderson's front-row desk, turning to the sports page.

"Look," he says, pointing to a story about last Friday's basketball game. "Here's the story about the big game. The reporter tells you how the score went back and forth and how the crowd went wild when Keith Browning made that shot in the last three seconds. That's the narrative, the story, complete with all the drama and excitement. Then, here, in a box at the bottom of the page, you see the stats for the two teams: that's analysis. Now, that's clear, isn't it, Melissa?" he says, handing her back her newspaper and giving her an expectant look. "Clear?"

Melissa glances sideways at Jerome, an athletic eighteen-year-old, who is mimicking a free throw. "Yes. I guess so." Melissa says. "Just like you say: there's the story and the numbers. They're different."

"Okay," Susan says. "I think it's time to just jump right into your small-group discussions."

Susan and Sam watch the students drag their chairs from the usual rows into five-person circles for small-group discussions. The students finally settle in their seats and begin to read the handout.

"This silence is eerie," Susan whispers to Sam as the students read. "I'm always afraid they won't have anything to say."

But just moments later, they hear a voice in the back of the room, then another from the group by the windows. In no time at all, the noise level rises and discussion is underway.

"Let's circulate," Susan suggests. "I sort of like to listen in to what's happening. I want to make sure this group thing makes a difference." Sam nods and heads for a group toward the back of the room as Susan takes off for the other corner.

Do We Have to Know This for the Test?

As Sam squeezes between groups on his way toward the back of the room, a hand flies out in front of him, madly waving: it's Melissa. He tries to duck, but she has him; there's no escape.

"Dr. Marston? Can I ask you something? Dr. Marston?" Sam nods. "I was just wondering about the midterm. Are we going to have to know about this Kiev protest? And what about that paragraph we looked at last week about the Gulf War?" The other members of Melissa's group look up at Sam expectantly, one of them, Sam thinks, smiling an ironic smile.

"Well, Melissa," he offers, trying not to sound impatient, "the Kiev incident is just an example, really. Like the Gulf War. I mean we expect you to know some examples and to be able to use them to illustrate your argument, but their value is as examples, not main ideas."

Eager to divert attention from the "history as events and facts" school of thought, Sam reminds the group that the midterm will be an essay and short-answer exam, calling more for analysis and interpretation than for dates and facts. "We'll talk about the midterm at the end of the hour. Okay?" Sam says to Melissa, wondering all the while how the point of the course could be so difficult for these students to get. He and Susan have been drilling it into them since day one, he thinks in frustration—it's not facts but ways of interpreting facts. How can it be so hard?

Brian's Group

Meanwhile, Susan has stopped at a group toward the back of the room that includes Brian and two other older students, Rosa and Tobias, as well as Marcy, a talkative, earnest young woman who had, if Susan's memory serves her, gotten a good solid B on the first exam.

"I don't know how we're supposed to evaluate this," Marcy announces to Susan with evident frustration. "Are we just supposed to say what we think? I've never even heard of Kiev University."

"But we're all students," Brian insists. "We know about student protests. Remember the protests about tuition last year? We need more of that kind of thing around here . . . to shake things up a little bit."

"Well, I don't know about that," says Rosa. "I thought those affirmative action demonstrations down at city hall last month got way out of hand. All those arrests. It was frightening."

"Yeah," Brian challenges, "but those protests drew some attention to the issue, didn't they, Rosa?"

Susan cocks her head and listens. It's important for students to connect the course with things they care about, she thinks, and one of the goals of the class has to do with values, but certainly they are "off task" at this point. Susan moves closer and asks, in what she hopes is an innocent tone of voice, "Making progress?"

Marcy looks up and shrugs again.

"Well, keep at it," Susan urges. "I think you're making progress."

After Susan walks away, Tobias volunteers his perspective: "I think it's analytical—it describes the number of students who were arrested."

"Yeah, you're probably right," says Brian.

"Well, okay, I guess we're done," says Marcy. "Rosa, can I look at your notes from Monday's lecture? I want to make sure I didn't miss any important details for the midterm."

Rosa shares her notes, but does not look convinced that the group's conclusion made sense. "Is this the blind leading the blind?" she asks in a barely audible voice. The rest of the group starts talking about things other than modes of analysis.

It Has to Be One or the Other, Right?

"No contest," Jerome is saying in the next group on Sam's circuit. "Of course the answer is narrative. One thing following another. A story. It's obvious. Just like Dr. M. said at the beginning of the class."

Gina, a student in her second year at the college responds, "Well, you're entitled to your opinion, Jerome, but I think the passage could be either narrative or analytical, I mean, does it have to be one thing or the other? Why not both?"

Sharee, another student in the group, is the first person in her family to go to college. With a family and a full-time job as grocery store cashier, she takes only two courses each semester but always manages to complete the assigned reading. Sharee tries to get the discussion going, saying, "Okay, let's carefully consider the definitions of analytical and narrative, and think about the paragraph, before we decide on an answer." After a silence, she asks: "Hasn't anyone else done the reading?"

Jerome shakes his head in disgust and rolls his eyes. He and the other students notice Sam nearby. All eyes turn to the professor. "The answer is narrative, right?" Jerome says to Sam. "Right? I mean, it has to be."

"Talk about it among yourselves. I have to move on, folks," Sam says, backing up. "I've got a couple more groups to visit."

"Aw, come on," says Jerome. "You're the teacher, tell us the answer."

Off the Track

When Susan discovers that the next group is talking about their weekend plans—something about the basketball game—she makes a U-turn and circles back around to catch Sam between groups. "I think we better break in," she says. "They're getting off the track. And I think some of them are really confused."

"Maybe so," Sam says. "But now we've really got some conversations going. Let's let them continue a couple more minutes."

"Well, all right," Susan agrees, "but does talking guarantee learning?"

Closing Discussion

A couple minutes later, Susan and Sam position themselves in front of the room and call the class back together. "So, what do you think?" Sam asks the class.

In no time at all, discussion is rolling, with views on both sides—narrative and analytical—being loudly put forward.

Sam loves a good battle, Susan thinks, watching, smiling.

"We thought it was analytical," Marcy volunteered.

"No way!" Jerome shouts out, "it's narrative." Marcy reddens.

"You seem pretty sure, Jerome," Sam says back. "But I bet someone else has a different idea."

"Our group talked about civil demonstrations and how important it is for students to take a stand," Brian says from his usual back-of-the-room seat. "It was a really good discussion."

"That's an interesting connection," Susan says, relieved to see Brian entering into the discussion in good spirit, even if somewhat off the subject.

"And you're probably right," Sam adds. "But we really can't get off on that right now. We only have a couple more minutes, and I want to be sure that the main point of the session is clear. What we're interested in here is the method of analysis."

Sam turns to Susan, who continues. "That's right," she says loudly, over the shuffling of books and bags as students start packing up to leave at the final click of the clock above the door. "And what we've seen today in this discussion is that the approaches we've been talking about aren't neat closed boxes. They aren't pure. One kind of analysis leaks over into another so that in today's example, for instance, we have several different modes of thought operating at once."

Glancing at Melissa in the front row, Sam jumps in. "Some of you asked about the midterm, which is in a week and a half. Being able to identify modes of thought and explain your reasoning, which we didn't really have a chance to do in this short final discussion, is what we'll be after there. We'll talk more about that next week when we have more time."

"Well, what was *that* all about? Like, what are we supposed to study?" Susan hears Marcy ask Melissa on the way out.

"Yeah, I know," Melissa answers. "I still don't know what the answer was."

"Those groups were really lively today." Sam chuckles, as the students file out of the room.

"Yes," Susan says, scrunching her forehead. "But is it working?"

CASE ANALYSIS

The case just presented is different from the others in this book in that it is a researched case study. The case author observed this class in the fall of 1990, and as a supplement to the case itself, we have available an exceptionally rich store of research about it. This research consists of interviews (telephone and face-to-face with students and one of the teachers), course documents (the syllabus, assignments, and exam questions), notes from class observations, and written student responses to questions about the class.

Thus, in this case analysis, instead of highlighting the learning issues as we have done in the previous case analyses, we present the raw data collected by the case author. We suggest that you study the data, individually or in discussion groups, to identify the learning issues revealed in the research. Following this section, we revert to our established pattern for this book, presenting a literature review of some relevant background research. We hope, however, that your analysis will reveal other learning issues than those the review addresses and that these further issues will motivate your further exploration of the literature and what it has to contribute to your understanding of the learning issues in this case.

All the data presented here are actual data from the study, usually presented as direct quotes from students and teachers or from notes made about documents and interviews. (The case author's notes on class observations were incorporated into the case presentation.)

Syllabus Excerpts

The syllabus was a nine-page document describing course goals and objectives, course requirements, criteria for evaluation (including information about plagiarism and the late assignment policy), the class agenda, the assignments, and the due dates. It contained these statements:

- We take as our starting premise the view that what we believe happened in the past—whether true or not—has a tremendous influence on what we believe we see today and what we decide to do in the future.
- This course will explore some aspects of the theory and

practice (both contemporary and historical) of the study of the past; it will focus on the ways in which:

1. Our thinking is affected by our personal experience and our beliefs about what happened in the past.
2. We can reconstruct and explain the past.
3. We can arrive at moral evaluations of the past.
4. We can organize and present knowledge and views of the past.
5. We can analyze and critically evaluate what others argue are "lessons of the past."

- Among the course goals are these:
  1. Know about the historical and philosophical traditions that shape the Western world.
  2. Consider the significance of evidence that sheds light on the experience of people and the ideas of civilizations.
  3. Understand moral and ethical reasoning.
  4. Use historical and philosophical methods to examine and assess evidence, draw conclusions, and evaluate the meaning of these conclusions.

Instructor Interview Notes

In an interview with one of the instructors conducted during the semester, the following viewpoints were presented:

- The point is to get students to let go of the notion of historical objectivity, of simple facts. This is very difficult for them. They think in great antipodes—with scientific truth on one end, mere opinion on the other—nothing in between.
- We want to get students to see how different it looks from different points of view; to develop confidence in their ability to make sense of things.
- Learning this kind of self-consciousness about thinking is like learning to ride a bike. You have it or you don't, and once you get it, you wonder what all the fuss was about.
- I can't figure out a way not to trade depth for coverage. For me, the change will have to be very incremental.

End-of-Term Essay Assignment Excerpts

The handout describing the end-of-term essay was four pages long and included the due date, assignments, and criteria for grading the essay. It included this statement:

What we believe about the past influences our perceptions of contemporary events and our recommendations about future courses of action. In the End-of-Term Essay, you are to demonstrate your understanding of the material covered in this course by discussing a current issue and applying to it the methods and models of analysis you have learned this semester.

You are to present your work in the form of a well-organized and well-written essay of about 5–7 pages (typewritten, double-spaced, with proper margins). Your essay is to be a policy memorandum and recommendation to an important adviser to the President of the United States; specifically you are being asked to inform the Presidential adviser how to go about determining the so-called "lessons of the past" to use in formulating the best policy for the United States to follow on a critical issue. [A list of fifteen suggested topics follows ("the problem of the homeless," for example), along with a list of seven specific questions to be addressed in the essay: for example, "What kinds of questions about the past, as it pertains to your issue, should policy-makers get answers to in order to arrive at intelligent decisions about the best future course of action?"

Student Expanded Minute Papers Excerpts

About midway through the fall semester, and with the permission of the instructors, Hutchings asked students to write their answers to five questions about the class. Excerpts from student responses to three of the questions follow. To the question, "What do you take to be the purpose of studying this topic or issue. That is, why is it important?" students wrote:

- To understand how history includes both facts and interpretation of facts.
- It is important to know which way a historian is looking at history in order to be able to look at his ideas critically and with understanding.
- [To] teach us how to be more truthful and precise about what we are saying.
- To not make assumptions based on what people say.
- I'm not sure if it really is important. I don't think I will see this info again in my academic or non-academic career.
- Truthfully, I find it irrelevant. Most of us at this point have already decided on how we think the world works. There is a trivia quality alone to the subject, i.e., need to hear about it.

To the question, "What was the most important thing you learned in today's class?" students wrote:

- Everyone has different opinions on quantitative concepts (the numerical value).
- How unreliable quantitative history can be without reference and backup.
- I really don't get
- The reason why historians are forced to specialize.

To the question, "What has surprised you most in this course?" students wrote:

- I honestly thought this class dealt with more "book" history, rather than historical analysis. It's an OK class.

- A very different way of learning about history. (Not history as such, but study of explaining history.)
- Much more fun and cooperative learning styles are approached than I thought would be.
- How overwhelmingly annoying it is.
- How far the name and course description are from the actual subject matter of the course . . . yin and yang.
- When I first took this course, I was expecting it to be a course in history. The fact that I am learning how to think critically greatly surprises me.

End-of-Course Telephone Interviews: Major Issues

The end-of-course telephone interviews with students covered a wide range of topics. Because the instructors seemed to be especially interested in getting students to look at history in a new way, we have selected from the notes of the interviewer, comments that revealed whether the course was accomplishing that purpose, that is, is it working?

One of the questions posed by the interviewer asked directly, "Do you think differently in any way because you have taken this course?" The interviewer recorded the following student responses:

- [I'm] aware of more things—causal models.
- No. Not at all. One day spent saying there is no such thing as facts.
- No. Maybe for future situations.
- Yes. See the concept of history differently. Comes from individual perspectives.
- Yes. Gave exact way to argue and use critical thinking.
- No, not really. Content did not really impress enough to be useful or appealing.
- Yes, somewhat. Chance to rewrite was excellent and gave me a chance to really learn stuff.
- Yes, more open to alternatives and drawing conclusions.
- Yes, look more at how someone is presenting an argument.

Another question that is closely related to seeing history in a new light asked students, "What was the most significant moment in the course for you? For example, was there a class where you suddenly realized the meaning behind a difficult concept? Or, on the other hand, was there a moment in the course where you got lost or puzzled?"

- Causal model hard at first, but not now.
- Content taught fairly well.
- Kind of. Three or four classes on "facts." Still don't know what [the instructor] was trying to say to us.
- What a fact is—they said no facts. Got lost there. Only affected that class, not rest of the course.

- Causal models and syllogisms. Good to sit in class and use brain; sometimes out of focus, but worked back to clarity.
- Difficult class and never quite sure that I was doing things right. Worked with another class member to understand.
- One class similar to logic section of SAT. Teaches why you think like you do.
- Once understood objective of class, got into it more.
- Last couple weeks could see whole picture.

Case Analysis Conclusion

Two things stand out in this case: First, the instructors are trying to get students to think in new ways about history, and second, they are apparently succeeding with some students, but others remain baffled and frustrated—even "overwhelmingly" annoyed. It is apparent, especially in the research data, that there is a gulf between the students who think that history is about events and dates and these instructors, who want to get across the message that history depends on who is interpreting it.

Bridging that gap is not easy. Indeed, by the end of the semester, some students still "just don't get it," despite heroic efforts on the part of the instructors to make their intentions clear. The syllabus—all nine pages of it—appears to be exceptionally clear about the course orientation. And the interview with one of the instructors pictures her as clear in her goals and very articulate in expressing them. The question for study is, Why should it be so hard to get this message across to students? The following literature review and the suggestions for Classroom Assessment and Classroom Research will address this question. Note that the literature review for our overall question for investigation, Is it working? is divided into two sections: literature on peer learning groups and literature on intellectual development and critical thinking. Each review is followed by a recommended reading section.

A QUESTION FOR INVESTIGATION

Is It Working?

REVIEWING
THE LITERATURE

What Do We Know from Research and Theory About Peer Learning Groups?

Introduction. The key question asked by the instructors in this case is, Is it working? Susan and Sam wonder if small-group discussions are helping students understand the task at hand—determining the mode of historical analysis—and more importantly, are they helping students progress from an understanding of history as a collection of facts to seeing historical methods as a way of understanding and critically evaluating different explanations of the past.

Susan and Sam have made a commitment to co-teach this history class and to experiment with the technique of assigning students to work in small groups in an effort to "force students to be involved" and become "independent thinkers." During this first semester that they have used a peer learning group approach, their observations of student behaviors and comments have raised questions about the effectiveness of small-group discussions to enhance students' understanding of course concepts. Although the students appear engaged in their small-group discussions, Susan wonders, "does talking guarantee learning?"

Susan is in good company, a number of faculty are somewhat skeptical about the effectiveness of collaborative student work. Even some advocates of cooperative learning share these words of caution: "Simply placing individuals in groups and telling them to work together does not in and of itself promote higher achievement and greater productivity" (Johnson, Johnson, and Smith, 1994, p. 317).

This review of the literature will address the following questions: What are the features of peer learning groups? What general conclusions does research offer about the effectiveness of peer learning methods? And what are the implications for practice in college classrooms?

Features of Peer Learning Groups. Peer learning groups involve two or more students working together toward a common learning goal. The rationale for learning groups is to encourage active learning and involvement, to provide peer motivation and support, and to provide opportunities for students to elaborate or rehearse new concepts in their peer conversations.

For the purposes of this literature review, the term *peer group learning* encompasses a broad array of learning activities, including collaborative learning; cooperative learning; paired student discussion; small-group discussion; peer tutoring; reciprocal teaching; informal study groups; small groups assigned to work on case studies, course assignments, or research projects; and so on. Most instructors are familiar with the terms collaborative and cooperative learning, and many use these terms interchangeably.

Proponents of collaborative learning (Bruffee, 1995) and cooperative learning (Cooper, Robinson, and McKinney, 1994) in higher education agree that these two forms of peer learning are closely related but also that they differ in significant ways. Cooperative learning, first developed for use in K–12 classrooms, is highly structured by the teacher, with an emphasis on group and individual accountability, the development of learners' social skills, and the elimination of classroom competition. Collaborative learning, more prevalent in higher education settings, emphasizes a shift of authority from teacher to students. In collaborative-learning groups, students' roles and tasks are less structured by the teacher, although students are typically asked to report out on the group's discussion. In cooperative learning, some part of each students' grade usually depends on the performance of the group, but in collaborative learning, grades may depend on individual performance only. In cooperative learning, with its emphasis on the development of teamwork, it is common for the teacher to monitor the group process of the learning groups closely and pay explicit attention to students' social skills. Instructors in collaborative-learning settings tend to stand back from the action, as Susan and Sam did in the case, to encourage students to work out group and content issues on their own. Bruffee (1995) concludes that collaborative learning and cooperative learning are similar in their strengths—enabling students to learn through the sharing of ideas—but that they differ in their liabilities. Collaborative learning promotes peer-governed relations, at the expense of accountability, whereas cooperative learning guarantees accountability, although leaving the authority of the classroom with the teacher.

In the investigation of this case, we will use the terms collaborative, cooperative, and peer group learning interchangeably to describe the approach used by Susan and Sam.

Are Peer Learning Groups an Effective Use of Class Time?
Although the idea of requiring students to interact with one another to apply and elaborate on course material is appealing, a logical objection to peer learning by many teachers is the time that it takes from covering course content. One response to this objection is that because it is never possible to cover all the important points in a given discipline, it may be a better use of time to teach main ideas and then encourage students to apply them (Cooper, Robinson, and McKinney, 1994). Susan and Sam seem resigned to this realistic response and are more concerned about teaching the broad principles of historical methods rather than a set of discrete facts.

As instructors decide whether to make time in class for student learning groups, James Cooper, a leading author on cooperative learning in higher education, suggests they ask the question, "Who does most of the complicated, difficult thinking in the classroom?" (1995, p. 8). In the lecture class, it is the teacher rather than the student who benefits from the organization and analysis required to plan a lecture. The syllabus excerpts included in the case analysis indicate that History and Its Methods balances lecture and discussion. Based on the amount of effort Sam and Susan invested in developing this course, it is safe to assume they enjoy the intellectual endeavor of preparing and delivering lectures but that their goal is to leave some of the thinking work for their students.

Recently a university biology professor at a Classroom Assessment workshop commented that she has always enjoyed lecturing and has considered her lectures a gift to her students, because of the time she took to organize materials, make connections between concepts, and share brilliant new insights. But over time, she had come to realize that this gift she planned so carefully was not always received with understanding or enthusiasm. Cooper explains that "in lectures, students often hear a highly skilled problem-solver resolve complicated issues without hearing the diversity of ideas that went into the lecturer's ultimate resolution" (1995, p. 7). Without the benefit of hearing the thought process behind the "product" of the lecture, students are left only with the task of memorization and have little chance of improving their ability to think through a challenging problem.

In peer learning groups, some of the thinking and construction of knowledge is left to the students. Students listen to each other as they struggle with new ideas, and the thinking process is made public. Thus, the role of the teacher shifts from dissemination of information to facilitation of learning. Teachers who use collaborative methods think of themselves less as "expert transmitters of knowledge to students and more as expert designers of intellectual experiences for students" (Smith and MacGregor, 1992, p. 10).

This change in teaching methods requires changes in students' classroom roles as well, and these changes may be met with some resistance. In peer learning groups, students must be active contributors, not passive takers of information, and they must shift from being a private to a public presence in the classroom (MacGregor, 1992). In large lecture classes, being prepared for a class session and even attending at all are largely a matter of personal choice. When ongoing group work is required, however, preparation and attendance become part of a responsibility to other students.

"The task of the successful student in peer learning" according to McKeachie, "is to question, explain, express opinions, admit confusion, and reveal misconceptions; but at the same time the student must listen to peers, respond to their questions, question their opinions, and share information or concepts that will clear up their confusion" (1994, p. 149). Working in small groups, students are more likely to ask and respond to each other's questions. Student questioners and explainers alike have the opportunity for cognitive rehearsal, organization of material, and synthesis of new concepts. This is not, however, a case of "faster" learners helping "slower" learners grasp the material. In these interactions, "both the confused and unconfused benefit" from engaging with course material (McKeachie, 1994, p. 149).

Benefits of Peer Learning Groups. McKeachie's description of the cognitive tasks for students in groups implies the first benefit of peer groups—active and involved learning. A consistent finding of research on peer learning groups is improved involvement and gains in achievement (Cooper and Mueck, 1992; Cooper, Robinson, and McKinney, 1994; Johnson and others, 1981; Slavin, 1983).

The social nature of peer learning groups has implications for increasing student involvement and retention. In *What Matters in College? Four Critical Years Revisited,* Astin (1992) reported on results of research on students from over two hundred colleges that suggests that student-student and student-faculty interactions are key predictors of student cognitive and attitudinal changes in college. Student peer groups guarantee student-student interactions.

Cognitive and attitudinal changes result when students have an opportunity to hear different perspectives and take in new ideas that challenge their own. Joyce McNeill reports that traditional-age and even older college students in cooperative groups realize "there's a much bigger world out there than my world" (1996). In heterogeneous learning groups, students are likely to experience conflict and cognitive disequilibrium (Cooper, 1995). The attempt to resolve such cognitive conflicts by gathering more information promotes intellectual development. (See the second literature review in this chapter, which concerns intellectual development and cognitive skills.)

One of the challenges faced by students in the historical methods class in the case study is the unfamiliar disciplinary conventions, which require them to analyze explanations for events of the past rather than to recite a list of historical facts. It takes time for students to understand and participate in the "normal discourse" of a discipline (Bruffee, 1984). Group work is one means to make tacit disciplinary conventions explicit to students. Faculty, with years of experience in their fields, have internalized the modes of thinking required by their disciplines, making it difficult for them to explain these modes to students. Craig Nelson, a professor of biology and of public and environmental affairs observes, "Often we do not notice when we have stopped speaking plain English" (1994, p. 50). He reports, for example, on a colleague who found that the grades of students in discussion sections taught by advanced undergraduates were higher than in those taught by faculty. Nelson suspects that the undergraduate instructors, who are newer to the discipline, are better able to break down disciplinary concepts and conventions for other students. This view is in keeping with Vygotsky's description (1978) of learners' "zones of proximal development," or their limited area of developmental readiness for learning new things. Thus, slightly more advanced peers, or near peers, may be more helpful than faculty for promoting student progress to the next level of understanding, because these near peers do not expect the students to leap beyond their zone of developmental readiness.

Some of the research on peer learning addresses specific collaborative-learning techniques, such as peer questioning and peer teaching. Alison King (1990), for example, investigated student reciprocal peer questioning procedures. Some students were taught to pose questions that promote critical thinking about course topics. These students asked deeper-level questions, as opposed to simple recall questions, and gave more elaborated responses than students participating in regular small-group discussions or in unguided peer questioning groups. King concluded that training students in reciprocal questioning techniques increased the quality of their questions and thus student responses and discussion. (Examples of King's questioning strategies appear on page 194 of the next literature review, on intellectual development and cognitive skills.)

In another study (Benware and Deci, 1984), students in an introductory psychology class were invited to participate in an experiment on learning. They were divided into two groups, and all were asked to take home an article to read and study. Members of the experimental group were told they should read the material in preparation for teaching it to another student. Students in the control group were told to read the article in preparation for an exam. The results suggested that students who engaged in learning in order to teach material to others were more intrinsically motivated, had higher conceptual learning scores, and perceived themselves as more actively engaged (Benware and Deci, 1984). McKeachie summarizes the research on peer learning in this way: "pay to be a tutor, not to be tutored" (1994, p. 146).

Putting Peer Learning Groups into Practice. How can college faculty use peer group learning most productively? Some guidelines for practice come from the literature on cooperative learning, which constitutes only one subset of peer learning activities. Because cooperative learning is more highly structured than other forms of peer group learning, the literature contains more prescriptions for its practice. These guidelines are presented here not as rules but rather as points for consideration by faculty interested in setting up various kinds of group learning experiences.

Cooperative learning is distinguished from other forms of peer learning groups by the requirements of positive interdependence among group members, with each member responsible for the learning of the others, and individual accountability. In addition, cooperative learning places explicit emphasis on the instructor's role in developing group-work skills.

Positive interdependence. In cooperative learning, the challenge for the instructor is to promote the feeling of individual responsibility for the successful learning of others in the group. Positive interdependence requires the group to work toward a common goal that requires the learning and understanding of each member. This does not mean that the brightest, most efficient, or most responsible student does the work for the rest of the group. In the history class, this concern was raised by Sharee, the student who asked if she was the only one who did the reading. One strategy for building interdependence is to assign each student in a group to learn a different portion of the material and then teach it to the others. In the case of a group research project, each student is assigned to research and complete a part of the work that the other members' work depends upon. These strategies have been called the jigsaw technique, because each student's contribution fits with others to complete the task.

Individual accountability. The potential for some students to take advantage of the work of others is a troubling aspect of peer learning for faculty and students alike. Students who receive information, credit, or grades based on the diligent efforts of others have been called *freeloaders* and *free riders.* Cooperative learning requires individual accountability in grading, to reduce the possibility of freeloading and to instill confidence in the fairness of the process (Cooper, Robinson, and McKinney, 1994).

In cooperative-learning settings, a major portion of each student's course grade is based on independent work on exams, quizzes, and written papers. In addition, a number of strategies exist to prevent the free rider phenomenon. Sociology instructors at Illinois State University, for example, report assigning worksheets prior to small-group discussions to ensure that students prepare for class (Rau and Heyl, 1990). Students turn in a written worksheet at the beginning of class as their "ticket to ride" (p. 147), that is, to participate in the small-group discussion. In some cases, student groups receive credit for participating in or completing a product from a group discussion. However, even when, as in Sam and Susan's history class, grades or credit are not involved in peer learning groups, students who have prepared for class resent it if they must spend time getting others up to speed on the reading before the group can start in on a discussion or assignment.

In some courses, instructors structure the group task so that students take turns in different roles: as group leader, recorder, reporter, writer, presenter, and so forth. Not only does this prevent freeloading, it reduces the potential for more able or more assertive students to dominate the group. In full-class and small-group discussions, students are often so busy formulating their own responses that they do not listen to their peers. One strategy to encourage students to learn from other students' contributions is the round-robin discussion format, in which each student presents his or her ideas and explicitly states what he or she has learned from the comments of other students (Nelson, 1994). This is an example of using explicit role structuring for formal cooperative learning.

Attention to student teamwork skills. One reason for the current interest in small-group work in college classrooms is the relevance of group skills to business and industry. Ongoing cooperative experience has been found to enhance students' ability to work in a group, which may make them more prepared for teamwork on the job (Sharan, 1980). Explicit attention to student teamwork skills is a feature of structured cooperative learning that may or may not be emphasized in other types of group learning. Many faculty who assign peer learning activities take for granted that students will know how to work productively in a small group by the time they get to college, but this is not necessarily so.

Bosworth (1994, pp. 27–28) has organized group-work skills into the following taxonomy:

- Interpersonal skills: being friendly, listening to others, using eye contact, and speaking positively without using put-downs or other harmful forms of communication.

- Group management skills: organizing the work of the task, keeping members on task, and taking the time for group processing and analysis of effectiveness.

- Inquiry skills: asking clarifying questions, probing for additional information, critiquing ideas, probing assumptions, and eliciting the views of other group members (these inquiry skills are needed to promote intellectual development and critical thinking).

- Conflict prevention, mediation, and resolution skills.

- Presentation skills: oral and written communication, including summarizing, synthesizing, and speaking before a group.

To help student groups function more effectively, Bosworth recommends that at the very least, faculty make students aware of the skills that enhance cooperative work. For more advanced students, simply identifying important skills will be enough for students to implement them. In other classes, faculty will have to demonstrate, model, and talk through these skills.

Assignment of students to groups. A final feature of structured cooperative-learning activities is the role of the instructor in assigning students to heterogeneous groups (Cooper, Robinson, and McKinney, 1994; Cooper and Mueck, 1992; Johnson, Johnson, and Smith, 1994). Factors to consider when putting groups together include students' majors, ages, and relative abilities (as shown by past GPAs).

In a study of students' most positive and negative group experiences, groups that were formed by students themselves were more likely to be listed by students as their worst group experiences, because the students had not considered the demands of the learning task when choosing their fellow group members (Fiechtner and Davis, 1992). For example, one student commented about a self-selected group, "When we formed our group, we didn't realize how important it would be to have someone who was good on the computer, so we were always at a disadvantage" (p. 61). This study of students' positive and negative group experiences also suggested that it is preferable to keep group membership consistent over the semester, in order to develop a sense of interdependence among group members and to provide time for students to work through conflicts rather than always be moving on to a new set of students and potential conflicts. One student commented about a frustrating group-work experience: "Group members were not the same for each project. Every time I learned someone's name and phone number [the teacher] changed groups on us" (p. 61).

Guidelines for Implementing Peer Learning Groups. We conclude this literature review with some general guidelines for implementing peer learning, adapted from the research- and practice-based recommendations of Cooper, Robinson, and McKinney (1994, pp. 82–84).

1. *Start small.* Before radically restructuring a course, start small by using group work in one class meeting, such as a pre-exam review session. Or break up a lecture by pausing to ask students to share questions or application ideas with the student sitting next to them. A concern many faculty have about using group activities is the time it will take them to develop assignments. Activities that do not require a lot of background work include assigning student groups to develop test questions or clarify confusing points for each other. Old exam or homework questions can also be used as learning activities for small groups.

2. *Explain why peer learning groups are productive and valuable.* To

smooth the way for collaborative assignments, you can explain to students the goals and rationale behind your use of group work. Anticipate student resistance and nip it in the bud by explaining the benefits of group learning and the system in place for fair grading. Reduce student resistance by requiring minimal, if any, student group work outside of class. The logistics of scheduling out-of-class meeting times, especially for adult students juggling work and child-care responsibilities, can overshadow the benefits of collaborative learning. Out-of-class time, however, is ideal for voluntary student study groups.

3. *Be organized and explicit.* Somehow even the clearest of instructions get lost in the shuffle when students move into groups. How often have you observed or been part of a small faculty or student group that eagerly assembles, only to pause and ask "now what were we supposed to do?" The basic rule is that you can never be too explicit when providing instructions for small-group work. Peer learning activities require defined tasks, clear instructions, and spelled-out expectations. Instructions and assignments will need to be more structured at the beginning of the semester than as time goes on.

4. *Consider grading issues.* Competition is a significant barrier to the success of peer learning groups. Students who end up in college classrooms are by and large those who have been successfully competitive in high school (Bosworth, 1994). Grading on a curve is at cross-purposes with fostering cooperation. When grading is a zero-sum game, grades act as a disincentive for helping other students learn.

In general, grades from peer group work should make up only a small part of the overall course grade. When group-work grades make up a large percentage of overall grades, students will likely have more anxiety about freeloaders and complaints about fairness.

5. *"Structure collaborative activities so students will learn something, not just do something"* (Cooper, Robinson, and McKinney, 1994, p. 93). If the collaborative task is simply to fill out a worksheet, students may rush through the assignment without concern for other group members' understanding of the concepts. There was some indication of this behavior in the history class, when students rushed to decide on the mode of historical analysis without discussing the concepts in depth. To avoid surface approaches to group work, instructors can test mastery of the content beyond the group worksheet or product and can communicate "the ethic that the team's work is never done until all members have mastered the skills that underlie the cooperative learning activity" (Cooper, Robinson, and McKinney, 1994, p. 84). Of course, the assigned task

should be relevant to the content of the course. Compare the following two responses from the study of students' negative and positive group-work experiences (Fiechtner and Davis, 1992, p. 65):

> In one class the assignments were just "busy work"—there was nothing relevant to gain.
>
> She [the instructor] researched organizations and came up with real questions and problems, not just something to keep us busy.

These comments reveal the continuum of effectiveness in peer learning groups. At the low end, groups are merely an approach to keep students busy. At the high end, peer learning groups are used to engage students in relevant application of course concepts.

RECOMMENDED READING

Peer Learning Groups

Bosworth, K., and Hamilton, S. J. *Collaborative Learning: Underlying Processes and Effective Techniques.* New Directions for Teaching and Learning, no. 59. San Francisco: Jossey-Bass, 1994.

This volume on collaborative learning is suitable for readers interested in the rationale and guidelines for group learning methods in college classrooms. Individual chapters that might provoke discussion within a faculty group are Chapter Two, by James Flannery, which addresses the roles of students and teachers in constructing knowledge, and Chapter Four, by Craig Nelson, which explains the connection between collaborative learning and critical thinking. Readers interested in developing the collaborative skills of college students should see Chapter Three, written by Kris Bosworth.

Cooper, J. L., Robinson, P. R., and McKinney, M. "Cooperative Learning in the Classroom." In D. F. Halpern and Associates, *Changing College Classrooms: New Teaching and Learning Strategies for an Increasingly Complex World.* San Francisco: Jossey-Bass, 1994.

This short but comprehensive chapter is practice focused and research based. James Cooper, of the Network for Cooperative Learning in Higher Education, and his colleagues review key features of cooperative learning, confront objections to the method, and provide recommendations for implementation. This brief chapter packs enough information for a reader to make real changes in classroom practices.

Davis, B. G. *Tools for Teaching.* San Francisco: Jossey-Bass, 1993.

Barbara Gross Davis's book is a complete tool kit for all aspects of college teaching, including delivering lectures, leading discussions, using instructional media, designing tests, and grading students' work. In Chapter Five, "Collaborative and Experiential Strategies," Davis provides practical ideas for forming and sustaining in-class cooperative-learning activities and general study groups to promote successful learning.

Goodsell, A., Maher, M., and Tinto, V. (eds.). *Collaborative Learning: A Sourcebook for Higher Education.* University Park, Pa.: National Center on Postsecondary Teaching, Learning, and Assessment (NCTLA), 1992.

This NCTLA sourcebook could serve as an introductory text on collaborative learning for a graduate class or a faculty group. Barbara Leigh Smith and Jean T. MacGregor of the Washington Center for Improving the Quality of Undergraduate Education introduce underlying principles, definitions, goals, and varied examples of collaborative-learning methods. Contributors to this volume are Kenneth Bruffee, James Cooper, David and Roger Johnson, Karl Smith, Robert Slavin, and more. The sourcebook contains an extensive annotated bibliography, plus a resource guide on institutions using collaborative learning. (To order the sourcebook, send $23.00 to the National Center on Postsecondary Teaching, Learning, and Assessment, Pennsylvania State University, 403 South Allen St., Suite 104, University Park, PA 16801–5252; telephone 1–814–865–5917.)

REVIEWING
THE LITERATURE

*What Do We Know from Research and Theory
About Intellectual Development and Critical Thinking?*

Introduction. We selected the case study "Is It Working?" for inclusion in this book because it illustrates how much is involved in the "simple" teaching of a disciplinary concept such as modes of thought in the writing of history. In this second review of the relevant literature, we address two major issues highlighted in the case: stages of intellectual development and critical thinking. (In order to relate this literature review to the case, it is important that you read the case analysis as well as the case itself, because the data revealed in the analysis contain important elements of student reactions to the course.)

Intellectual Development. This case presents a beautiful real-life illustration of the great diversity in intellectual development that exists today in almost any college classroom. The students in this class, all presumably exposed to the same syllabus, assignments, discussions, and lectures for half a semester, have received very different messages about what they are expected to learn. In students' written responses to the questions posed by Hutchings midway through the semester, we find everything from quite accurate interpretations ("to understand how history includes both facts and interpretations of facts"), to confusion ("the reason why historians are forced to specialize"), to doubt ("I'm not sure if it really is important"), to "overwhelming" annoyance. Students do not seem to be getting the message that Susan and Sam hoped they were sending. He and Susan "have been drilling it into them since day one," Sam thinks; "It's not facts, but ways of interpreting facts. How can it be so hard?"

Although students' persistent misunderstandings of what teachers feel to be clearly stated expectations are frustrating and mystifying to many teachers, psychologists are exploring explanations for these highly individualistic interpretations, through research and theory building about intellectual development. Students mature at different rates intellectually as well as physically and emotionally. Some students enter college with very inadequate understandings of what learning is all about, whereas others demonstrate levels of development and understanding likely to be in accord with faculty perceptions.

In this case, Melissa and Jerome are concerned about getting the "right" answers. Will it be on the midterm? and, Do we have to know it? are familiar questions that annoy many college teachers who hope they are teaching ways of thinking about their discipline and skills in analysis and critical thinking. Some students, however, see the learning task as product rather than process, as facts rather than skill development. They seek "the answers," and to them, ambiguities and uncertainties represent a lack of knowledge. As these students see it, Sam and Susan are the experts or authorities in history, and it is their duty to provide students with, in the words of one theorist, "the truth, the right answers, in assimilable, graduated doses. [The student's] duty is to 'absorb' them by honest hard work known as 'study.' Then the teacher will 'ask for them back' in the same form in which they were originally given. [The student's] responsibility is then to re-present them unmodified and unabridged for the teacher's inspection" (Perry, 1985, p. 6).

This frustrating picture is a rather typical developmentalist description of an early stage of intellectual development. William G. Perry, Jr., a counselor at Harvard in the 1950s and 1960s, is perhaps the best-known developmental stage theorist in higher education, despite the fact that his model has some serious shortcomings in addressing diversity in the student body. He derived his model from interviews with Harvard male undergraduates, that is, young white upper-class males, and recent scholars have questioned the validity of his model for a wide range of nontraditional students including women (Belenky, Clinchy, Goldberger, and Tarule, 1986;

Clinchy, 1994a; Gilligan, 1977, 1982) and minorities (Cross, 1971; Helms, 1990).

According to Perry, the progress in intellectual growth of the Harvard students looked something like this: students at a low level of development looked to an outside authority (teacher) for the "right" answer. Gradually, they began to discover that authorities disagree and that the values of fellow students differed from their own. In an effort to resolve the differences between equally credible people, they moved to the next level of development, concluding that there is no one right answer and that everyone has a right to his or her own opinion. As they proceeded through college, some students began to see that they must find the answers for themselves, through a process of reasoning and learning in a relativistic world. From these interviews, Perry identified nine levels or positions of development, along with a number of "transition" stages. For our purposes here, we combine and simplify the definitions into three major categories. (The interested reader will find complete definitions and alternative labels and groupings in Cross, 1976; Kurfiss, 1988; Pascarella and Terenzini, 1991; and Perry, 1970, 1981).

1. *Absolutist or dualist (positions 1, 2, and 3).* The student at this level of intellectual development sees the world in polar terms—right or wrong, good or bad. "Authority" knows the answers, and it is the business of people in authority to teach the right answers to students. Moving toward position 3, the student sees some diversity of opinion but attributes these differences to the uncertain state of the knowledge. Authority has not found "the answer"—*yet.*

2. *Multiplicity or problematic (positions 4, 5, and 6).* At position 4, students perceive legitimate uncertainty and conclude that everyone has a right to his or her own opinion. Moving toward position 6, students begin to perceive that not everything has an answer and that they need to look at the evidence and come to the conclusion that seems most reasonable to them.

3. *Commitment (positions 7, 8, and 9).* At this level of intellectual development, students make their own decisions, based on a consideration of alternatives. In the process of making initial commitments to certain ideas and positions and experiencing the implications, they recognize commitment as an activity through which they express their responsibilities and establish their identities (King, 1978).

Perhaps without realizing it, in her interview with Hutchings, Susan makes a remarkably insightful comment about intellectual development when she says, "The point is to get students to let go of the notion of historical objectivity, of simple facts. This is very difficult for them. They think in great antipodes—with scientific truth on one end, mere opinion on the other—nothing in between."

In his research, Perry found that most freshmen entered Harvard at positions 3, 4, and 5, and perhaps 75 percent of them graduated in positions 6, 7, and 8. Subsequent research, however, found virtually no students scoring in positions 7, 8, and 9 (Pascarella and Terenzini, 1991, p. 30) and Perry admitted that position 9 was almost never observed in college students. It, like position 1 at the other extreme, is a logical extrapolation of the limits of the definition.

Magolda (1992) conducted a more recent study, using a research design very similar to Perry's but with a more representative sample, consisting of roughly equal numbers of men and women. She followed seventy students through college (Miami University in Ohio) and postcollege experiences and arrived at categories similar to Perry's. Like Perry, Magolda is concerned with epistemology, that is, how students perceive the nature of knowledge. She found four "ways of knowing" that illustrate a general progression from respecting what authorities say to developing one's own perspective. Her categories are helpful in suggesting the rough percentages of students that might fall in each position.

1. *Absolute knowing.* Students categorized as absolute knowers viewed knowledge as certain; answers *do* exist in all areas of knowledge, and uncertainty arises only because students do not yet have access to absolute knowledge. Absolute knowing was prevalent among freshmen (68 percent), becoming less common as students proceeded through college (46 percent of sophomores, 11 percent of juniors, and 2 percent of seniors).

2. *Transitional knowing.* Transitional knowers still believe that absolute knowledge exists in some areas but accept that uncertainty may exist in others. Students are beginning to believe that understanding is more important than acquiring and remembering information. Transitional knowing is characteristic of only 32 percent of the freshmen, but rises to a peak of 83 percent of juniors and 80 percent of seniors, dropping to 31 percent in the year following graduation.

3. *Independent knowing.* In this way of knowing, authorities are no longer the source of knowledge, and students begin to create their own perspectives, thinking through and expressing their own views as well as hearing out those of others. Independent knowers believe that the nature of knowledge is uncertain but that teachers should reward independent thinking and should not penalize those who hold views that differ from those of the teachers or authors of texts. In this phase, students stress the virtue of open-mindedness. Independent knowing is not common among college

students, rising from zero in the freshman year to only 16 percent in the senior year, but making a very substantial jump to 57 percent in the year following graduation from college.

4. *Contextual knowing.* Contextual knowing, like Perry's highest levels of development, is rarely evident in college students. In Magolda's study, it appeared in only 12 percent of the students interviewed and then only in the year following graduation. At this stage, perceptions of learning change from valuing thinking independently to valuing thinking through problems and integrating and applying knowledge in context in the light of evidence.

Magolda, writing in a time of high criticism of education, is somewhat more likely than Perry to look for characteristics of traditional education that inhibit learning, whereas Perry, writing in the glory days of higher education, is more likely to look for the growth-enhancing experiences of education. Ironically, perhaps, this difference in the perspectives of the two authors is testimony to the convictions of both that knowledge is contextual and socially constructed.

Magolda sees the traditional dominance of objectivist perspectives in education as extending students' reliance on authority for knowledge. She also faults traditional education for distorting peer and teacher relationships and for producing the low degree to which minorities and women feel validated as knowers in a male-dominated academic culture. "Students who are subordinated on two levels—first, as students and, second, as women or minorities (or both)—may be less likely to see their own voices as valid or to express them than those students who experience less subordination" (p. 208).

Although Magolda's research supports Perry's, her sample made a substantial improvement in the gender balance. She did then find some gender differences, but she concluded (reluctantly, she says) that there were more similarities than differences in men's and women's ways of knowing. Belenky, Clinchy, Goldberger, and Tarule (1986), however, claim some important gender differences. Where Perry and Magolda are concerned with the *nature* of knowledge, the authors of *Women's Ways of Knowing* are concerned with the *source* of knowledge. Clinchy (1994b, p. 34) notes that their interview questions consisted of questions like these: "How does the woman conceive of herself as a knower?" "Is knowledge seen as originating outside or inside the self?" "Can it be passed down intact from one person to another, or does it well up from within?" "Does knowledge appear effortlessly in the form of intuition or revelation, or is it attained only through an arduous procedure of construction?" These are questions that go to the very heart of what Susan and Sam are trying to get students to think about in the way history is presented.

Clinchy (1994b, p. 34) compares the insights from their research on women with those of Perry and finds that "received knowledge" is similar to Perry's dualism. Students relying on received knowledge depend on authorities to supply the right answers. "Truth, for them, is external. They can ingest it but not evaluate it or create it for themselves." A second mode of knowing is "subjectivism," which is similar to Perry's multiplicity. Subjective knowers look inside themselves for knowledge. For them, truth is internal—you have your truths, and I have mine. Clinchy says both positions have limitations. Drawing on her personal experience, she describes the dilemma for teachers as follows:

> When I am teaching Child Development, for example, I do not want students to swallow unthinkingly Piaget's interpretations of his observations, but I do want them to pay close attention to what he has to say. I do not want them simply to spout off their own interpretations and ignore the data. Students who rely exclusively on received or subjective knowledge are in some sense not really thinking. The received knower's ideas come from the authority; the subjectivist's opinions are "just there." Neither has any procedures for developing new ideas or testing their validity. As a teacher, I want to help these students develop systematic, deliberate procedures for understanding and evaluating ideas [p. 35].

Perry and Magolda would agree. Their schemes aim for growth up the developmental ladder. Developmental theory, as it is used in research and theory today, implies growth in a positive direction. Thus, the study of intellectual development has to be based on theory that posits a model of desirable development. And therein lies much of the controversy surrounding the notion of a common and desirable model of human development. Most developmental theory assumes that "every human being passes through the same stages; no stage can be skipped; each stage is more complex than the preceding one; and each stage is based on the preceding one and prepares the individual for the succeeding one" (Cross, 1976, p. 152).

These assumptions are constantly being tested, and they gain credibility as research shows similar patterns across different areas of study. For example, there is substantial agreement among scholars studying all kinds of human development—intellectual development, ego development, moral development—that development involves the whole person in a series of transformations, sometimes called stages, that move the person to ever higher levels of development. The desirable goal is the highest level attainable, which not many people achieve. Indeed, some people become "stuck" at quite low levels of development, and most people experience "plateaus," where no growth occurs. It is presumably not possible for a person to understand a level of development higher than his or her own. Thus, we cannot describe or explain a higher level of development to students and hope that they can emulate it; they must experience it for themselves. Susan grasps this in her interview with Hutchings when she says, "Learning this kind of self-consciousness about thinking is like learning to ride a bike. You have it or you don't, and once you get it, you wonder what all the fuss was about." Developmentalists believe that cognitive development cannot be given to students; they must find it for themselves. And the way they find it is in interaction with an environment that demands active learning. Instructors can, however, introduce *cognitive conflict*, which challenges students to move to a higher plane of reasoning.

This sort of theorizing explains, in part at least, the annoyance expressed by several of the students in the history class. If they believe that learning consists of learning the facts of history, then teachers' assertions that (in the understanding of several students) "there is no such thing as facts" is understandably upsetting, even leading to bitterness. Perry listened patiently to one absolutist Harvard student complain, "This place is all full of bull. They don't want anything really honest from you. If you turn in something, a speech that's well written, whether it's got one single fact in it or not is beside the point" (1981, p. 83).

Most developmental theorists adopt a general model that posits a hierarchy of stages with the pathway of development moving "from simplicity and absolutism to complexity and relativism, from concreteness to abstractness, and from external to internal regulation of behavior" (Kurfiss, 1994, p. 175). There is some evidence that this general pattern of growth conforms to the changes in college students documented by researchers studying change rather than development per se. Seniors are less likely than freshmen to make simple and moralistic judgments; they are more flexible and able to cope with complexity and ambiguity; and they are more autonomous and integrated, with a clearer perception of identity (Pascarella and Terenzini, 1991).

The major contribution of the developmentalists to the improvement of teaching and learning lies not so much in the specifics (their definitions of stages) as in their testing of assumptions and their efforts to create models to guide research and theory building. Developmental theorists are, first and foremost, interactionists, who assume that human beings are actively involved in their own development (Mines and Kitchener, 1986). The richer and more challenging the environment, the greater the potential for growth. Thus, the aim of education is to stretch the cognitive structure to accommodate new ideas—to stimulate students to search for organizational structures that will handle increasingly complex ideas and experiences. Perry tells the amusing story of a student who complained about a "sloppy, disorganized course," assuring the counselor that what learning he *did* experience had been "due *entirely to my own efforts*" (1981, p. 77).

It should be encouraging to college teachers, and to developmental theorists, that most research on young adults shows that higher education appears to be a positive environment for engaging students in the kinds of experiences that promote development along the hierarchical lines posited by developmental theory (Basseches, 1986). In fact, there is research evidence that formal education (number of years in school) is a more powerful predictor of the level of development than age or any other demographic variable (Rest, 1986). Pascarella and Terenzini, after a thorough review of the research on the growth of cognitive skills during college, conclude that "compared to freshmen, seniors have better oral and written communication skills, are better abstract reasoners or critical thinkers, are more skilled at using reason and evidence to address ill-structured problems for which there are no verifiably correct answers, have greater intellectual flexibility in that they are better able to understand more than one side of a complex issue, and can develop more sophisticated abstract frameworks to deal with complexity" (1991, p. 155). Thus, research to date gives high credibility to the general effectiveness of college in stimulating intellectual development and, in particular, to the importance of enriched environments. The intention to foster intellectual development remains somewhat controversial because it involves structural transformation rather than changes in specific capabilities or competencies. But the general growth posited for intellectual development has much in common with the current high interest in critical thinking, reflective judgment, higher-order thinking skills, and the like.

Critical Thinking. Although almost everyone is in favor of teaching students to think critically, definitions—and no doubt perceptions—of this cognitive ability range from those based primarily in scientific positivism calling for analysis, logic, and problem solving to broader definitions including the functions of problem recognition, identification of main ideas, support of conclusions, and the like. Most people would probably agree with the definition used by Pascarella and Terenzini in their review of the impact of college on critical thinking: "critical thinking appears to stress the individual's ability to interpret, evaluate, and make informed judgments about the adequacy of arguments, data, and conclusions" (1991, p. 118). Many theorists also insist that the *disposition* to apply these cognitive skills is just as important to critical thinking as is the possession of the skills. Thus, King asserts that "the hallmark of a critical thinker is an inquiring mind" (1995, p. 13). And Angelo concludes that "most formal definitions of critical thinking include the *intentional* application of rational, higher-order thinking skills such as analysis, synthesis, problem recognition and problem solving, inference, and evaluation" (1995, p. 6, emphasis added). Glaser provides an inclusive concept of critical thinking, contending that critical thinking involves these three critical elements: an *attitude* or disposition to approach problems in a thoughtful, analytical way, *knowledge* of the methods of inquiry and reasoning, and *skill* in applying the methods (1985, p. 24).

One of the goals of Susan and Sam's course in history, according to the course syllabus, is to "analyze and critically evaluate what others argue are 'lessons of the past.'" One of the class sessions described is teaching the concepts of two modes of historical thought. Because there is abundant evidence that much factual material is forgotten soon after it is presented (Pascarella and Terenzini, 1991, p. 114), it is not very likely that a year from now students in this class will remember much about narrative and analytical modes of thought in history. But according to their syllabus, Susan and Sam are not really interested in that. They hope that students will learn something about using evidence, evaluating meaning, drawing conclusions, and using other cognitive skills that are associated with critical thinking.

There is consistent evidence that college students do make significant gains in these cognitive skills—and indeed were showing such gains even before critical thinking became a buzz word in higher education. A comprehensive study done more than forty years ago showed significant gains during students' first year of college on a general test of critical thinking that measured ability to define a problem, select information pertinent to the problem, recognize assumptions, formulate relevant hypotheses, and draw valid conclusions (Dressel and Mayhew, 1954). Many other studies since then have shown significant gains in what instructors now call critical-thinking ability, and it appears that even though substantial gains are made during the four years of college, in general the greatest gains seem to be made during the first year and in areas related to the student's major. After a thorough review of the literature on critical thinking, Pascarella and Terenzini conclude that "the weight of evidence clearly supports the notion that college has a net positive influence on the development of critical thinking" (1991, p. 129).

Although there seems to be widespread agreement on the desirability and possibility of increasing the critical-thinking ability of college students, the goal is not without critics. Clinchy suggests that college educators might well "put more emphasis on a form of *un*critical thinking that we call *connected learning*" (1994b, p. 33). Feminists distinguish between connected learning (more characteristic of women) and separate learning (more characteristic of men). "Separate knowing," says Clinchy, "we could just as easily call *critical thinking*. Some just call it *thinking*. It requires detachment and objectivity. The separate knower holds herself aloof from the object she is trying to analyze. She takes an impersonal stance. She follows certain rules or procedures to ensure that her judgments are unbiased" (p. 36). In contrast, "Connected knowers are not dispassionate, unbiased observers. They deliberately bias themselves in favor of what they are examining. They try to get inside it and form an intimate attachment to it. The heart of connected knowing is imaginative attachment: trying to get behind the other person's eyes and 'look at it from that person's point of view.'. . . In this sense, connected knowing is uncritical. But it is not unthinking" (p. 39).

Clinchy maintains that both separate and connected ways of knowing are necessary and that students should become proficient in both. Without separate knowing, we could not criticize our own or other people's thinking. Argument is a powerful (and certainly common) form of discourse in higher education. But Belenky, Gilligan, Clinchy, and other scholars studying gender issues found in their interviews that many women do not like to argue, and Tobias (1990) found that the competitive, argumentative, adversarial climate in many science classrooms turns many women away from careers in science. Clinchy relates the experience of a male colleague at Smith College who complained that "he has trouble getting a class discussion off the ground because the students refuse to argue, either with him—when he tries to lure them by taking a devil's advocate position—or with each other" (p. 37).

What should teachers do to offer some balance to the "technical rationality" that Schön (1983) and others complain dominates academic approaches to knowledge? Clinchy suggests that many women would rather think with someone than against them. She argues against an "unnecessarily constricted view of thinking as analytic, detached, divorced from feeling" and proposes instead an integrated approach that starts with trying to understand *why* someone holds a particular point of view and only then takes up a critical attitude. She says:

> I am trying to learn to be this kind of teacher; I have not found it easy. It is easier for me to tell a student what is wrong with her

paper than what is right. I can write good specific criticism in the margins; my praise tends to be global and bland; "good point." Connected teaching means working hard to discern precisely what is "good"—what my colleague Mary Belenky calls the "growing edge"—in a student's thinking. . . .

When we asked women to describe classes that had helped them grow, they described classes that took the form not of debates but of what we called "connected conversations" and the women called "real talk." In these classes, each person serves as a midwife to each other's thoughts, drawing out others' ideas, entering into them, elaborating upon them, even arguing passionately, and building together a truth none could have achieved alone [1994b, p. 41].

Although investigation into what teachers can do to improve critical thinking is somewhat sparse, it is not inconsistent with Clinchy's advice. One study found that three teacher behaviors were related to student gains in critical thinking: the degree to which faculty encouraged, praised, or used student ideas; the degree to which students participated in class and the cognitive level of that participation; and the degree to which peer-to-peer interaction occurred in the class (Smith, 1977). This theme of the desirability of supportive, challenging, interactive environments prevails in the research. McKeachie, Pintrich, Lin, and Smith (1986) concluded, after a sophisticated statistical reanalysis of twenty-seven studies that looked at instructional approaches to critical thinking, that instruction that stresses student discussion, with an explicit emphasis on problem-solving procedures, may be effective in enhancing critical thinking. After a comprehensive review of the research on intellectual growth and cognitive skills, Pascarella and Terenzini concluded that "substantial evidence exists to suggest that interactions with major socializing agents (faculty and peers) are, in fact, significantly linked to the development of general cognitive skills during college" (1991, p. 149).

Given these research conclusions, Susan and Sam appear to be using class activities that encourage intellectual growth. The use of small groups requires peer-to-peer interaction, and the instructors appear to have respect for student ideas. To what extent the assigned topic of narrative versus analytical modes of thought is cognitively demanding is hard to discern, but King (1995) suggests that discussion can be oriented toward critical thinking by asking students to develop their own critical-thinking questions. The problem is that when students are asked to write essay exam questions or discussion questions, they often pose factual rather than thought-provoking questions. To help students generate questions that encourage critical thinking, King (p. 14) offers a list of question stems, including the following:

What are the strengths and weaknesses of _____?
What is the difference between _____ and _____?
Explain why _____. (Explain how _____)
What would happen if _____?
What is a new example of _____?
What are the implications of _____?
What do we already know about _____?
Why is _____ important?
How does _____ apply to everyday life?
What is the counterargument for _____?

The assignment given by Sam and Susan is to "decide whether the short account of the student revolts in Kiev is narrative or analytical and be prepared to explain why." Although the instruction to explain why is consistent with King's list of question stems, students in this class interpret the message to mean that they are to decide which is the correct answer. One of the strengths of the small peer discussion groups, of course, is that students will encounter different ideas as they try to decide which is the correct answer. But King suggests that the discussion groups would be more productive and more likely to require critical thinking if students went into their groups with at least one thought-provoking question formulated. Incidentally, King notes that when she assigns students the task of writing out a discussion question for use in the class discussion, she learns a great deal about the students' understanding of the material covered. This is an excellent example of a useful CAT that meets the major requirements for Classroom Assessment: it requires students to think and the feedback informs teachers about the level of student learning.

RECOMMENDED READING

Intellectual Development and Critical Thinking

Clinchy, B. M. "On Critical Thinking and Connected Knowing." In K. S. Walters (ed.), *Re-Thinking Reason: New Perspectives in Critical Thinking.* Albany: State University of New York Press, 1994.

This chapter is one of the most articulate and readable pieces of work on the feminist perspective on ways of knowing. It is succinct and summarizes very nicely for the general reader the major arguments and positions of the feminists for more attention to connected ways of knowing. In this brief chapter (ten pages), Clinchy draws on the study reported in Belenky, Clinchy, Goldberger, and Tarule (1986), but distills for us the nature of the findings and their implications for teaching.

Halpern, D. F. "Assessing the Effectiveness of Critical-Thinking Instruction." *Journal of General Education*, 1993, 42(4), 238–254.

Halpern discusses the current research advocating courses in critical-thinking skills for college students. She includes research results on the effectiveness of different instructional strategies to improve critical thinking and concludes that appropriate instruction can improve students' thinking skills.

King, A. "Inquiring Minds Really Do Want to Know: Using Questioning to Teach Critical Thinking." *Teaching of Psychology,* 1995, 22(1), 13–17.

This brief and very practical article presents Alison King's approach to promoting critical thinking. The model emphasizes helping students develop a habit of inquiry by learning to ask thoughtful questions—of themselves and each other—about what they read in their textbooks and hear in class. An especially useful section gives examples of several dozen question stems, some of which we listed earlier, that help students (and teachers, we would add) formulate thought-provoking questions for discussion. Question stems are classified by the type of thinking skill they are thought to require—analysis, evaluation, provision of evidence, and the like.

Kurfiss, J. "Intellectual, Psychosocial, and Moral Development in College: Four Major Theories." In K. A. Feldman and M. B. Paulsen (eds.), *Teaching and Learning in the College Classroom.* ASHE Reader Series. New York: Ginn, 1994. (Originally published in J. P. Bales and J. R. Judy [eds.], *A Handbook on Values and Development and the Lutheran Church-Related College.* Greenville, Pa.: Thiel College, 1988.)

This is a chapter for the moderately advanced reader who would like to pursue the literature on intellectual development in more depth than is presented here. It differentiates among Piaget's cognitive development, Perry's epistemological development, Erikson's psychosocial development, and Kohlberg's moral development. Kurfiss does a nice job of synthesizing and explaining the theory of each, presenting in some detail the various stages of development. The description of each theory is followed by a penetrating critique and a useful section on "teaching implications."

Pascarella, E. T., and Terenzini, P. T. *How College Affects Students: Findings and Insights from Twenty Years of Research.* San Francisco: Jossey-Bass, 1991.

Chapter Two, "Theories and Models of Student Change in College," and Chapter Four, "Cognitive Skills and Intellectual Growth," especially, present an extensive review of research on cognitive skills and intellectual development and the impact of college upon them. They are written for readers with moderate, but not extensive, knowledge of educational research. The authors are sophisticated researchers themselves and ably evaluate methodology and conclusions. This book is the most current, comprehensive, and authoritative review that exists on the impact of college on student growth and development. It is well worth having for reference in a library of faculty development materials but, overall, probably too detailed and research oriented for most teaching faculty.

Perry, W. G., Jr. "Cognitive and Ethical Growth: The Making of Meaning." In A. W. Chickering and Associates, *The Modern American College: Responding to the New Realities of Diverse Students and a Changing Society.* San Francisco: Jossey-Bass, 1981.

This chapter is probably the most comprehensive summary of Perry's work from the 1970s. It tells the general reader all he or she needs to know about the Perry scheme of intellectual development on which his later work is based (Perry, 1970). It is more technical and theoretical (forty pages) and not as compelling as a later shorter piece (Perry, 1985, seventeen pages), which is amusingly written and strikes a note of familiarity with most college teachers, but it is probably easier for most readers to obtain.

CLASSROOM ASSESSMENT

Collecting Further Information

Introduction. The question that Susan and Sam would like an answer to is, Is this course working? There are really two parts to that question: First, are students learning what the instructors are trying to teach? Second, how are students responding to the teaching methods that the instructors are using?

One CAT that we might suggest has already been effectively used in this class, when halfway into the semester the case study author collected student responses to an expanded version of the Minute Paper. Responses to that inquiry, as described earlier, were decidedly mixed. Some students got it; a few clearly did not. In this case, the "it" was the constructivist message of history as interpretation. Even by the end of the term, the telephone interviews with students showed that some students really had not learned what Susan and Sam felt it most important to teach.

But what about the smaller day-to-day lessons of the class? Are students learning the difference between the narrative and analytical descriptions of history? How are they responding to the small-group discussions that, on the face of it, at least, Sam and Susan think are working? To find some answers to those questions, we suggest two CATs: the Defining Features Matrix, for information about whether students learned the difference between narrative and analytical presentations of history, and the Group-Work

Evaluation, for information about how effective the students thought the small-group discussions were.

Example 1: Defining Features Matrix. (See CAT 9 in Angelo and Cross, 1993, pp. 164–167.) The purpose of the Defining Features Matrix is to find out how well students can distinguish the similarities and differences among two or more concepts. In this case, the lesson for the day consisted of applying the criteria for narrative and analytical styles in presenting history. In preparing the matrix, the instructors would need to make a list of the defining features of the two styles, asking students to check the presence or absence of the characteristics after their small-group discussions or at the end of the class period. Table 4.1 illustrates how a Defining Features Matrix (with answers) might look for the topic of narrative and analytical styles.

Students might score their own papers, or this CAT might be handed in as a mini-test. In keeping with the philosophy of Classroom Assessment, however, the tests would not be graded but would be handed in anonymously to help teachers—and students—monitor the learning of the class. A report back on the performance at the next class period would function as a quick review of an important concept and might also serve as a bridge to the next class session. This CAT could come as welcome relief to students seeking some answers in a class that is more about the nature of history as a discipline than about the "facts" of history. At the same time, the instructors in this course would probably want stu-

Table 4.1.

Defining Features Matrix for Narrative and Analytical Styles.

Features	Narrative	Analytical
Aims to capture the uniqueness of a historical event	x	
Aims to draw conclusions or formulate hypotheses about cause and effect		x
Assumes certain values, theories, points of view	x	x
Preserves detail and concreteness	x	
Tells a story	x	
Weighs arguments		x
Enhances understanding of history	x	x

dents to understand that the purpose of the class exercise and the matrix is to help them see important patterns rather than to test their recall of discrete facts.

Example 2: Group-Work Evaluations. (See CAT 47 in Angelo & Cross, 1993, pp. 349–351.) Group-Work Evaluation forms are simple questionnaires used to collect feedback on students' reactions to cooperative learning, where students work in structured groups toward an agreed-upon learning goal. This CAT can help both teachers and students see what is going well and what needs attention, and it can also be used to gain insight into group process. The questionnaire should be constructed with both ends in mind: What do the instructors want to know about the functioning of the group and what do they want students to notice about what contributes to effective and ineffective group work? A sample of a general group-work evaluation form appears in Exhibit 4.2.

The more specific the questions are to the group assignments, the more useful the responses will be. In this case, for example, Susan and Sam feared that some groups were getting off the topic. Thus, they might choose to include a group-work evaluation question asking how much of the time spent in small groups was maximally productive—none, a fourth, a half, or all.

Exhibit 4.2.
Sample of a Group-Work Evaluation Form.

Group-Work Evaluation Form

1. Overall, how effectively did your group work together on the assignment?

   Poorly   Adequately   Well   Extremely well

2. Out of the five group members, how many participated actively most of the time?

   None   One   Two   Three   Four   Five

3. Out of the five group members, how many were fully prepared for the activity?

   None   One   Two   Three   Four   Five

4. Give one specific example of *something you learned from the group* that you probably wouldn't have learned working alone?

5. Give one specific example of *something other group members learned from you* that they probably wouldn't have learned otherwise.

6. Suggest one change the group could make to improve its performance.

Source: Angelo and Cross, 1993, p. 350.

CLASSROOM
RESEARCH

Explorations for Understanding

Introduction. There are some things that traditional educational researchers can do far better than Classroom Researchers, and there are other things that Classroom Researchers can do far better than educational researchers. Research into intellectual development and critical thinking illustrates some of the important differences.

It is perhaps no accident that much of the interest in intellectual development in college students was initiated by a nonresearcher, William Perry. As a counselor interested in students' reactions to their education, Perry interviewed students, relying on sensitive and insightful observation, to launch his hypotheses about intellectual development (see the discussion in the review of the literature earlier in this chapter). Classroom Researchers have an opportunity not usually available to educational researchers to observe students in the process of learning. Moreover, because learning occurs in the presence of something to be learned, a sensitive observer who knows the discipline is likely to be alert to special learning problems and nuances within the discipline. Conversely, the critical element that Classroom Researchers usually lack is familiarity with the literature on intellectual development, which makes it hard for them to know what to look for and hard for them to see common patterns. The following suggestion for Classroom Research tries to capitalize on the strengths of classroom teachers in the study of intellectual development.

Example 1: Collaborative Research on Intellectual Development. Collaborative investigations have proved not only popular but very productive among teachers using Classroom Assessment. They may have even more appeal in Classroom Research projects. A faculty study group that takes the literature on intellectual development as a semester-long topic for review and discussion offers an opportunity for some interesting collaborative research. The literature review plus the recommended readings suggested in this chapter offer a brief introduction to the literature on research and theory about the intellectual development of college students. These readings, or others that the study group might identify, could serve as a common reading assignment for all members of the group while specific individuals take on the assignment of reading in depth and leading the discussion on particular topics. Occasional guest lecturers from campus and local university departments of education, psychology, and the like might serve to stimulate interest, identify relevant literature, and answer questions for the group. Such study would heighten the interest of group members in observing the intellectual development of students, and the opportunity for exchanging observations with colleagues would add focus and direction to the study.

In the present case study, for example, and indeed, in the cases throughout this book, there is evidence of different levels of intellectual development among the students described. The evidence is most apparent in this case in the research data collected by the case author. Compare, for example, these student comments to the descriptions presented in the literature review on intellectual development.

> Truthfully, I find it irrelevant. Most of us at this point have already decided on how we think the world works.
> Everyone has different opinions on quantitative concepts.
> Three or four classes on "facts." Still don't know what [the instructor] was trying to say to us.
> Difficult class and never quite sure that I was doing things right.
> When I first took this course, I was expecting it to be a course in history. The fact that I am learning how to think critically greatly surprises me.

Data collected by members of the study group from their own classes, using CATs or other methods, would make fascinating material for discussion in the context of the literature on intellectual development. For example, a collaborative research group might undertake the study of students in the absolutist stages of development. A study of what the literature has to say about this stage, followed by examples gleaned from the classes of group members, followed by discussion and experimentation about how best to help these students move to a higher level of intellectual development would make a productive semester-long investigation.

Similarly, a collaborative Classroom Research group might take up the study of gender issues. There is now an excellent literature on the topic, and the issues for observation are abundant. In this case, for example, Susan and Sam might observe the operation of the groups. Do many women students (and some men) try to avoid argument? Do many women use connected modes of thinking, trying to put themselves in the place of the other? Rather than simply circulating among the groups to see if students are on task, Classroom Researchers might enrich their own understanding of the learning process by focused observation and by sharing their observations with colleagues making similar classroom observations.

Once members of the study group have learned what to look for, they might turn their attention to discussion of how to create the kind of learning environments that challenge students to grow intellectually. Theory suggests that one way to help students move to the next level of intellectual development is to design environments that question old ways of thinking and require new approaches. Classroom teachers probably know better than anyone else the issues of challenge in their disciplines. A further agenda for the study group might consist of the exchange of information about what seems to work. We say "seems to work" because there are probably no hard criteria for making a determination. Intellectual development is not something that is likely to occur in measurable amounts within the short time span of a single semester and in the relatively narrow intellectual band of a single class. But it is individual "aha" experiences that occur in single classrooms that eventually add up to the advances in intellectual development evident in the research that shows the general effectiveness of challenging college environments in spurring intellectual development.

Even though the specific observations and discussions recommended here for Classroom Research are not traditional research methods, the kind of collaboration we are recommending has become the working environment of choice for even the largest and most traditional research groups. Collecting data in one's own area of expertise, placing it in the context of what is known about the subject, and sharing insights and interpretations with colleagues is research in the best and most sophisticated sense of the word. Moreover, if a study group's concept of research includes making findings available to the wider community, the group might wish to write about members' findings in order to share them with others in the discipline via the Internet or publication in a teaching journal.

The research questions for studying intellectual development in a systematic way might be summed up as follows: What do we know from the literature on intellectual development? How closely does what we can observe in our classes conform to what the literature says? Do colleagues from different disciplines find different examples, or do the observations support the theory of common patterns or stages of intellectual development? How do students at various levels of intellectual development react to such various types of situations as ambiguity and ill-defined problems, ethical issues, taking responsibility for coming to a reasoned conclusion, and dealing with complexity and uncertainty? How do students in different stages of development encourage or discourage growth in other students? What kinds of questions do students raise in class or on a written assignment in preparation for class discussion? What kinds of questions are submitted when students are invited to formulate questions for possible use in tests? How do student responses to various CATs differ by level of intellectual development: for example, can students be grouped by the nature of their responses to CATs like the Minute Paper?

Other questions group members might formulate might concern methodology: How can we best study students in various stages of intellectual development? What are the opportunities for natural observations in interviews, class discussion, work on projects, and small-group work? Can special requests for individual help during office hours provide opportunities for in-depth conversations with students about their approaches to study and learning?

Still other researchable questions might concern application and assessment: What constitutes a challenging environment for different types of students? How do students in different stages of intellectual development respond to various teaching approaches such as frequent versus infrequent exams, essay or multiple-choice exams, and different types of homework assignments, for example, a request for *summaries* versus a request for *syntheses* of required readings?

The point is that Classroom Research on intellectual development should consist of far more than trying to identify the various stages present in any college classroom, and certainly, it should not have a primary objective of labeling students. The unique opportunity for Classroom Researchers is that in their continuing relationship with students, they can observe manifold orientations to learning and reactions to teaching.

Example 2: Classroom Research on Critical Thinking. The question that Susan posed at the end of the case study was, Is it working? A more specific question for investigation is, Are students learning critical-thinking skills in the small discussion groups? Or are the small groups effective in teaching critical-thinking skills? Those are slightly different questions. But in either instance, one thinks first of the need for a criterion measure. How does an instructor know whether students are gaining critical-thinking skills?

There is an understandable temptation to seek measures of critical thinking by rather conventional means—pre- and posttests, for instance, using some such instrument as the Watson-Glaser Critical Thinking Appraisal (see Pascarella and Terenzini, 1991, p. 143). We are not especially enthusiastic about encouraging classroom teachers to use tests of generic critical thinking as a criterion measure in their Classroom Research, for the following reasons.

First, research to date suggests that growth in generic critical thinking is unlikely to show up in a single class over the short time span of a semester. It is not very likely that classroom teachers will find "significant" or even interesting results on published tests of general critical thinking. Second, trying to construct a criterion-based test of critical-thinking ability is probably not a feasible activity for most Classroom Researchers. As Pascarella and Terenzini note, "The reliable and valid measurement of general cognitive competencies and skills is often a difficult and highly complex psychometric task" (1991, p. 115). It is probably a task best left to trained researchers and program evaluators with the resources, research skills, and grounding in the research and literature of critical thinking. And third, research of this nature, although important in institutional studies, is not very consistent with the purposes and philosophy of Classroom Research because it is perceived as an extra activity for the class rather than part of the ongoing instruction. Students, for instance, have little to gain from taking a general test of critical thinking, and thus, such a test may be a dubious use of class time for the average instructor.[1]

These caveats, however, do not mean that critical thinking is not a rich and important field for inquiry by Classroom Researchers. In fact, there are strong arguments that of all the people who need to be concerned and knowledgeable about critical thinking, teachers and students are the foremost. Moreover, different disciplines foster unique aspects of critical thinking, and discipline-oriented teachers are in an excellent position to define critical thinking for their own field of study. Cromwell, for example, observes that "areas in the humanities share the idea that 'problems' tend to have ambiguous and even open-ended 'solutions,' whereas the sciences tend to have a much more systematic view of problem solving" (1992, p. 40). In her view, it is not only feasible for classroom teachers to assess critical thinking, it is absolutely necessary that they do so. Lucy Cromwell is a professor of English at Alverno College who has worked with classroom teachers in the context of the well-known Alverno College assessment program, which integrates assessment and instruction. She has written a very helpful chapter (Cromwell, 1992) addressed specifically to college teachers. The essence of her message is that college teachers know what critical thinking is in their disciplines, and they can and should measure it continuously in their own assignments and tests.

Even though most teachers undoubtedly know critical thinking when they see it, they do not make concerted efforts to measure it. The evidence is strong that the majority of classroom tests call for simple factual information and little else. Even when teachers *think* their tests tap complex cognitive skills, independent judgments of test questions reveal far less call for critical thinking than teachers think they are requiring (Milton, Pollio, and Eison, 1986, pp. 20–21). Thus, one of the first requirements of Classroom Research on critical thinking is that instructors develop the criteria for evidence of critical thinking in their own disciplines and classrooms. That means establishing clear goals and then developing the appropriate assessments. Both the goals and the assessments (those proposed as well as those completed) should be shared with students.

Assuming appropriate discipline-based criterion measures for critical thinking, then, we return to Susan's research question: Is it working? Are students learning critical-thinking skills in the small discussion groups? And are the small groups effective in teaching critical-thinking skills? The two questions are very similar, but the first question involves an evaluation of student learning, the second an evaluation of the effectiveness of the groups.

In the case presented here, it is not clear that Susan and Sam have defined the goals of the small-group work very clearly. Their one stated criterion for assessing whether the groups are working is that students will be talking. "I'm always afraid they won't have anything to say," says Susan. Although students' talking is not a sufficient criterion for determining the effectiveness of the groups, it is necessary to get students actively involved in debating an issue with one another. Thus, one way to evaluate what students are learning is to observe the groups in action, that is, what kind of talking is going on? Are students challenging one another to support their answers? Or are they simply seeking agreement on the "right" answer? The assignment might be interpreted by some students as a charge to find the "right" answer or to develop group consensus. Are the groups engaged in active analysis?

Another way to evaluate what students are learning is to ask them. A request for a brief written response, immediately following the group meetings, might ask for the student's own conclusion plus supporting reasons for his or her answer. Such a request has the added advantage of alerting those students who have a tendency to let the group do the work to their individual responsibilities. The rationale for this post-group-work quiz should be made clear to students, and to be consistent with the premises of Classroom Research, it should not be graded. Students as well as teachers stand to gain from this type of research. The time it takes for each student to reflect on his or her answer and to write it out is probably time very well spent, and the data collected about what is happening to each student in the groups will be of high interest and value to the instructors.

The second question regarding the effectiveness of the groups might follow a similar methodology—observation and written response—but in this instance, the written response might take the form of a targeted group evaluation, asking students to respond to such questions as, In what way was the group helpful to you? What was the most important question raised in the group, and who raised it? Was there a debatable issue, and how many group members entered into the debate? Did your group come to a conclusion quickly or was there extended discussion? (This question also evaluates the effectiveness of the assigned task; a too simple task results in wasted time and little intellectual challenge, whereas a too complex assignment results in lack of focus and diffused arguments).

There are many ways to address this universal question for teachers, Is it working? The problem comes only in failing to raise the question as an investigative possibility. Some teachers think that they can "feel" whether "it" is working; others believe that in the absence of rigorous criteria, the question is simply too complicated to investigate. The most realistic answer probably lies somewhere in between. A systematic and sensitive observation of what is happening in the class may well lead to legitimate feelings that all is going well, but formulating questions, targeting inquiry, and collecting data will not only verify teachers' feelings, but also add to their knowledge about teaching and learning.

CHAPTER 5

"The Challenge"

Designing Your Own Classroom Research

Like the other cases you have read in this book, "The Challenge" sets the stage for discussion of teaching and learning, Classroom Assessment, and Classroom Research. However, unlike the other chapters, this chapter does not include the formulation of hypotheses about learning issues, reviews of the relevant literature, or suggestions for Classroom Assessment and Classroom Research. That is up to you, the readers, to develop. We do give you this clue: this case was specifically written to illustrate most of the learning issues discussed throughout this book. The challenge is for you to identify the learning issues, suggest Classroom Assessment projects to assess the learning of students in the class, and invent and develop Classroom Research projects that will shed further light on learning issues as they appear in college classrooms.

CASE STUDY _____

"Well, this article is bound to start a lively discussion," Professor Elena Diaz thought to herself as she looked over the assigned readings for today's Motivation and Learning class. Elena had found last week's discussion of the reading on motivation theory very disappointing. Even her highly motivated teacher education students seemed to have processed the information on only the most surface level. In response to her carefully crafted discussion questions, they merely read aloud from their notes excerpts from the assigned reading. Because most students simply listed points from the readings, she rarely heard students discuss the theoretical concepts in their own words. This week, Elena had tried a new strategy. She had asked students to develop questions they would like the class to discuss. She hoped this assignment would engage students in self-questioning and comprehension monitoring while reading.

Before becoming a faculty member in the education department of the state university, Elena had been an elementary school teacher and administrator for over ten years. The students in the teacher education program appreciated her connection to the classroom, and her anecdotes from experience helped bring theory to life. Her course reading lists often included a mix of articles from research journals and practitioner-oriented publications. Although last week's readings were primarily theoretical, this week's assignment was more closely connected to motivation in the classroom. One of today's readings was decidedly controversial, and Elena expected it to involve students more personally with the material. Students were asked to read and develop questions based on an abridged version of an interview by Ron Brandt, executive editor of *Educational Leadership,* of Alfie Kohn, author of the 1993 book *Punished by Rewards.* (See Exhibit 5.1 for the abridged interview the students read.)

After reviewing the reading, Elena took a last sip of her coffee, gathered her materials, and headed for the seminar room where her senior-level Motivation and Learning course was about to meet. She greeted the students as they arrived just in time for the four o'clock class. Many were exhausted after a full day of student teaching and slumped in their chairs around the large conference table. Fifteen of the twenty students were education majors in the middle of their first semester of student teaching. Motivation and Learning is a required course for their teacher education program. However, not all of Elena's students are currently working as student teachers. Three are senior psychology majors preparing for graduate programs, and there are also two sophomore women who have special permission to take the course as part of a teaching careers exploration program.

Recognizing that the students were overwhelmed with their student-teaching assignments or work for other classes, Elena worked hard to engage her class in the subject matter and keep the discussion moving. Today, after taking care of a few housekeeping details, Elena begins by saying: "Your assignment for today was to prepare a question, based on the readings, that you would like the class to discuss. Who'd like to start?"

She looks around the room and catches the alert eye of Joe Alvarez, a former engineering major who decided in his junior year

Exhibit 5.1.

Case Study Reading Assignment.

Punished by Rewards?
A Conversation with Alfie Kohn

by Ron Brandt

RB: *Alfie, we educators use punishment quite a lot, but we've come to understand that it's not a very effective motivator. We've been convinced that it's much better to use rewards instead. But now you come along and say that's wrong, too. Why?*

AK: First, let's make sure we agree on your first premise, which is that punishment is destructive. A number of people seem to think if we call it "consequences" or insert the modifier "logical," then it's okay. "Logical consequences" is an example of what I call "punishment lite," a kinder, gentler way of doing things *to* children instead of working *with* them. Having said that, I'll move on to rewards. Rewards and punishments are both ways of manipulating behavior.

RB: *And you're saying rewards are just as undesirable as punishment?*

AK: By virtue of being controlling, they're likely to be experienced as aversive in the long run. The reason is that while students would certainly like to have the goody itself—the pizza or money or gold star—none of us enjoys having the very things we desire used as levers to control our behavior.

RB: *You're saying that's the case even for kids who find a certain task rewarding for its own sake?*

AK: Rewards are *most* damaging to interest when the task is already intrinsically motivating. This may be simply because there is that much more interest to lose when extrinsics are introduced; if you're doing something boring, your interest may already be rock bottom. However, that doesn't give us license to treat kids like pets when the task is uninteresting. Instead, we need to examine the task itself, the content of the curriculum, to see how it can be made more engaging.

RB: *In* Punished by Rewards *you cite a lot of research on points like that. You're saying this is not just your opinion.*

AK: That's right. There are at least 70 studies showing that extrinsic motivators—including A's, sometimes praise, sometimes other rewards—are not merely ineffective over the long haul but counterproductive with respect to the things that concern us most: desire to learn, commitment to good values, and so on.

RB: *That seems so contrary to our everyday experience. Everybody is used to getting rewards and giving them. As educators we think it's only right to give rewards; kids who do good things deserve rewards.*

AK: What kids deserve is an engaging curriculum and a caring atmosphere so they can act on their natural desire to find out about stuff. No kid deserves to be manipulated with extrinsics so as to comply with what others want.

Exhibit 5.1. *Continued.*

It's remarkable how often educators use the word *motivation* when what they mean is *compliance.* Indeed, one of the fundamental myths in this area is that it's possible to motivate someone else. Whenever you see an article or a seminar entitled "How to Motivate Your Students," I recommend you ignore it. You can't motivate another person, so framing the issue that way virtually guarantees the use of controlling devices.

Moreover, motivation is something that kids start out with. You don't have to bribe a young child to show you how she can count to a thousand million or decode signs on the highway. But research shows that by the middle—or certainly by the end—of elementary school, this intrinsic motivation starts to tail off sharply—by an extraordinary coincidence, around the time that grades have started to kick in.

RB: *Surely it's unrealistic to expect that all kids will find all the curriculum intrinsically motivating. There are some things that kids just have to slog through, aren't there?*

AK: Well, a given child is likely to be more interested in some things than others, but we're not talking about putting something on the chalkboard and expecting kids to jump up and down and say, "I can't wait to get at this." Skillful teaching involves facilitating the process by which kids come to grapple with complex ideas—and those ideas, as John Dewey has told us, have to emerge organically from the real-life interests and concerns of the kids.

In the context of a task that matters to students, the specific skills we care about can be taught naturally without sugarcoating, without games, and above all without offering kids little doggie biscuits for doing what we tell them.

RB: *Let me ask about praise, which is particularly tricky, because it's not a tangible reward. If I tell one of my staff members that he or she did a terrific job on something, am I giving a reward at that point?*

AK: That's an interesting question, and I wish more educators would ask it, regardless of what the answer turns out to be.

Positive feedback that is perceived as information is not in itself destructive and indeed can be quite constructive, educationally speaking. And encouragement—helping people feel acknowledged so that their interest in a task is redoubled—is not a bad thing. But most praise given to children is given in the form of a verbal reward.

A typical example is the elementary school teacher who is taught to say, "I like the way Cecilia is sitting so nice and quiet and ready to work." I have multiple objections to this practice.

RB: *Why?*

AK: First, the teacher hasn't done Cecilia any favors. You can imagine one of the other kids coming up to her after class: "Miss 'nice and quiet' dork!"

Second, the teacher has just turned a learning experience into a quest for triumph. She has introduced competition into the classroom. It's now a contest to see who is the nicest, quietest child—and the rest of you just lost.

Exhibit 5.1. *Continued.*

Third, this is a fundamentally fraudulent interaction. The teacher is pretending to speak to Cecilia, but she's really using Cecilia to manipulate the behavior of the other people in the room—and that's simply not a nice way to deal with human beings.

Fourth, and possibly most important, I ask you to reflect on what is the most important word in that expression. I believe it's *I*. Even if such a practice "works," it has worked only to get Cecilia and the other people watching to be concerned about what I demand, regardless of what reasons I may or may not have for asking her to do something. Cecilia is not helped one iota to reflect on how her experience affects other people in the room or what kind of person she wants to be.

RB: *What about less successful students? A lot of educators feel strongly that they need even more praise than other kids. They need to be praised when they make the slightest bit of progress.*

AK: No research supports the idea that praising children for inching up the adult-constructed ladder helps them develop a sense of competence.

Indeed, praise for success at relatively easy tasks sends a message that this child must not be very bright. Moreover, children are not helped to find the material itself important or interesting if they are praised for doing it."

RB: *What you're saying is not going to be readily accepted by most people. It seems to go against our everyday experience.*

AK: It does and it doesn't. For example, parents come up to me and say things like, "You know it's funny you say this, because just yesterday I asked my kid to clear the table after dinner and he said, 'What are you going to give me for it?'" What I find remarkable about that is not what the child said, but that the parent is asking me to shake my head and commiserate about These Kids Today. What I want to ask is "Where do you think the kid learned this?" And if I do ask that, with very little prompting, people understand.

RB: *All the same, it's a different way to think about things. For example, I like it when people recognize me for an accomplishment of some kind.*

AK: Yes, of course. We all want to be appreciated, encouraged and loved. The question is whether that need must take the form of what often looks like a patronizing pat on the head and saying "good boy," to which I believe the most logical response is "Woof!" . . . I'm struck by teachers who say over and over to me, "You don't understand the kind of backgrounds and home lives these kids have, they come from loveless, sometimes brutal places, and you're telling me not to praise them?" My answer is, "Yes." What these kids need is unconditional support and encouragement and love. Praise is not just different from that; it's the *opposite* of that. Praise is, "Jump through my hoops, and only then will I tell you what a great job you did and how proud I am of you." And that can be problematic. Of course, with positive feedback, it's a matter of nuance and emphasis and implementation. That

Exhibit 5.1. *Continued.*

---

is not the case with gold stars, candy bars, and A's, which I believe are inherently destructive.

The kind of motivation elicited by extrinsic inducements isn't just less effective than intrinsic motivation; it threatens to erode that intrinsic motivation, that excitement about what one is doing.

RB: *So what are you suggesting instead?*

AK: I sometimes talk about the three C's of motivation. The first C is *content.* Far less interesting to me than whether a student has learned what he was supposed to is the question, "Has the child been given something to do worth learning?" If you ask me what to do about a kid being "off task"—one of our favorite buzzwords,—my first response is going to be, "What's the task?" If you're giving them garbage to do, yes, you may have to bribe them to do it. If the kids have to endlessly fill in the blanks on dittos, you're not going to get rid of rewards any time soon.

The second C is *community:* not only cooperative learning but helping kids feel part of a safe environment in which they feel free to ask for help, in which they come to care about one another as opposed to having to be manipulated to share or not be mean.

The third C is *choice:* making sure that kids are asked to think about what they're doing and how and with whom and why. You know, kids learn to make good choices not by following directions but by making choices.

You show me a school that really has those three C's in place—where students are working with one another in a caring environment to engage with interesting tasks that they have some say in choosing—and I'll show you a place where you don't need to use punishments or rewards.

Source: Brandt, 1995, pp. 13–16.

to switch to education. He wanted to use his science background and his ability to speak both Spanish and English to teach science to elementary school kids in the urban community where he grew up.

Joe starts off the class with his question: "Well, okay. I thought we had a good discussion last week on theories of motivation, and we tried to apply that to motivating our students. So now this week we read something by a guy who says, 'whenever you see an article or seminar called How to Motivate Your Students, I recommend that you ignore it. You can't motivate another person,' he says. 'Motivation is something kids start out with.' I'm confused here—the kids in the sixth-grade class I'm working in do not seem to be motivating themselves. What am I supposed to do? Can teachers motivate kids, or not?"

"Thanks, Joe, you got right to the heart of the matter. Before we start our discussion let's hear a few more questions. Who has another one? How about yours, Grace?" Elena asks.

Grace Lee is a sophomore psychology major with a nearly perfect grade point average. She is very intelligent, but is somewhat intimidated by the other students' confident and informal interaction with each other and the professor in this discussion format. She is captivated by the older students' stories from their student-teaching assignments. In her soft voice, Grace reads a question from her spiral notebook: "List three reasons why Alfie Kohn recommends against using rewards in the classroom."

"Geez, what's this, the Psych 101 midterm?" mutters Jake Webber to one of the other psychology majors. Jake is a senior who has already been admitted to a graduate program in psychology.

Elena, hoping that Grace has not heard Jake's scornful comment, quickly asks, "Did you want to read your question, Jake?" At the same time, Elena is wondering how she can help Grace and others develop the ability to ask questions that require more thought than regurgitating facts from the reading.

"All right," Jake replied, "I was wondering how Kohn takes into account the work of B. F. Skinner, who claimed that learning is really conditioning, and teaching is accomplished through the skillful use of reward and punishment. Reward what you want to happen; punish what you want to discourage."

"That's right," interjects Carla Roland, a confident older teacher education student in her mid-thirties. "What was that book of Skinner's that blew it all out of the water—?"

There was a slight pause, as students seemed to search their memories. Carla could see Grace light up as if she knew the title, but only after Carla turned to her directly, did Grace respond tentatively, "I think we just learned about it in one of my psych classes—*Beyond Freedom and Dignity*?"

Carla continued, "Thanks Grace, that's it. As I remember, his thesis was that you can control anyone by conditioning—people, pigeons, rats, it's all the same. Reward behavior that you want to see repeated, and you will gain control over that person."

Joe, the former engineering major leaned over to Holly Bailey, a sophomore, like Grace, and asked: "Who the heck is B. F. Skinner? What's this about rewarding a rat, and what does it have to do with this class?"

Holly whispers a reply: "Skinner's a famous behavioral psychologist—really important in conditioned learning. I know what you mean, though, aren't we getting off the topic?"

Janet Hollister, another older teacher education student, picks up where Carla left off, "Well, what I think that Kohn means by saying that we don't have license to treat kids like pets is—"

Jake Webber jumps in, "Yeah—whatever, kids aren't pets—but it's absurd that Kohn can ignore an entire tradition of research on the relationship of reward to behavior!"

Janet sat back in her chair and fell silent, as if she, rather than Kohn's position, had been attacked.

Jake continues: "Condition, control, socialization—whatever. What's the difference? Parents and teachers have to be able to socialize the kids they're responsible for, and I don't see how you can do that without using rewards."

Laurie Nelson furrows her brow in thought. She has wanted to be a teacher for as long as she can remember. But her experience as a student teacher in an inner-city school is causing her to rethink her career goals. She had always believed that she could make a difference in the lives of children through education. But among the children in her fifth-grade class, few can read at grade level, many come to school hungry, many are withdrawn, and others cannot even sit still for a half-hour lesson.

"I have to admit," Laurie agreed, "that this time last year I would have agreed with Kohn. But now I find myself relying more on rewards and punishments. These kids are so shaped by their environment that they do not find intrinsic rewards in school learning. What I mean is that finishing your math problems only feels good if you've been socialized to believe doing well in school is a good thing. By the time these kids in my school get to fifth grade, they are not filled with pride and joy by finishing their math problems, if they can finish them at all. The only way I can get them to be quiet long enough to get through a lesson is to bribe them with M&Ms."

"I see your point," says Holly tentatively. "Maybe it just depends. What is right in one situation will never work somewhere else."

Elena pushes gently: "Surely, some ways of using rewards are better than others—"

Grace responds with a question: "Kohn says there is evidence from some seventy studies that extrinsic motivation is ineffective in the long run. Doesn't that mean teachers shouldn't use extrinsic motivators?"

Holly, who has not yet been a student teacher, looks thoughtful and responds, "I'm not sure. Research never seems to come to any clear-cut answers. What if there are another seventy studies somewhere that show 'no significant difference' or maybe even that extrinsic motivators are effective?"

"Well," Joe contributes, "you'd need to look at the research methodology to determine the credibility of the studies."

Jake, geared for debate, replies, "Sure, but the criteria for good methodology change from decade to decade. Were those older studies contextually valid? And do some of the more recent studies sacrifice rigor for the sake of relevance?"

Carla rolls her eyes, "Come on, you guys, before you get into a big argument about methodology, let's figure out where Kohn's coming from, and how this is relevant to our teaching. He makes an interesting point about ruining something for learners by rewarding them for something they already enjoy doing. Most of us have some experience with kids. What do you all think about this?"

"I don't know, my own kids seem to appreciate it when I praise them, and they sure respond to rewards. It's amazing how clean their rooms get with the promise of pizza for dinner!" contributes Janet Hollister, a mother of three who returned to college for a teaching credential after her youngest child entered kindergarten. "I don't know what to make of this. Is Kohn talking mainly about school learning? Do his recommendations make sense for my students, or my own kids? Are parents supposed to follow his advice, too?"

Janet, in her mid-thirties like Carla, lacks Carla's confidence in the college classroom. Still, she has a knack for drawing others into the conversation: "Laurie, what's your experience from student teaching?"

Laurie replies, "Well, theoretically Kohn's ideas sound fine, but it's pretty hard not to reward the kids who are doing what you want them to and, in the process, setting a good example for others. Especially since that's such a rare occurrence in my classes. It's hard not to praise, or to bribe, for that matter."

Chris Warner, exhausted from a long day of teaching sixth-grade social studies, has not said much today, but is starting to get impatient: "This is a great discussion, but I'm already starting to burn out on student teaching, and it's only my first semester. I don't need a debate about theory, I need someone to tell me what I'm supposed to do with these kids in my class!"

"You know, Chris," says Janet, "that's related to the question I prepared for today: How do Kohn's recommendations apply to our future work as teachers? And do they make sense based on our experience?"

"Yes," replies Joe, "I wonder if Kohn has ever taught? Make content engaging, yeah, sure. Act on kids' natural desire to find out about stuff? I was pissed when he said that if the students are 'off task' then the task was probably 'garbage,' like it's the teacher's fault. I set up these great experiments for the kids to do, and they act like it's about as interesting as reading software documentation. All my kids are intrinsically motivated to learn is stuff adults don't want them to know. What is the bottom line on motivating kids, or getting them to motivate themselves? I kind of miss being an engineering major. We got some answers in those classes. No offense, Professor Diaz," he adds good-naturedly.

"That's like my question for today," Chris adds, "Which is right, what we learned about motivation last week, or what we learned about motivation this week?"

"What about asking the question this way, Chris?" Elena interjects: "Compare and contrast Kohn's view of the role of rewards and punishments for motivating learners with theories we studied earlier in the course."

"Yeah, that does sound like a good way to ask the question. That's a tough one; will that be on the midterm?" Knowing this question is a pet peeve of the instructor, Chris adds, "Just kidding! But even with all this discussion, I'm still left wondering what to do."

Carla says, thoughtfully, "I think the point of this discussion is that there is no simple answer. Although this guy, Kohn, talks as though he has 'The Answer,' I think the message is that you shouldn't try to find a reward for everything you want to encourage. You should think about the implications."

"Okay," Chris concedes. "But if every teacher has to figure out what to do in each individual classroom with each individual student, then why are we spending so much time on this stuff? There's so much reading to begin with, and the articles seem to contradict one another. Isn't anybody going to teach me how to teach?" Chris challenged.

THE READER'S CHALLENGE

The case you have just read is a composite of the learning issues that have been discussed throughout this book. We have included "The Challenge" as an opportunity for readers to *apply* what they have learned about the identification of learning issues in a classroom setting and about the formulation of Classroom Assessment and Classroom Research projects to deepen their understanding of teaching and learning issues. The discussion of this case might begin with some questions about what is happening in this classroom, from the perspectives of both teacher and students.

That analysis should lead to the identification of hypotheses and questions about learning issues in the case. The learning issues illustrated in the case come directly from the literature reviews in Chapters Two, Three, and Four. They include issues of motivation, deep and surface approaches to learning, metacognition and learning strategies, schema theory, gender, intellectual development, and critical thinking. No doubt experienced teachers will be able to identify other learning issues.

Identification of the learning issues, however, is just the beginning. C. Roland Christensen, master teacher of the case method at the Harvard Business School says, "The minimum end product of a case discussion is an understanding of what needs to be done and how it can be accomplished" (1987a, p. 30). In this book, case discussions serve as the launching point for Classroom Assessment and Classroom Research projects. Case discussions lead to hypotheses or questions and the in-depth study of learning issues. And the end product of the case discussions is the design and implementation of Classroom Assessment and Classroom Research projects.

The rest of this chapter offers guiding questions for discussing the case study and a series of exercises for defining learning issues and developing Classroom Research projects. Some readers will wish to take advantage of these case analysis activities, whereas others will prefer to pursue case analysis and Classroom Research projects independently. In either case, we wish you success in your explorations of teaching and learning.

GUIDING QUESTIONS

Case Discussion and Analysis

The following discussion questions for analysis of "The Challenge" are grouped according to learning issue. These questions apply specifically to the case presented in this chapter, but they model questions that you can adapt to the other cases in this book or to cases you develop on your own.

Opening the Discussion

- How would Elena Diaz describe the discussion taking place in her classroom? What does she hope students are learning?
- Take the role of one of the students portrayed [in order of appearance, they are Joe, Grace, Jake, Carla, Janet, Holly, and Chris] and describe your reactions to Professor Diaz's Motivation and Learning class.
- What are the key learning issues revealed in this case?
- Are there learning issues in the case that are similar to issues present in the courses that you teach or have taught?
- What useful additional information about the background or current learning of students in this class could you gather using Classroom Assessment Techniques?

Schemata and the Role of Prior Knowledge

- What evidence is there in this case of the role of schemata or prior knowledge?

- Does it matter that Joe is unfamiliar with B. F. Skinner and his work on conditioning and rewards? Would student knowledge about the work of other theorists on rewards be helpful to a good classroom discussion of the ideas presented in the Kohn interview? Why or why not?

- How could the instructor use Classroom Assessment Techniques to determine what students know about the literature on rewards and punishments as motivators?

- Are there necessary prerequisites for a course on motivation and learning in a teacher education program? If so, what are they?

- What questions, if any, does this case raise for you about the role of prior knowledge? What would you like to investigate further? How might you investigate your questions? Formulate a Classroom Research project for "The Challenge." For example, do students' performances in this course vary according to whether or not each student is currently a student teacher or a parent?

Approaches to Learning and Cognitive Learning Strategies

- Is there any evidence in this case of students using a surface approach to learning? What conditions would encourage a surface approach?

- What do you think is the rationale behind Elena's strategy of asking students to generate questions for discussion based on the assigned reading? Is this constructive? Why or why not?

- What might Elena do to encourage good reading skills and learning strategies in her students?

- What Classroom Assessment Techniques could be used to collect information on students' approaches to learning and use of learning strategies?

- What CATs could be used to encourage deeper approaches to learning and foster students' use of learning strategies?

- What questions, if any, does this case raise for you about the students' approaches to learning and/or learning strategies? What would you like to investigate further? How might you investigate your questions? Formulate a Classroom Research project for "The Challenge." For example, design a simple Classroom Research project to investigate any differences between the learning strategies of "good" and "poor" students.

Intellectual Development, Critical Thinking, and Gender Issues

- Why do you think Elena assigned this controversial article? What does it "teach" students?

- What do the discussion questions that students prepared tell you about the learners in the class?

- Select one student in the case and describe what that student's comments reveal about his or her intellectual development.

- Why are some students finding competing theories of motivation so frustrating?

- How might Elena help students deal with ambiguous learning tasks such as making decisions when confronted with conflicting information?

- Is there evidence that critical thinking is going on in this class? What is that evidence?

- How might Elena promote critical thinking?

- Which students seem most comfortable in this class? Why?

- Are any students feeling uncomfortable in this discussion? Why?

- In your classes, do patterns of student discussion (who talks and when) change depending on the classroom activity (whole-class discussions, group work, paired discussions, and so forth)?

- Are any gender issues revealed in this case? Where?

- What Classroom Assessment Techniques might you use to get further information about students' comfort level in this class?

- What questions, if any, does this case raise for you about intellectual development, critical thinking, and gender? What would you like to investigate further? How might you investigate your questions? Formulate Classroom Research projects for "The Challenge." For example, design a simple Classroom Research project to investigate patterns of student interaction in the classroom.

Motivation

- Why are students taking Motivation and Learning? What might be the goals and expectations of different students in the class?

- How might students' reasons for taking this course affect their motivations? What do you think are the particular needs and interests of the preprofessional students? How might these needs be met?

- What role, if any, does students' self-confidence play in their learning in this class? Does self-confidence have a role in their success as pre-service and eventually in-service teachers?

- What Classroom Assessment Techniques could be used to answer questions about student expectations for this course?

- Is the Kohn interview a motivating assignment for these students? Why or why not?

- Are the motivational issues that emerged in the Kohn interview relevant to teaching in college classrooms?

- What questions, if any, does this case raise for you about an instructor's use of motivation? What would you like to investigate further? How might you investigate your questions? Formulate a Classroom Research project for "The Challenge." For example, design a simple Classroom Research project dealing with the motivational issues of preprofessional students.

ACTIVITIES AND EXERCISES

Classroom Research Project Design

By now, you have discussed the case and become familiar with the relevant learning issues. Next, we offer several activities and exercises designed to help you clarify learning issues of interest and develop a Classroom Research project plan. Some readers may wish to work through these exercises on their own or with colleagues, whereas others may move straight to designing their own Classroom Research projects.

Many of the following activities are based on Classroom Assessment Techniques. They focus on "The Challenge," but like the discussion questions presented earlier, they can be adapted to a Classroom Research project based on another case or on your own classes.

Focused Listing

(CAT 2 in Angelo and Cross, 1993, pp. 126–131.)

Instructions: Take three minutes to brainstorm and list any learning issues that stand out in this case. Then circle any that you would be interested in investigating further through Classroom Assessment or Classroom Research.

1. _____
2. _____
3. _____
4. _____
5. _____
6. _____
7. _____
8. _____
9. _____
10. _____

Freewriting

Instructions. Write out a few brief sentences on any hypotheses or questions about the learning issue(s) that you are interested in investigating further.

_____

_____

_____

_____

_____

CAT Planning

Instructions. What additional information could you collect using Classroom Assessment to help you define your questions for investigation? Use the following chart to record the information that you need, and the CATs you will use to get it.

Information Needed	CATs	Notes
Example: Why are students taking this class?	*Example:* Course Goals Inventory	*Example:* Do early in term.

Using the Literature

Whether you have already developed a question or project or need help getting started in doing so, it is valuable at this point to deepen your understanding of the learning issue you have identified, through the use of existing research and theory. Here are some suggestions:

- Use the table of contents of this book to identify topic areas and then return to the literature reviews that are relevant to the learning issues you wish to investigate further.
- Read the relevant recommended readings that follow each of the literature reviews in this book.
- Take special note of any additional works cited in that recommended reading that you would like to get and read.
- Conduct a library search for information on your selected topic. Use your school library's electronic card catalog, browse the ERIC (Educational Resources Information Center) database, or do an on-line search from home via the Internet.
- Talk with some colleagues about forming a study group on a particular issue.

Using Applications Cards

(CAT 24 in Angelo and Cross, 1993, pp. 236–239.)

Instructions. Explain in a few sentences (say, the space available on an index card) how a particular concept from your reading is applicable to the learning issues in the case.

_____

_____

_____

_____

_____

Using Directed Paraphrasing

(CAT 23 in Angelo and Cross, 1993, pp. 232–235.)

Instructions. After reading the literature reviews and the recommended readings or other literature you found relevant, paraphrase in a few sentences what you read about any learning theory concept.

First, paraphrase the information so that it would be understood and considered relevant by other faculty in your discipline.

_____

_____

_____

_____

_____

Second, paraphrase the information so that you could translate and convey it to students to help them learn how to learn.

_____

_____

_____

_____

_____

Discovering the Muddiest Point

(CAT 7 in Angelo and Cross, 1993, pp. 154–158.)

Instructions. What in this case is the most puzzling issue that you are interested in investigating? Does the literature that you reviewed illuminate or confuse the issue? What does not make sense? If you have any hunches or clues that might lead to clarification of this issue, note them here.

_____

_____

_____

_____

_____

Developing a Classroom Research Project Prospectus

(Based on CAT 27 in Angelo and Cross, 1993, pp. 248–253.) This exercise offers several prompts to help you develop an initial Classroom Research project prospectus. The prospectus is only a plan and will probably change considerably before you complete your project.

The prompts will encourage you to consider how your question might be investigated through Classroom Assessment and Classroom Research. Sometimes it will first be necessary to conduct Classroom Assessment to get further information before you can develop a question or hypothesis for Classroom Research. Of course, some questions can be answered through Classroom Assessment alone. At other times, you may begin with a Classroom Research question and use CATs, or any number of other research methods, to carry out the investigation.

Classroom Researchers often consult with other faculty members about their project designs. You may share your prospectus with a colleague for feedback and additional ideas for data collection, analysis, and using the results.

Here are a few questions to keep in mind while answering the prompts and designing your project: What is your research question? Is it of real interest to you? How will you investigate this question? How will you analyze the data or information you gather? How will this Classroom Research project further your understanding of teaching and learning? (If you cannot answer this question, then the project probably is not worth the effort.)

Instructions. To design your project, respond to the following prompts.

Class:

Learning issue:

Related literature:

Purpose of project:

Major question(s) you hope to answer:

Work calendar (timeline for data collection, analysis, and so on):

Data collection methods to be used, including any CATs:

Data analysis methods to be used:

How you will involve or inform students? Does participating in this project benefit students:

Resources needed (materials, information, colleagues for consultation):

Concerns or questions about this project:

What will you do with the results of this investigation? Is this information significant to you?

Case Writing: The Minute Case and Expanding the Case

This book is about Classroom Research, not about writing or discussing case studies, and it is not necessary to write a case study to design a Classroom Research project. However, you may find case writing a useful strategy for clarifying learning issues in your own classes. Therefore, we present two case writing exercises here. In addition, some case writing guidelines are presented in Exhibit 5.2.

Exhibit 5.2.

Things to Keep in Mind When Writing Cases.

The Content

- Limit the scope.
- Base the case on a real classroom event or issue.
- Keep student learning in the forefront.
- Address fundamental teaching and learning issues.
- Raise questions.
- Select an instructor with whom faculty can identify.
- Experiment with format: try drama, dialogue, and so on.
- Include concrete details.
- Make it realistic and believable.

The Process

- Set aside time and space for collaborative efforts.
- Share drafts; give and get feedback.
- Plan to write multiple drafts.
- Connect case writing to other faculty interests, such as Classroom Assessment and Classroom Research.
- Address issues of confidentiality when writing about real events.
- Value the process.

Source: Based on Hutchings, 1993, pp. 43–45.

The first case writing exercise is the Minute Case. (Based on CAT 6 in Angelo and Cross, 1993, pp. 148–153.)

Instructions. Select and read any one of the cases in Chapters Two, Three, or Four. Reflect on a learning problem that you have observed in one of your classes, or that you have encountered as a learner, that is similar to a learning issue presented in the case. Take about five minutes to write a Minute Case, no longer than three paragraphs, that briefly describes your experience. If you wish, share and discuss your Minute Case with others.

The second case writing exercise is Expanding the Case.

Instructions. After further study of the literature relevant to the learning issue in your case, expand your Minute Case into a case of several pages. Include important details, provide background about the course, and describe the context of the classroom. Include enough detail to highlight the important learning issues (see Exhibit 5.2).

If possible, share and discuss your case with other faculty. Take advantage of feedback from others to expand and refine your case. A detailed case based on one of your courses may clarify important learning issues to get you

Exhibit 5.3.

Things to Keep in Mind About Classroom Assessment.

> - Start small.
> - Set limits on the time and effort you will invest.
> - Try the technique on yourself before administering it to students.
> - Get students actively involved. Make the *purpose* and the *process* clear to students. Expect students to need time and practice for participating in Classroom Assessment.
> - Plan ahead how you will analyze the data.
> - Be flexible and willing to change.
> - Don't ask what you don't want to know.
> - Work with other faculty who share your interests.
> - Share feedback from assessment results with students.

Source: Based on Angelo and Cross, 1993, pp. 58–59.

Exhibit 5.4.

Things to Keep in Mind When Planning a Classroom Research Project.

> - Formulate a question about the learning of students in your class that is important to you in your teaching.
> - Keep your question simple, realistic, and focused on your own experience. Follow your hunches; predict what might happen.
> - Inform yourself about what is known about the learning issue you have selected. Read with focus—not necessarily exhaustively or exhaustingly. Form a study group to share the load.
> - Reformulate your question into a researchable question. What do you want to know?
> - Work with other faculty to discuss, design, cooperate on, and interpret your Classroom Research projects.
> - Think through how students will benefit; how they can be included in the research; what issues are too sensitive for the teacher-student relationship.
> - Decide how you will investigate your question. (Avoid the temptation to use an instrument because it is there or to collect data that have no clear purpose.)
> - Conduct a pilot study, with yourself and colleagues as respondents.
> - Estimate the time needed for student response and for analysis of the data.
> - Even if you have no plans to publish, write up your results to clarify for yourself what you have learned—about doing research, about learning, about your teaching.

started on a Classroom Research project. A group of faculty might collaborate on writing a case, reviewing the literature, and carrying out a Classroom Research project. In a graduate course, a term paper might take the form of a written case, accompanied by analysis, a literature review, and a Classroom Research project prospectus.

Things to Keep in Mind When Planning Classroom Assessment and Classroom Research

Throughout this book, we have discussed ideas and guidelines for planning and carrying out Classroom Assessment and Classroom Research projects. In the first three case study chapters ("The Leslies," "The Captive Audience," and "But Is It Working?"), we offered detailed examples of both types of projects, specifically targeted to the learning issues in each case. In your own classrooms, you are likely to encounter learning problems similar to those in the case studies, as well as a host of others not covered here. Recognizing that there are diverse areas for inquiry that you may choose to pursue, we provide in Exhibits 5.3 and 5.4 some general suggestions for launching your Classroom Assessment and Classroom Research endeavors.

RESOURCES

Classroom Assessment, Classroom Research, and Case Studies for College Faculty

Angelo, T. A. "Faculty Development for Learning: The Promise of Classroom Research." In S. Kahn (ed.), *To Improve the Academy*. Stillwater, Okla.: New Forums Press, 1989.

Angelo, T. A. (ed.). *Classroom Research: Early Lessons from Success*. New Directions for Teaching and Learning, no. 46. San Francisco: Jossey-Bass, 1991.

Angelo, T. A. "Classroom Assessment for Critical Thinking." *Teaching of Psychology*, 1995, 22(1), 6–7.

Angelo, T. A., and Cross, K. P. "Classroom Research for Teaching Assistants." In J. D. Nyquist, R. D. Abbott, and D. H. Wulff (eds.), *Teaching Assistant Training in the 1990s.* New Directions for Teaching and Learning, no. 39. San Francisco: Jossey-Bass, 1989.

Angelo, T. A., and Cross, K. P. *Classroom Assessment Techniques: A Handbook for College Teachers*. (2nd ed.) San Francisco: Jossey-Bass,

1993. (See especially pp. 407–408 for additional resources, including publications and videotapes.)

Boehrer, J., and Linsky, M. "Teaching With Cases: Learning to Question." In M. D. Svinicki (ed.), *The Changing Face of College Teaching*. New Directions for Teaching and Learning, no. 42. San Francisco: Jossey-Bass, 1990.

Case Writing Group of The Washington Center for Improving the Quality of Undergraduate Education. *Washington Center Casebook on Collaborative Teaching and Learning*. Olympia, Wash.: Evergreen State College, 1993. (To order, send a check for $10.00, to cover postage and handling, to Evergreen State College, Attention: Bookstore, Olympia, WA 98505–0002.)

Catlin, A., and Kalina, M. *How to Institute the Cross/Angelo Classroom Assessment Training Program on a College Campus or How to Create a Dynamic Teaching/Learning Partnership Between Teachers and Students*. Napa Valley College, 1993. (To order, send a check for $18.00, to cover postage and handling, to Napa Valley College Bookstore, 2277 Napa-Vallejo Highway, CA 94558.)

Christensen, C. R., with Hansen, A. J. *Teaching and the Case Method*. Boston, Mass.: Harvard Business School, 1987.

Christensen, C. R., with Hansen, A. J., and Moore, J. F. *Teaching and the Case Method Instructor's Guide*. Boston, Mass.: Harvard Business School, 1987.

Cross, K. P. "The Rising Tide of School Reform Reports." *Phi Delta Kappan*, 1984, *66*(3), 167–172.

Cross, K. P. "A Proposal to Improve Teaching." *AAHE Bulletin*, 1986, *39*(1), 9–15.

Cross, K. P. "The Adventures of Education in Wonderland: Implementing Educational Reform." *Phi Delta Kappan*, 1987, *68*(7), 496–502.

Cross, K. P. "Teaching for Learning." *AAHE Bulletin*, Apr. 1987, *39*, 3–7.

Cross, K. P. "In Search of Zippers." *AAHE Bulletin*, June 1988, *40*, 3–7.

Cross, K. P. "Classroom Research: Helping Professors Learn More About Teaching and Learning." In P. Seldin (ed.), *How Administrators Can Improve Teaching*. San Francisco: Jossey-Bass, 1990.

Cross, K. P. "Teaching to Improve Learning." *Journal on Excellence in College Teaching*, 1990, *1*, 9–22.

Cross, K. P. "College Teaching: What Do We Know About It?" *Innovative Higher Education*, 1991, *16*(1), 7–25.

Cross, K. P. "On College Teaching." *Journal of Engineering Education*. Jan. 1993, pp. 1–12.

Cross, K. P. "Improving the Quality of Instruction." In A. Levine (ed.), *Higher Learning in America: 1980–2000.* Baltimore: Johns Hopkins University Press, 1993.

Cross, K. P., and Angelo, T. A. *Classroom Assessment Techniques: A Handbook for Faculty.* Ann Arbor: National Center for Research to Improve Postsecondary Teaching and Learning, University of Michigan, 1988.

Cross, K. P., and Fideler, E. F. "Assessment in the Classroom." *Community/Junior College Quarterly of Research and Practice*, 1988, *12*(4), 275–285.

Fideler, E. F. (ed.). *Educational Forum.* (Fall ed.). Wellesley Hills, Mass.: Massachusetts Bay Community College Press, 1991.

Hutchings, P. *Using Cases to Improve College Teaching: A Guide to More Reflective Practice.* Washington, D.C.: American Association for Higher Education, 1993. (For ordering information, contact American Association for Higher Education, One Dupont Circle, Suite 360, Washington, DC 20036–1110; telephone (202) 293–6550.)

Hutchings, P. "Windows on Practice. Cases about Teaching and Learning." *Change*, 1993, *25*(6), 14–21.

Kelly, D. "Classroom Research and Interactive Learning: Assessing the Impact on Adult Learners and Faculty." Unpublished doctoral dissertation, Claremont Graduate School, 1993.

Kelly, D. K. *The Effects of Classroom Research by Part-Time Faculty Upon the Retention of Adult Learners.* New York: National Center on Adult Learning, Empire State College, 1991.

Kort, M. S. "Classroom Research and Composition Classes." *Teaching English in the Two-Year College*, May 1991.

Mosteller, F. "The Muddiest Point in the Lecture as a Feedback Device." *On Teaching and Learning: The Journal of the Harvard-Danforth Center*, Apr. 1989, pp. 10–21.

Silverman, R., and Welty, W. "The Case of Edwina Armstrong." *To Improve the Academy*, 1992, *11*, 265–270.

Steadman, M. H. "Implementation and Impact of Classroom Assessment Techniques in Community Colleges." Unpublished Ed.D. dissertation, University of California, Berkeley, 1994. (UMI Microform no. 9528688.)

Weimer, M., Parrett, J. L., and Kearns, M-M. *How Am I Teaching? Forms and Activities for Acquiring Instructional Input.* Madison, Wis.: Magna Publications, 1988.

Wilkerson, L., and Boehrer, J. "Using Cases About Teaching for Faculty Development." *To Improve the Academy*, 1992, *11*, 253–262.

Videotapes

Classroom Research: Empowering Teachers. 18 min. Catalogue no. 38022. University of California Extension Media Center, 2000 Center St., Suite 400, Berkeley, CA 94704; telephone (510) 642–0460. (Rental or purchase)

K. Patricia Cross on Classroom Research. 25 min. Catalogue no. 38023. University of California Extension Media Center, 2000 Center St., Suite 400, Berkeley, CA 94704; telephone (510) 642–0460. (Rental or purchase)

Preface

1. All names used in the case studies are pseudonyms.

Chapter Two

1. This Concept Map example and the related discussion include comments on some ideas presented in later literature reviews. Readers may wish to flag the page in order to return to it to reinforce their own understanding of the hypotheses in the Leslies case.

2. A traditional researcher might also use such a four-way matrix, but the Classroom Researcher will probably analyze the data differently.

3. Where the decision to exclude students can be made as departmental policy, it may indeed be less costly and more efficient to exclude underprepared students from a class, but that is an option that most instructors and many departments do not have. As a matter of information, Jerry Evensky, the author of the Leslies case, concluded after many conversations with students and colleagues that the generic Leslies who show up in introductory economics courses without adequate background generate high costs and waste everyone's time. Thus, over a period of three semesters and with high expertise in psychometrics, Evensky and his colleagues at Syracuse constructed a pre-screening test that they felt gave them good information

about students who were "ready," "not-ready," and "readiable" for economics. Moreover, they found that readiable students would voluntarily take a specially designed tune-up course that prepared students who had understood geometry when they took it in tenth grade but whose skills had atrophied.

4. Expectancy/Value theory, reviewed in the literature review for hypothesis 1 of the Captive Audience Case (Chapter Three), includes several elements of each of these three theories and may also be useful for examining the motivation issues in the Leslies case.

Chapter Three

1. To preserve student anonymity but allow the matching of evaluation instruments from the first and the last week of a class, students can be asked to code their papers with their birth date, social security number, or some other number they are likely to remember.

2. This brochure is available from the Oxford Centre for Staff Development, Oxford Brookes University, Headington, Oxford, OX3 OBP, England.

3. Remember that when modifications are made in an existing instrument, the advantages of the instrument's psychometric properties are sacrificed to relevance to the particular situation.

4. Academics have a penchant for arguing endlessly about terminology. Cashin (1988, p. 1) prefers the term ratings over evaluations on the grounds that student input consists of data that need to be interpreted before the teaching can be evaluated. Weimer (1990, p. 56) notes that student rating forms should be considered in the context of describing rather than judging. We agree with these observations but have used interchangeably student ratings, observations, reactions, and perceptions.

Chapter Four

1. For teachers who are especially interested in the measurement of critical thinking despite our reservations, we recommend starting with Chapter Four, "Cognitive Skills and Intellectual Growth," in Pascarella and Terenzini (1991).

These two authors caution that critical thinking is defined by whatever is measured by the many and various instruments that have been devised over the years, but their chapter very nicely covers brief descriptions of the major instruments used and a synthesis of the research findings.

REFERENCES

Ames, C. "The Enhancement of Student Motivation." In M. L. Maehr and D. A. Kleiber (eds.), *Advances in Motivation and Achievement: Enhancing Motivation.* Greenwich, Conn.: JAI Press, 1987.

Ames, C. "Classrooms: Goals, Structures, and Student Motivation." *Journal of Educational Psychology,* 1992, *84,* 261–271.

Anderson, J. R. *Cognitive Psychology and Its Implications.* New York: Freeman, 1985.

Angelo, T. A. (ed.). *Classroom Research: Early Lessons from Success.* New Directions for Teaching and Learning, no. 46. San Francisco: Jossey-Bass, 1991.

Angelo, T. A. "Classroom Assessment for Critical Thinking." *Teaching of Psychology,* 1995, *22*(1), 6–7.

Angelo, T. A., and Cross, K. P. *Classroom Assessment Techniques: A Handbook for College Teachers.* (2nd ed.) San Francisco: Jossey-Bass, 1993.

Arreola, R. A., and Aleamoni, L. M. "Practical Decisions in Developing and Operating a Faculty Evaluation System." In M. Theall and J. Franklin (eds.), *Student Ratings of Instruction: Issues for Improving Practice.* New Directions for Teaching and Learning, no. 43. San Francisco: Jossey-Bass, 1990.

Astin, A. W. *What Matters in College: Four Critical Years Revisited.* San Francisco: Jossey-Bass, 1992.

Atkinson, J. W. *An Introduction to Motivation.* New York: Van Nostrand Reinhold, 1964.

Atkinson, J. W., and Feather, N. T. *A Theory of Achievement Motivation.* New York: Wiley, 1966.

Atkinson, J. W., and Litwin, G. H. "Achievement Motive and Test Anxiety Conceived as Motive to Approach Success and

Motive to Avoid Failure." *Journal of Abnormal and Social Psychology,* 1960, *60,* 52–63.

Ausubel, D. P. *The Psychology of Meaningful Verbal Learning.* Philadelphia: Grune & Stratton, 1963.

Ausubel, D. P. *Educational Psychology: A Cognitive View.* Austin, Tex.: Holt, Rinehart and Winston, 1968.

Bandura, A. "Self-Efficacy: Toward a Unifying Theory of Behavioral Change." *Psychological Review,* 1977, *84*(1), 191–215.

Bandura, A. "Self-Efficacy Mechanism in Human Agency." *American Psychologist,* 1982, *37*(2), 122–147.

Bartlett, F. C. *Remembering: A Study in Experimental and Social Psychology.* Cambridge, England: Cambridge University Press, 1932.

Basseches, M. "Dialectical Thinking and Young Adult Cognition." In R. A. Mines and K. S. Kitchener (eds.), *Adult Cognitive Development: Methods and Models.* Westport, Conn.: Greenwood Press, 1986.

Becker, H. S., Geer, B., and Hughes, E. C. *Making the Grade: The Academic Side of College Life.* New York: Wiley, 1968.

Belenky, M. F., Clinchy, B. M., Goldberger, N. R., and Tarule, J. M. *Women's Ways of Knowing: The Development of Self, Voice, and Mind.* New York: Basic Books, 1986.

Benware, C. A., and Deci, E. L. "Quality of Learning with an Active Versus Passive Motivational Set." *American Educational Research Journal,* 1984, *21,* 755–765.

Berliner, D. C. "The Half-Full Glass: A Review of Research on Teaching." In P. L. Hosford (ed.), *Using What We Know About Teaching.* Alexandria, Va.: Association for Supervision and Curriculum Development, 1984.

Biggs, J. B. "Approaches to the Enhancement of Tertiary Teaching." *Higher Education Research and Development,* 1989, *8,* 7–25.

Biggs, J. B., and Collis, K. F. *Evaluating the Quality of Learning: The SOLO Taxonomy.* Orlando, Fla.: Academic Press, 1982.

Block, J. H. (ed.). *Mastery Learning: Theory and Practice.* New York: Henry Holt, 1971.

Bloom, B. S. "Mastery Learning." In J. H. Block (ed.), *Mastery Learning: Theory and Practice.* New York: Henry Holt, 1971.

Bloom, B. S. "The New Direction in Educational Research: Alterable Variables." *Phi Delta Kappan,* Feb. 1980, pp. 382–385.

Bloom, B. S., Englehard, M., Furst, E., Hill, W., and Krathwohl, D. *Taxonomy of Educational Objectives, Handbook I: Cognitive Domain.* New York: McKay, 1956.

Boehrer, J., and Linsky, M. "Teaching with Cases: Learning to Question." In M. D. Svinicki (ed.), *The Changing Face of College Teaching.* New Directions for Teaching and Learning, no 42. San Francisco: Jossey-Bass, 1990.

Bornholdt, L. Foreword. In O. Milton, H. R. Pollio, and J. A. Eison, *Making Sense of College Grades: Why the Grading System Does Not Work and What Can Be Done About It.* San Francisco: Jossey-Bass, 1986.

Bosworth, K. "Developing Collaborative Skills in College Students." In K. Bosworth and S. J. Hamilton (eds.), *Collaborative Learning: Underlying Processes and Effective Techniques.* New Directions for Teaching and Learning, no. 59. San Francisco: Jossey-Bass, 1994.

Boyer, E. L. *Scholarship Reconsidered: Priorities of the Professoriate.* Princeton, N.J.: Carnegie Foundation for the Advancement of Teaching, 1990.

Brandt, R. "Punished by Rewards? A Conversation with Alfie Kohn." *Educational Leadership,* Sept. 1995, pp. 13–16.

Bransford, J. D., and Johnson, M. K. "Contextual Prerequisites for Understanding: Some Investigations of Comprehension and Recall." *Journal of Verbal Learning and Verbal Behavior,* 1972. *11,* 717–726.

Brophy, J. "Socializing Students' Motivation to Learn." In M. L. Maehr and D. A. Kleiber (eds.), *Advances in Motivation and Achievement: Enhancing Motivation.* Greenwich, Conn.: JAI Press, 1987.

Brown, A. L. "Metacognition, Executive Control, Self-Regulation, and Other More Mysterious Mechanisms." In F. E. Weinert and R. H. Kluwe (eds.), *Metacognition, Motivation, and Understanding.* Hillsdale, N.J.: Erlbaum, 1987.

Brown, A. L., Bransford, J. D., Ferrara, R. A., and Campione, J. C. "Learning, Remembering, and Understanding." In J. H. Flavell and E. M. Markman (eds.), *Handbook of Child Psychology,* Vol. 3: *Cognitive Development.* New York: Wiley, 1983.

Brown, J., and Weiner, B. "Affective Consequences of Ability Versus Effort Ascriptions: Controversies, Resolutions, and Quandaries." *Journal of Educational Psychology,* 1984, *76,* 146–158.

Bruffee, K. A. "Collaborative Learning and the Conversation of Mankind." *College English,* 1984, *46,* 635–652.

Bruffee, K. A. "Sharing Our Toys: Cooperative Learning Versus Collaborative Learning." *Change,* 1995, *27*(19), 12–18.

Carey, S. "Cognitive Science and Science Education." *American Psychologist,* 1986, *48*(10), 1123–1130.

Carnegie Foundation for the Advancement of Teaching. "National Survey of Faculty, 1989." In E. L. Boyer (ed.), *Scholarship Reconsidered.* Princeton, N.J.: Carnegie Foundation for the Advancement of Teaching, 1990.

Case Writing Group of the Washington Center for Improving the Quality of Undergraduate Education. *Washington Center Case-*

book on Collaborative Teaching and Learning. Olympia, Wash.: Evergreen State College, 1993.

Cashin, W. E. *Student Ratings of Teaching: A Summary of the Research.* IDEA Paper no. 20. Manhattan: Center for Faculty Evaluation and Development, Kansas State University, 1988.

Cashin, W. E. "Assessing Teaching Effectiveness." In P. Seldin (ed.), *How Administrators Can Improve Teaching: Moving from Talk to Action in Higher Education.* San Francisco: Jossey-Bass, 1990.

Catlin, A., and Kalina, M. *How to Institute the Cross/Angelo Classroom Assessment Training Program on a College Campus or How to Create a Dynamic Teaching/Learning Partnership Between Teachers and Students.* Napa, Calif.: Napa Valley College, 1993.

Cattell, R. B. "Theory of Fluid and Crystallized Intelligence." *Journal of Educational Psychology,* 1963, *54*(1), 1–22.

Centra, J. A. "Effectiveness of Student Feedback in Modifying College Instruction." *Journal of Educational Psychology,* 1973a, *65*(3), 395–401.

Centra, J. A. "Self-Ratings of College Teachers: A Comparison with Student Ratings." *Journal of Educational Measurement,* 1973b, *10*(4), 287–295.

Centra, J. A. *Faculty Development Practices in U.S. Colleges and Universities.* Project Report 76–30. Princeton, N.J.: Educational Testing Service, 1976.

Centra, J. A. *Reflective Faculty Evaluation: Enhancing Teaching and Determining Faculty Effectiveness.* San Francisco: Jossey-Bass, 1993.

Chi, M.T.H., Glaser, R., and Rees, E. "Expertise in Problem Solving." In R. Sternberg (ed.), *Advances in the Psychology of Human Intelligence.* Hillsdale, N.J.: Erlbaum, 1982.

Chickering, A. W., and Gamson, Z. F. "Seven Principles for Good Practice in Undergraduate Education." *AAHE Bulletin,* Mar. 1987, pp. 3–7.

Chickering, A. W., and Gamson, Z. F. (eds). *Applying the Seven Principles for Good Practice in Undergraduate Education.* New Directions for Teaching and Learning, no. 47. San Francisco: Jossey-Bass, 1991.

Chiesi, H. L., Spilich, G. J., and Voss, J. F. "Acquisition of Domain-Related Information in Relation to High and Low Domain Knowledge." *Journal of Verbal Learning and Verbal Behavior,* 1979, *18,* 257–274.

Chomsky, N. *Language and Responsibility.* New York: Pantheon, 1977.

Christensen, C. R., with Hansen, A. J. *Teaching and the Case Method.* Boston: Harvard Business School, 1987.

Christensen, C. R., Hansen, A. J., and Moore, J. F. *Teaching and the*

Case Method Instructor's Guide. Boston: Harvard Business School, 1987.

Clinchy, B. "Issues of Gender in Teaching and Learning." In K. A. Feldman and M. B. Paulsen (eds.), *Teaching and Learning in the College Classroom.* ASHE Reader Series. New York: Ginn, 1994a.

Clinchy, B. "On Critical Thinking and Connected Knowing." In K. S. Walters (ed.), *Re-Thinking Reason: New Perspectives in Critical Thinking.* Albany: State University of New York Press, 1994b.

Cohen, J. *Statistical Power Analysis for the Behavioral Sciences.* (2nd ed.) Hillsdale, N.J.: Erlbaum, 1988.

Cohen, P. A. "Effectiveness of Student Rating Feedback for Improving College Instruction: A Meta-Analysis of Findings." *Research in Higher Education,* 1980, *13*(4).

Cohen, P. A. "Student Ratings of Instruction and Student Achievement: A Meta-Analysis of Multisection Validity Studies." *Review of Educational Research,* 1981, *51,* 281–309.

Cohen, P. A. "Bringing Research into Practice." In M. Theall and J. Franklin (eds.), *Student Ratings of Instruction: Issues for Improving Practice.* New Directions for Teaching and Learning, no. 43. San Francisco: Jossey-Bass, 1990.

Cooper, J. L. "Cooperative Learning and Critical Thinking." *Teaching of Psychology,* 1995, *22*(1), 7–9.

Cooper, J. L., and Mueck, R. "Student Involvement in Learning: Cooperative Learning and College Instruction." In A. Goodsell, M. Maher, and V. Tinto (eds.), *Collaborative Learning: A Sourcebook for Higher Education.* University Park, Pa.: National Center on Postsecondary Teaching, Learning, and Assessment, 1992.

Cooper, J. L., Robinson, P. R., and McKinney, M. "Cooperative Learning in the Classroom." In D. F. Halpern and Associates, *Changing College Classrooms: New Teaching and Learning Strategies for an Increasingly Complex World.* San Francisco: Jossey-Bass, 1994.

Corno, L., and Mandinach, E. B. "The Role of Cognitive Engagement in Classroom Learning and Motivation." *Educational Psychologist,* 1983, *18*(2), 88–108.

Corno, L., and Rohrkemper, M. M. "The Intrinsic Motivation to Learn in Classrooms." In C. Ames and R. Ames (eds.), *Research on Motivation in Education,* Vol. 2: *The Classroom Milieu.* Orlando, Fla.: Academic Press, 1985.

Costin, F. "A Graduate Course in the Teaching of Psychology: Description and Evaluation." *Journal of Teacher Education,* 1968, *19,* 425–432.

Covington, M. V. "Self-Esteem and Failure in School: Analysis and Policy Implications." In A. M. Mecca, N. J. Smelser, and J.

Vasconcellos (eds.), *The Social Importance of Self-Esteem.* Berkeley: University of California Press, 1989.

Covington, M. V. "A Motivational Analysis of Academic Life in College." In J. C. Smart (ed.), *Higher Education: Handbook of Theory and Research,* Vol. 9. New York: Agathon Press, 1993.

Covington, M. V., and Berry, R. G. *Self-Worth and School Learning.* Austin, Tex.: Holt, Rinehart and Winston, 1976.

Covington, M. V., and Omelich, C. L. "Effort: The Double-Edged Sword in School Achievement." *Journal of Educational Psychology,* 1979, 71(2), 169–182.

Covington, M. V., and Omelich, C. L. "Need Achievement Revisited: Verification of Atkinson's Original 2 x 2 Model." In C. D. Spielberger, I. G. Sarason, Z. Kalcsar, and G. L. Van Heck (eds.), *Stress and Emotion,* Vol. 14: *Anxiety, Anger, and Curiosity.* Bristol, Pa.: Hemisphere, 1991.

Crawford, M., and Chaffin, R. "The Reader's Construction of Meaning: Cognitive Research on Gender and Comprehension." In E. A. Flynn and P. P. Schweickart (eds.), *Gender and Reading: Essays on Readers, Texts, and Contexts.* Baltimore: Johns Hopkins University Press, 1986.

Cromwell, L. "Assessing Critical Thinking." In C. A. Barnes (ed.), *Critical Thinking: Educational Imperative.* New Directions for Community Colleges, no. 77. San Francisco: Jossey-Bass, 1992.

Cronbach, L. J. "Beyond the Two Disciplines of Scientific Psychology." *American Psychologist,* 1975, 30, 116–127.

Cross, K. P. *Accent on Learning: Improving Instruction and Reshaping the Curriculum.* San Francisco: Jossey-Bass, 1976.

Cross, K. P. "A Proposal to Improve Teaching." *AAHE Bulletin,* Sept. 1986, pp. 9–15.

Cross, K. P. *Feedback in the Classroom: Making Assessment Matter.* Washington, D.C.: American Association for Higher Education, 1988a.

Cross, K. P. "In Search of Zippers." *AAHE Bulletin,* June 1988b, pp. 3–7.

Cross, K. P., and Angelo, T. A. *Classroom Assessment Techniques: A Handbook for Faculty.* Ann Arbor: National Center for Research to Improve Postsecondary Teaching and Learning, University of Michigan, 1988.

Cross, W., Jr. "Discovering the Black Referent: The Psychology of Black Liberation." In J. Dixon and B. Foster (eds.), *Beyond Black or White.* New York: Little, Brown, 1971.

Dansereau, D. F. "Cooperative Learning Strategies." In C. E. Weinstein, E. T. Goetz, and P. A. Alexander (eds.), *Learning and Study Strategies.* Orlando, Fla.: Academic Press, 1988.

Davis, B. G. *Tools for Teaching.* San Francisco: Jossey-Bass. 1993.

de Groot, A. "Perception and Memory Versus Thought: Some Old Ideas and Recent Findings." In B. Kleinmuntz (ed.), *Problem Solving.* New York: Wiley, 1966.

"Deep Learning, Surface Learning." *AAHE Bulletin,* Apr. 1993, pp. 10–11.

Dewey, J. *The Sources of a Science of Education.* New York: Liveright, 1929.

Diener, C. I., and Dweck, C. S. "An Analysis of Learned Helplessness: Continuous Changes in Performance, Strategy, and Achievement Cognitions Following Failure." *Journal of Personality and Social Psychology,* 1978, *36,* 451–462.

Diener, C. I., and Dweck, C. S. "An Analysis of Learned Helplessness. II: The Processing of Success." *Journal of Personality and Social Psychology,* 1980, *39,* 940–952.

Dressel, P. L., and Mayhew, L. *General Education: Explorations in Evaluation.* Westport, Conn.: Greenwood Press, 1954.

Dweck, C. S., and Bempechat, J. "Children's Theories of Intelligence: Consequences for Learning." In S. Paris, G. Olson, and H. Stevenson (eds.), *Learning and Motivation in the Classroom.* Hillsdale, N.J.: Erlbaum, 1983.

Dweck, C. S., and Leggett, E. L. "A Social-Cognitive Approach to Motivation and Personality." *Psychological Review,* 1988, *95*(2), 256–273.

Eble, K. E. *The Aims of College Teaching.* San Francisco: Jossey-Bass, 1983.

Eccles, J. "Expectancies, Values, and Academic Behaviors." In J. T. Spence (ed.), *Achievement and Achievement Motives.* New York: Freeman, 1983.

Eccles, J., and Wigfield, A. "Teacher Expectancies and Student Motivation." In J. B. Dusek (ed.), *Teacher Expectancies,* Hillsdale, N.J.: Erlbaum, 1985.

Edgerton, R., Hutchings, P., and Quinlan, K. *The Teaching Portfolio: Capturing the Scholarship in Teaching.* Washington, D.C.: American Association for Higher Education, 1991.

Eisner, E. *The Art of Educational Evaluation: A Personal View.* Bristol, Pa.: Falmer Press, 1984.

Eison, J. A., Janzow, F., and Pollio, H. R. *LOGO F: A User's Manual.* Cape Girardeau: Center for Teaching and Learning, Southeast Missouri State University, 1989.

Eison, J. A., Pollio, H. R., and Milton, O. "Educational and Personal Characteristics of Four Different Types of Learning- and Grade-Oriented Students." *Contemporary Educational Psychology,* 1986, *11,* 54–67.

Elliott, E. S., and Dweck, C. S. "Children's Achievement Goals as Determinants of Learned Helplessness and Mastery Oriented Achievement Patterns: An Experimental Analysis." Unpublished manuscript, Harvard University, 1981.

Entwistle, N. *Styles of Learning and Teaching: An Integrated Outline of Educational Psychology for Students, Teachers, and Lecturers.* New York: Wiley, 1981.

Entwistle, N., Hanley, M., and Housell, D. "Identifying Distinctive Approaches to Studying." *Higher Education,* 1979, *8,* 365–380.

Feather, N. T. "Human Values and the Prediction of Action: An Expectancy-Valence Analysis." In N. T. Feather (ed.), *Expectations and Actions: Expectancy-Value Models in Psychology.* Hillsdale, N.J.: Erlbaum, 1982.

Feather, N. T. "Values, Valences, and Course Enrollment: Testing the Role of Personal Values Within an Expectancy-Value Framework." *Journal of Educational Psychology,* 1988, *69,* 579–585.

Feldman, K. A., and Paulsen, M. B. (eds.). *Teaching and Learning in the College Classroom.* ASHE Reader Series. New York: Ginn, 1994.

Fetterman, D. M. "In Response to Lee Sechrest's 1991 AEA Presidential Address." *Evaluation Practice,* 1992, *13,* 171–172.

Fiechtner, S. B., and Davis, E. A. "Why Some Groups Fail: A Survey of Students' Experiences with Learning Groups." In A. Goodsell, M. Maher, and V. Tinto (eds.), *Collaborative Learning: A Sourcebook for Higher Education.* University Park, Pa.: National Center on Postsecondary Teaching, Learning, and Assessment, 1992.

Fischer, P. M., and Mandl, H. "Learner, Text Variables, and the Control of Text Comprehension and Recall." In H. Mandl, N. L. Stein, and T. Trabasso (eds.), *Learning and Comprehension of Text.* Hillsdale, N.J.: Erlbaum, 1984.

Flavell, J. H. "Developmental Studies of Mediated Memory." In H. W. Reese and L. P. Lipsitt (eds.), *Advances in Child Development and Behavior,* Vol. 5. Orlando, Fla.: Academic Press, 1970.

Flavell, J. H. "Metacognitive Aspects of Problem Solving." In B. C. Resnick (ed.), *The Nature of Intelligence.* Hillsdale, N.J.: Erlbaum, 1976.

Flavell, J. H. "Speculations About the Nature and Development of Metacognition." In F. E. Weinert and R. H. Kluwe (eds.), *Metacognition, Motivation, and Understanding.* Hillsdale, N.J.: Erlbaum, 1987.

Forsyth, D. R., and McMillan, J. H. "Practical Proposals for Motivating Students." In R. J. Menges and M. D. Svinicki (eds.), *College Teaching: From Theory to Practice.* New Directions for

Teaching and Learning, no. 45. San Francisco: Jossey-Bass, 1991.

Fox, P. W., and LeCount, J. "When More Is Less: Faculty Misestimation of Student Learning." Paper presented at the American Educational Research Association conference, Chicago, Apr. 1991.

Fransson, A. "On Qualitative Differences in Learning. IV: Effects of Intrinsic Motivation and Extrinsic Test Anxiety on Process and Outcome." *British Journal of Educational Psychology*, 1977, *47*, 244–257.

Fuhrman, B. S., and Grasha, A. F. *A Practical Handbook for College Teachers.* New York: Little, Brown, 1983.

Gagne, R. M., and Dick, W. "Instructional Psychology." *Annual Review of Psychology*, 1983, *34*, 261–395.

Ghatala, E. S. "Strategy-Monitoring Training Enables Young Learners to Select Effective Strategies." *Educational Psychologist*, 1986, *21*(1–2), 43–54.

Gibbs, G. "Changing Students' Approaches to Study Through Classroom Exercises." In R. M. Smith (ed.), *Helping Adults Learn How to Learn.* New Directions for Continuing Education, no. 19. San Francisco: Jossey-Bass, 1983.

Gibbs, G. "Improving the Quality of Student Learning." Bristol, England: Technical and Educational Services, 1992.

Gibbs, G. (ed.). *Improving Student Learning: Theory and Practice.* Oxford, England: Oxford Centre for Staff Development, Oxford Brookes University, 1994.

Gibbs, G., Habeshaw, S., and Habeshaw, T. *53 Interesting Ways to Appraise Your Teaching.* Bristol, England: Technical and Educational Services, 1988.

Gilligan, C. "In a Different Voice: Women's Conceptions of Self and of Morality." *Harvard Educational Review*, 1977, *47*, 481–517.

Gilligan, C. *In a Different Voice: Psychological Theory and Women's Development.* Cambridge, Mass.: Harvard University Press, 1982.

Glaser, E. M. "Critical Thinking: Educating for Responsible Citizenship in a Democracy." *Phi Kappa Phi Journal*, 1985, *65*(1), 24–27.

Gmelch, W. H., Lovrich, N. P., and Wilke, P. K. "Sources of Stress in Academe: A National Perspective." *Research in Higher Education*, 1984, *20*, 477–490.

Goetz, E. T., Alexander, P., and Burns, C. W. "Elaborative Strategies: Promises and Dilemmas for Instruction in Large College Classes." *Reading Research and Instruction*, 1988, *27*(2), 62–69.

Goldman, B. A., and Osborne, L. *Directory of Unpublished Experimental Mental Measures.* New York: Human Sciences Press, 1985.

Guba, E. "Naturalistic Inquiry." *Improving Human Performance Quarterly,* 1979, *8*(4), 268–276.

Halpern, D. F. "Assessing the Effectiveness of Critical-Thinking Instruction." *Journal of General Education,* 1993, *42*(4), 238–254.

Hansen, A. J. "Suggestions for Seminar Participants." In C. R. Christensen with A. J. Hansen, *Teaching and the Case Method.* Boston: Harvard Business School, 1987.

Helms, J. (ed.). *Black and White Racial Identity: Theory, Research, and Practice.* Westport, Conn.: Greenwood Press, 1990.

Hirsch, E. D., Jr. *Cultural Literacy.* Boston: Houghton Mifflin, 1987.

Hodgson, V. "Learning from Lectures." In F. Marton, D. Hounsell, and N. Entwistle (eds.), *The Experience of Learning.* Edinburgh: Scottish Academic Press, 1984.

Hoffmann, J., and Oseroff-Varnell, D. "Teacher Effectiveness and Student Ratings: Finding the Missing Link." Paper presented at the Second National Conference on the Training and Employment of Teaching Assistants, Seattle, Nov. 1989.

House, E. R. "Integrating the Quantitative and Qualitative." In C. S. Reichardt and S. F. Rallis (eds.), *The Qualitative-Quantitative Debate: New Perspectives.* New Directions for Program Evaluation, no. 61. San Francisco: Jossey-Bass, 1994.

Hutchings, P. *Using Cases to Improve College Teaching: A Guide to More Reflective Practice.* Washington, D.C.: American Association for Higher Education, 1993.

Jacobowitz, T. "AIM: A Metacognitive Strategy for Constructing the Main Idea of Text." *Journal of Reading,* 1990, *33*(8), 620–624.

Jacobs, L. C., and Chase, C. I. *Developing and Using Tests Effectively: A Guide for Faculty.* San Francisco: Jossey-Bass, 1992.

Janzow, F., and Eison, J. "Grades: Their Influence on Students and Faculty." In M. D. Svinicki (ed.), *The Changing Face of College Teaching.* New Directions for Teaching and Learning, no. 42. San Francisco: Jossey-Bass, 1990.

Johnson, D. W., Johnson, R. T., and Smith, K. A. "Basic Elements of Cooperative Learning." In K. A. Feldman and M. B. Paulsen (eds.), *Teaching and Learning in the College Classroom.* ASHE Reader Series. New York: Ginn, 1994.

Johnson, D. W., Maruyama, G., Johnson, R. T., Nelson, D., and Skon, L. "Effect of Cooperative, Competitive and Individualistic Goal Structures on Achievement: A Meta-Analysis." *Psychological Bulletin,* 1981, *89,* 47–62.

Keller, G. "Trees Without Fruit." *Change,* 1985, *17*(1), 7–10.

King, A. "Enhancing Peer Interaction and Learning in the Classroom Through Reciprocal Questioning." *American Educational Research Journal,* 1990, *27*(4), 664–687.

King, A. "Comparison of Self-Questioning, Summarizing, and

Notetaking-Review as Strategies for Learning from Lectures." *American Educational Research Journal,* 1992, *29*(2), 303–323.

King, A. "Inquiring Minds Really Do Want to Know: Using Questioning to Teach Critical Thinking." *Teaching of Psychology,* 1995, *22*(1), 13–17.

King, P. "William Perry's Theory of Intellectual and Ethical Development." In L. Knefelkamp, C. Widick, and C. A. Parker (eds.), *Applying New Developmental Findings.* New Directions for Student Services, no. 4. San Francisco: Jossey-Bass, 1978.

Kohlan, R. G. "A Comparison of Faculty Evaluations Early and Late in the Course." *Journal of Higher Education,* 1973, *44,* 587–595.

Kolb, D. "Learning Styles and Disciplinary Differences." In A. W. Chickering and Associates, *The Modern American College: Responding to the New Realities of Diverse Students and a Changing Society.* San Francisco: Jossey-Bass, 1981.

Kulik, C.-L., Kulik, J. A., and Bangert-Drowns, R. L. "Effectiveness of Mastery Learning Programs: A Meta-Analysis." *Review of Educational Research,* 1990, *60,* 265–299.

Kurfiss, J. G. "Cognitive Processes in Critical Thinking." *In Critical Thinking: Theory, Research, Practice, and Possibilities.* ASHE/ERIC Higher Education Report no. 2. Washington, D.C.: Association for the Study of Higher Education, 1988.

Kurfiss, J. G. "Intellectual, Psychosocial, and Moral Development in College: Four Major Theories." In K. A. Feldman and M. B. Paulsen (eds.), *Teaching and Learning in the College Classroom.* ASHE Reader Series. New York: Ginn, 1994.

Laurillard, D. "Learning from Problem Solving." In F. Marton, D. Hounsell, and N. Entwistle (eds.), *The Experience of Learning.* Edinburgh: Scottish Academic Press, 1984.

Lewis, K. G. "Gathering Data for the Improvement of Teaching: What Do I Need and How Do I Get It?" In M. Theall and J. Franklin (eds.), *Effective Practices for Improving Teaching.* New Directions for Teaching and Learning, no. 48. San Francisco: Jossey-Bass, 1991.

Lieberman, A. "Practices That Support Career Development. Transforming Conceptions of Professional Learning." *Phi Delta Kappan,* Apr. 1995, pp. 591–596.

Light, R. J. *The Harvard Assessment Seminars.* Cambridge, Mass.: Harvard University, 1990.

Light, R. J., Singer, J. D., and Willett, J. B. *By Design.* Cambridge, Mass.: Harvard University Press, 1990.

Lincoln, Y. S. "Trouble in the Land: The Paradigm Revolution in the Academic Disciplines." In J. C. Smart (ed.), *Higher Education: Handbook of Theory and Research.* New York: Agathon Press, 1989.

Lincoln, Y. S. "The Arts and Sciences of Program Evaluation." *Evaluation Practice*, 1991, *12*(1), 1–7.

Locke, E. A., and Latham, G. P.. "Work Motivation and Satisfaction: Light at the End of the Tunnel." *Psychological Science*, 1990, *1*(4), 240–246.

Locke, E. A., Shaw, K. N., Saari, L. M., and Latham, G. P. "Goal Setting and Task Performance: 1969–1980." *Psychological Bulletin*, 1981, *90*(1), 125–152.

Lowman, J. *Mastering the Techniques of Teaching.* San Francisco: Jossey-Bass, 1984.

MacGregor, J. T. "Collaborative Learning: Reframing the Classroom." In A. Goodsell, M. Maher, and V. Tinto (eds.), *Collaborative Learning: A Sourcebook for Higher Education.* University Park, Pa.: National Center on Postsecondary Teaching, Learning, and Assessment, 1992.

Magolda, M.B.B. *Knowing and Reasoning in College: Gender-Related Patterns in Students' Intellectual Development.* San Francisco: Jossey-Bass, 1992.

Marsh, H. W., Overall, J. U., and Kesler, S. P. "Validity of Student Evaluations of Instructional Effectiveness: A Comparison of Faculty Self-Evaluations and Evaluations by Their Students." *Journal of Educational Psychology*, 1980, *71*, 140–60.

Marton, F., and Saljo, R. "Approaches to Learning." In F. Marton, D. Hounsell, and N. Entwistle (eds.), *The Experience of Learning.* Edinburgh: Scottish Academic Press, 1984.

McKeachie, W. J. "Financial Incentives Are Ineffective for Faculty." In D. R. Lewis and W. E. Becker (eds.), *Academic Reward in Higher Education.* New York: Ballinger, 1979.

McKeachie, W. J. *Teaching Tips.* (9th ed.) Lexington, Mass.: Heath, 1994.

McKeachie, W. J., Pintrich, P. R., Lin, Y.-G., and Smith, D.A.F. *Teaching and Learning in the College Classroom: A Review of the Research Literature.* Ann Arbor: National Center for Research to Improve Postsecondary Teaching and Learning, University of Michigan, 1986.

McMillan, J. H. (ed.). *Assessing Students' Learning.* New Directions for Teaching and Learning, no. 34. San Francisco: Jossey-Bass, 1988.

McMillan, J. H., and Forsyth, D. R. "What Theories of Motivation Say About Why Learners Learn." In R. J. Menges and M. D. Svinicki (eds.), *College Teaching: From Theory to Practice.* New Directions for Teaching and Learning, no. 45. San Francisco: Jossey-Bass, 1991.

McNeill, J. "Cooperative Learning Groups at the College Level."

Paper presented at the Second International Conference on Classroom Research, Ana G. Mendez University System, San Juan, Puerto Rico, Jan. 25–27, 1996.

Miles, C. "Cognitive Learning Strategies: Implications for College Practice." In C. E. Weinstein, E. T. Goetz, and P. A. Alexander (eds.), *Learning Study Strategies: Issues in Assessment, Instruction, and Evaluation.* Orlando, Fla.: Academic Press, 1988.

Miller, C. D., Finley, J., and McKinley, D. L. "Learning Approaches and Motives: Male and Female Differences and Implications for Learning Assistance Programs." *Journal of College Student Development,* 1990, *31,* 147–154.

Milton, O., Pollio, H. R., and Eison, J. A. *Making Sense of College Grades: Why the Grading System Does Not Work and What Can Be Done About It.* San Francisco: Jossey-Bass, 1986.

Mines, R. A., and Kitchener, K. S. (eds.). *Adult Cognitive Development: Methods and Models.* Westport, Conn.: Greenwood Press, 1986.

Mishler, E. G. "Meaning in Context: Is There Any Other Kind?" *Harvard Educational Review,* 1979, *49*(1), 1–19.

Murray, H. G. "Classroom Teaching Behaviors Related to College Teaching Effectiveness." In J. G. Donald and A. M. Sullivan (eds.), *Using Research to Improve Teaching.* New Directions for Teaching and Learning, no. 23. San Francisco: Jossey-Bass, 1985.

Namenwirth, M. "Science Seen Through a Feminist Prism." In R. Bleier (ed.), *Feminist Approaches to Science.* New York: Pergamon, 1986.

National Commission on Excellence in Education. *A Nation at Risk.* Washington, D.C.: U.S. Department of Education, 1983.

National Governors' Association. *Time for Results.* Washington, D.C.: Center for Policy Research and Analysis, 1986.

Naveh-Benjamin, M., McKeachie, W. J., Lin, Y.-G., and Tucker, D. G. "Inferring Students' Cognitive Structures and Their Development Using the 'Ordered Tree Technique.'" *Journal of Education Psychology,* 1986, *78,* 130–140.

Nelson, C. E. "Critical Thinking and Collaborative Learning." In K. Bosworth and S. J. Hamilton (eds.), *Collaborative Learning: Underlying Processes and Effective Techniques.* New Directions for Teaching and Learning, no. 59. San Francisco: Jossey-Bass, 1994.

Newble, D. I., and Clark, R. M. "The Approaches to Learning of Students in a Traditional and in an Innovative Problem-Based Medical School." *Medical Education,* 1985, *20*(40), 267–273.

Norman, D.A., "What Goes on in the Mind of the Learner." In W. J. McKeachie (ed.). *Learning, Cognition, and College Teaching.* New

Directions for Teaching and Learning, no. 2. San Francisco: Jossey-Bass, 1980.

Norman, D., Gentner, D., and Stevens, A. "Comments on Learning Schemata and Memory Representation." In D. Klahr (ed.), *Cognition and Instruction.* Hillsdale, N.J.: Erlbaum, 1976.

Outcalt, D. L. (ed.). *Report of the Task Force on Teaching Evaluation.* Berkeley: University of California Press, 1980.

Oxford Centre for Staff Development. *Improving Student Learning.* Oxford, England: Oxford Centre for Staff Development, Oxford Brookes University, Mar. 1992.

Pascarella, E. T., and Terenzini, P. T. *How College Affects Students: Findings and Insights from Twenty Years of Research.* San Francisco: Jossey-Bass, 1991.

Perry, W. G., Jr. *Forms of Intellectual Development in the College Years.* New York: Henry Holt, 1970.

Perry, W. G., Jr. "Cognitive and Ethical Growth: The Making of Meaning." In A. W. Chickering and Associates, *The Modern American College: Responding to the New Realities of Diverse Students and a Changing Society.* San Francisco: Jossey-Bass, 1981.

Perry, W. G., Jr. "Different Worlds in the Same Classroom." In M. M. Gullette (ed.), *On Teaching and Learning.* Cambridge, Mass.: Harvard-Danforth Center for Teaching and Learning, 1985.

Pintrich, P. R. "Student Learning and College Teaching." In R. E. Young and K. E. Eble (eds.), *College Teaching and Learning: Preparing for New Commitments.* New Directions for Teaching and Learning, no. 33. San Francisco: Jossey-Bass, 1988a.

Pintrich, P. R. "Process-Oriented View of Student Motivation and Cognition." In J. S. Stark and L. A. Mets (eds.), *Improving Teaching and Learning Through Research.* New Directions for Institutional Research, no. 57. San Francisco: Jossey-Bass, 1988b.

Pintrich, P. R., Cross, D. R., Kozma, R. B., and McKeachie, W. J. "Instructional Psychology." *Annual Review of Psychology,* 1986, *37,* 611–651.

Pintrich, P. R., and Schunk, D. H. *Motivation in Education. Theory, Research, and Applications.* Upper Saddle River, N.J.: Prentice Hall, 1996.

Pintrich, P. R., Smith, D.A.F., Garcia, T., and McKeachie, W. J. *A Manual for the Use of the Motivated Strategies for Learning Questionnaire.* Technical Report no. 91-B-004. Ann Arbor: Regents of the University of Michigan School of Education, National Center for Research to Improve Postsecondary Teaching and Learning, 1991.

Pressley, M., Borkowski, J. G., and O'Sullivan, J. "Children's Metamemory and the Teaching of Memory Strategies." In

D. L. Forest-Pressley, G. E. MacKinnon, and T. G. Waller (eds.), *Metacognition, Cognition, and Human Performance,* Vol. 1. Orlando, Fla.: Academic Press, 1985.

Ramsden, P. "The Context of Learning." In F. Marton, D. Hounsell, and N. Entwistle (eds.), *The Experience of Learning.* Edinburgh: Scottish Academic Press, 1984.

Ramsden, P. *Learning to Teach in Higher Education.* New York: Routledge, 1992.

Rau, W., and Heyl, B. S. "Humanizing the College Classroom: Collaborative Learning and Social Organization Among Students." *Teaching Sociology,* 1990, *18,* 141–155.

Reichardt, C. S., and Rallis, S. F. (eds.). *The Qualitative-Quantitative Debate: New Perspectives.* New Directions for Program Evaluation, no. 61. San Francisco: Jossey-Bass, 1994.

Resnick, L. B. "Toward a Cognitive Theory of Instruction." In S. Paris, S. G. Olson, and H. Stevenson (eds.), *Learning and Motivation in the Classroom.* Hillsdale, N.J.: Erlbaum, 1983.

Resnick, L. B. "Cognition and Instruction: Recent Theories of Human Competence." In B. L. Hammond (ed.), *Psychology and Learning. The Master Lecture Series,* Vol. 4. Washington, D.C.: American Psychological Association, 1985.

Rest, J. R. "Moral Development in Young Adults." In R. A. Mines and K. S. Kitchener (eds.), *Adult Cognitive Development: Methods and Models.* Westport, Conn.: Greenwood Press, 1986.

Richardson, J.T.E. "Using Questionnaires to Evaluate Student Learning: Some Health Warnings." In G. Gibbs (ed.), *Improving Student Learning: Theory and Practice.* Oxford, England: Oxford Centre for Staff Development, Oxford Brookes University, 1994.

Robinson, J. P., and Shaver, P. R. *Measures of Social Attitudes.* Ann Arbor: Survey Research Center, Institute for Social Research, University of Michigan, 1973.

Robinson, J. P., Shaver, P. R., and Wrightsman, L. S. *Measures of Personality and Social Psychology Attitudes.* Orlando, Fla.: Academic Press, 1991.

Rossi, P. H. "The War Between the Quals and the Quants: Is a Lasting Peace Possible?" In C. S. Reichardt and S. F. Rallis (eds.), *The Qualitative-Quantitative Debate: New Perspectives.* New Directions for Program Evaluation, no. 61. San Francisco: Jossey-Bass, 1994.

Saljo, R. *Learning and Understanding: A Study of Differences in Constructing Meaning from a Text.* Gothenburg, Sweden: Aeta Universitatis Gothoburgensis, 1982.

Saljo, R. "Learning from Reading." In F. Marton, D. Hounsell, and N. Entwistle (eds.), *The Experience of Learning.* Edinburgh: Scottish Academic Press, 1984.

Schön, D. A. *The Reflective Practitioner.* New York: Basic Books, 1983.

Sechrest, L. "Roots: Back to Our First Generations." *Evaluation Practice,* 1992, *13*(1), 1–7.

Semb, G., and Spencer, R. "Beyond the Level of Recall: An Analysis of Higher Order Educational Tasks." In L. Fraley and E. Vargas (eds.), *Proceedings of the Third National Conference on Behavior and Technology in Higher Education,* Georgia State University, Atlanta, 1976.

Sharan, S. "Cooperative Learning in Small Groups: Recent Methods and Effects on Achievement, Attitudes, and Ethnic Relations." *Review of Educational Research,* 1980, *50*(2), 241–271.

Shulman, L. S. "Knowledge and Teaching: Foundations of the New Reform." *Harvard Educational Review,* Feb. 1987, *57,* 1–22.

Slavin, R. E. "When Does Cooperative Learning Increase Student Achievement?" *Psychological Bulletin,* 1983, *94,* 429–445.

Smith, B. L., and MacGregor, J. T. "What Is Collaborative Learning?" In A. Goodsell, M. Maher, and V. Tinto (eds.), *Collaborative Learning: A Sourcebook for Higher Education.* University Park, Pa.: National Center on Postsecondary Teaching, Learning, and Assessment, 1992.

Smith, D. "College Classroom Interactions and Critical Thinking." *Journal of Educational Psychology,* 1977, *69,* 180–190.

Sorcinelli, M. D. "Research Findings on the Seven Principles." In A. W. Chickering and Z. F. Gamson (eds.), *Applying the Seven Principles for Good Practice in Undergraduate Education.* New Directions for Teaching and Learning, no. 47. San Francisco: Jossey-Bass, 1991.

Stage, F. K. "Research on College Students: Commonality, Difference, and Direction." *Review of Higher Education,* 1990, *13*(3), 249–258.

Stark, J. S., Shaw, K. M., and Lowther, M. A. *Student Goals for College and Courses,* ASHE-ERIC Higher Education Report no. 6. Washington, D.C.: School of Education and Human Development, George Washington University, 1989.

Steadman, M. H. "Implementation and Impact of Classroom Assessment Techniques in Community Colleges." Unpublished Ed.D. dissertation, University of California, Berkeley, 1994. (UMI Microform no. 9528688.)

Sternberg, R. J. "Criteria for Intellectual Skills Training." *Educational Researcher,* 1983, *12,* 6–12, 26.

Study Group on the Conditions of Excellence in American Higher Education. *Involvement in Learning: Realizing the Potential of American Higher Education.* Washington, D.C.: National Institute of Education, 1984.

Terenzini, P. T., and Pascarella, E. T. "Living with Myths: Undergraduate Education in America." *Change,* 1994, *26*(1), 28–32.

Theall, M., and Franklin, J. "Student Ratings of Instruction in the Context of Complex Evaluation Systems." In M. Theall and J. Franklin (eds.), *Student Ratings of Instruction: Issues for Improving Practice.* New Directions for Teaching and Learning, no. 43. San Francisco: Jossey-Bass, 1990.

Tobias, S. *They're Not Dumb, They're Different: Stalking the Second Tier.* Tucson, Ariz.: Research Corp., 1990.

Turnbull, W. "Are They Learning Anything in College?" *Change,* 1985, *17*(6), 22–26.

Van Rossum, E. J., and Schenk, S. M. The Relationship Between Learning Conception, Study Strategy, and Learning Outcome. *British Journal of Educational Psychology,* 1984, *54,* 73–83.

Vygotsky, L. *Mind in Society: The Development of Higher Psychological Processes* (ed. M. Cole, V. John-Steiner, S. Scribner, and E. Souberman). Cambridge, Mass.: Harvard University Press, 1978.

Weimer, M. *Improving College Teaching: Strategies for Developing Instructional Effectiveness.* San Francisco: Jossey-Bass, 1990.

Weimer, M. "The Disciplinary Journals on Pedagogy." *Change,* 1993, *25*(4), 44–51.

Weiner, B. "A Theory of Motivation for Some Classroom Experiences." *Journal of Educational Psychology,* 1979, *71,* 3–25.

Weiner, B. "An Attributional Theory of Achievement Motivation and Emotion." *Psychological Review,* 1985, *92*(4), 548–573.

Weiner, B. *An Attributional Theory of Motivation and Motion.* New York: Springer-Verlag, 1986.

Weinstein, C. E. "Assessment and Training of Student Learning Strategies." In R. Schmeck (ed.), *Learning Strategies and Learning Styles.* New York: Plenum, 1988.

Weinstein, C. E., and Meyer, D., K. "Cognitive Learning Strategies and College Teaching." In R. J. Menges and M. D. Svinicki (eds.), *College Teaching: From Theory to Practice.* New Directions for Teaching and Learning, no. 45. San Francisco: Jossey-Bass, 1991.

Weinstein, C. E., and Underwood, V. "Learning Strategies: The How of Learning." In J. Segal, S. Chipman, and R. Glaser (eds.), *Thinking and Learning Skills: Relating Instruction to Research,* Vol. 1. Hillsdale, N.J.: Erlbaum, 1985.

Wellman, H. M. "The Origins of Metacognition." In D. L. Forest-Pressley, G. E. MacKinnon, and T. G. Waller (eds.), *Metacognition, Cognition, and Human Performance,* Vol. 1. Orlando, Fla.: Academic Press, 1985.

Wigfield, A. "The Role of Children's Achievement Values in the Self-Regulation of Their Learning Outcomes." In D. H. Schunk and B. J. Zimmerman (eds.), *Self-Regulation of Learning and Performance.* Hillsdale, N.J.: Erlbaum, 1994.

Wigfield, A., and Eccles, J. "The Development of Achievement Task Values: A Theoretical Analysis." *Developmental Review,* 1992, *12,* 265–310.

Wilson, R. C. "Improving Faculty Teaching; Effective Use of Student Evaluations and Consultants." *Journal of Higher Education,* 1986, *57,* 196–211.

Wilson, R. C., Gaff, J. G., Dienst, E. R., Wood, L., and Barry, J. L. *College Professors and Their Impact upon Students.* New York: Wiley, 1975.

Wittrock, M. C. "Learning as a Generative Process." *Educational Psychologist,* 1974, *11,* 977–95.

Yussen, S. R. "The Role of Metacognition in Contemporary Theories of Cognitive Development." In D. L. Forest-Pressley, G. E. MacKinnon, and T. G. Waller (eds.), *Metacognition, Cognition, and Human Performance,* Vol. 1. Orlando, Fla.: Academic Press, 1985.

Zimmerman, B. J., and Martinez Pons, M. "Development of a Structured Interview for Assessing Student Use of Self-Regulated Learning Strategies." *American Educational Research Journal,* 1986, *23*(4), 614–628.

INDEX

A

Ability, students' perceptions of own, 79–84. *See also* Self-confidence

Absolute knowing, 186

Absolutist level of intellectual development, 185

Academic learning time (ALT), 24–25

Academic performance: and schemata, 43; and self-regulatory strategies, 59–60

Accountability: and assessment movement, 8–9; in peer learning groups, 178–179

Active learning, 22; in peer learning groups, 176

Age, and learning approaches, 140

Agriculture extension model, 5

Aleamoni, L. M., 144

Alexander, P., 63

Alverno College, 203

American Evaluation Association (AEA), 15

Ames, C., 102, 104, 106, 120

Analytical versus narrative approaches, 191; Classroom Assessment of, 197–198; and peer learning, 176–177. *See also* "But Is It Working" case study; Critical thinking; Intellectual development

Anderson, J. R., 38

Angelo, T. A., 2, 7, 20, 22, 26, 45, 56, 63, 87, 107, 109, 133, 141, 149, 150, 152, 157, 191, 197, 198, 220, 222, 223, 225, 227, 229

Anxiety reduction, 78

Application, scholarship of, 27

Applications Cards (CAT 24), 222

Approaches to Studying Inventory (ASI), 132

Approaches to Studying Questionnaire (ASQ), 132, 133

Argument, 192

Arreola, R. A., 144

Ashcroft, J., 8

Assessment, and feedback, 9–10, 22–24. *See also* Classroom Assessment; Classroom Assessment Techniques; Grades; Student evaluation of instruction

Assessment-for-accountability, 8–11

Assessment-for-improvement, 8–11

Assessment movement, 4, 6; relationship of, to Classroom Assessment, 7–11. *See also* Classroom Assessment

Assessment of students: and cognitive levels, 136–137; consistency/inconsistency between, and teaching goals, 119–120, 135–140; and deep learning, 125, 128; and intellectual development stages, 202; as learners, 9–10. *See also* Test design

Assignment Assessments (CAT 49), 109–110

Astin, A. W., 176

Atkinson, J. W., 100, 101

Attainment value, 101–102

Attribution theory, 81–82

Ausubel, D. P., 60

Autobiographical sketches, 87–90

Automaticity, 38

B

Background knowledge: Classroom Assessment of, 45–50, 107–109; and relevance, 100; and schema theory, 40–44. *See also* Prerequisite knowledge/skills

Background Knowledge Probes (BKPs) (CAT 1), 46–47

Bandura, A., 80

Bangert-Drowns, R. L., 104

Bartlett, F. C., 38

Basseches, M., 190

Becker, H. S., 122

Belenky, M. F., 13, 140, 184, 187, 192

Bempechat, J., 80–81, 121, 122

Benware, C. A., 177
Berliner, D. C., 24
Berry, R. G., 25, 139
Bias, in Classroom Research, 78–79
Biggs, J. B., 122, 139
Block, J. H., 104
Bloom, B. S., 73, 104, 136–137
Boehrer, J., 228, 229
Borkowski, J. G., 61
Bornholdt, L. 115
Bosworth, K., 179, 181, 182
Boyer, E. L., 1, 4, 26–28
Brandt, R., 208, 209–212
Bransford, J. D., 41, 57, 64
Brophy, J., 85, 106
Brown, A. L., 57, 58, 63–64
Brown, J., 82
Bruffee, K. A., 173, 174, 176, 183
Building Bridges (CAT 16), 69–71
Burns, C. W., 63
"But Is It Working?" case study: case analysis of, 168–172; Classroom Assessment applied to, 196–198; Classroom Research applied to, 198–205; critical thinking and, 191–194; end-of-course telephone interviews from, 171–172; essay assignment excerpts from, 169–170; instructor interview from, 169; intellectual development issues and, 183–190; literature reviews in, 172–182, 183–194; Minute Papers excerpts from, 170–171; peer learning groups and, 172–182; presentation of, 161–168; recommended readings for, 182–183, 194–196; syllabus of, 168–169. *See also* Critical thinking; Peer learning groups
By Design (Light, Singer, Willett), 51, 135, 147–148

C

Campione, J. C., 57, 64
Campus culture, and cooperation, 21–22

Carey, S., 44
Carnegie Foundation for the Advancement of Teaching, 1, 4, 26–28, 142, 146
Case analysis: of "But Is It Working" case study, 168–172; and faculty development, 5; guiding questions for, in case study exercise, 217–220; procedures of, 36; of "The Captive Audience" case study, 97–98; of "The Challenge" case study, 216–220; of "The Leslies" case study, 33–36
Case discussion: in case study exercise, 216–217; guiding questions for, 217–220; opening of, 217; purpose of, 216–217
Case studies: "But Is It Working?" 161–168; procedures of, 36; resources for, 227–228; "The Captive Audience," 93–97; "The Challenge," 207–216; "The Leslies," 29–33. *See also* "But Is It Working" case study; "The Captive Audience" case study; "The Challenge" case study; "The Leslies" case study
Case writing: for Classroom Research project, 224–225, 226–227; content in, 225; Minute Case exercise for, 225; process of, 225
Case Writing Group of the Washington Center for Improving the Quality of Undergraduate Education, 228
Cashin, W. E., 142
Catlin, A., 228
Centra, J. A., 4, 23, 143, 144, 145–146, 147, 151, 153
Chaffin, R., 39, 40, 41, 44
Change, measurement of, 156–160
Chase, C. I., 136
Checklists, 154
Chess players, 41

Chi, M.T.H., 41
Chickering, A. W., 19–20, 154
Chiesi, H. L., 40
Chomsky, N., 15
Christensen, C. R., 216–217, 228
"Chunking" memorization strategies, 38
Civil war, 42–43
Clark, R. M., 105
Classroom Assessment, 2; defined, 7–8; and diverse teaching talents, 26; and feedback, 9–10, 23–24; general guidelines for, 226; and high expectations, 25; relationship of, to assessment movement, 7–11; and time on task, 24–25; use of questionnaires in, 132–133
Classroom Assessment Technique 1 (Background Knowledge Probe), 46–47
Classroom Assessment Technique 2 (Focused listing), 220–221
Classroom Assessment Technique 6 (Minute Papers), 20, 131, 133–134
Classroom Assessment Technique 7 (Discovering the Muddiest Point), 223
Classroom Assessment Technique 9 (Defining Features Matrix), 196, 197–198
Classroom Assessment Technique 16 (Concept Mapping), 47–50, 56; Building Bridges modification of, 69–71
Classroom Assessment Technique 23 (Directed Paraphrasing), 222–223
Classroom Assessment Technique 24 (Applications Cards), 222
Classroom Assessment Technique 27 (Prospectus), 223–224
Classroom Assessment Technique 32 (Course-Related Self-Confidence Surveys), 87
Classroom Assessment Technique 33 (Focused Autobio-

graphical Sketches), 87–90

Classroom Assessment Technique 34 (Interest/ Knowledge/ Skills Checklist), 107–109, 110–111

Classroom Assessment Technique 35 (Goals Ranking), 141

Classroom Assessment Technique 38 (Punctuated Lecture), 66–67

Classroom Assessment Technique 40 (Diagnostic Learning Logs), 67–69

Classroom Assessment Technique 42 (Electronic Mail Feedback), 150–151

Classroom Assessment Technique 44 (Group Instructional Feedback Technique), 149–150

Classroom Assessment Technique 47 (Group-Work Evaluations), 196–197, 198, 199

Classroom Assessment Technique 49 (Assignment Assessments), 109–110

Classroom Assessment Techniques (CATs): in "But Is It Working?" case study, 196–198; in Classroom Research methodology, 17, 56, 74, 90, 56, 74, 90, 220–227; for developing study methods, 63, 65–71; general guidelines for, 226, 227; for information collection about learning approaches, 131–134; for information collection about prerequisite knowledge, 45–50; for information collection about small-group learning, 198; for information collection about student feedback on teaching, 148–151; for information collection about student motivation, 86–90, 107–110; for information collection about students' understanding of narrative versus analytical presenta-

tions of history, 197–198; and intellectual development, 201; planning, in Classroom Research context, 221, 226, 227; resources for, 45, 227–228; and student-teacher interaction, 20; in "The Captive Audience" case study, 107–110, 131–134, 148–151; in "The Challenge" case study, 220–227; in "The Leslies" case study, 45–50, 65–71, 86–90

Classroom Assessment Techniques: A Handbook for College Teachers (Angelo, Cross), 45, 149, 152

Classroom Research: and Classroom Assessment, 2, 7–11, 23–24; Classroom Assessment Techniques in, 56, 74, 90, 220–227; characteristics of, 2–4; collaborative, 199–202; defined, 1–2, 7; design of, in "The Challenge" exercise, 207–227; and diverse teaching talents, 26; and high expectations, 25; and methodology, 14–18; versus other teaching/learning improvement approaches, 6–28; premise of, 6; relationship of, to faculty development, 18–26; relationship of, to the scholarship of teaching, 26–28; relationship of, to traditional educational research, 11–18, 54–55, 76, 198–199; resources for, 227–228; roots of, 4–6; and stakeholders, 16; and time on task, 24–25; traditional educational research approach in, 52; and traditional educational research designs, 71–74; use of, for critical thinking research, 202–203; use of, for intellectual development research, 198–202; use of existing instruments in, 138–141. *See also* "The Challenge" case

study; Educational research, traditional

Classroom Research projects: in "But Is It Working?" case study, 198–205; on competence and confidence, 110–112; on critical thinking, 202–204; design of, in case study exercise, 220–227; for design of student rating instruments, 151–156; general guidelines for, 226; on grades and student learning, 134–138; on intellectual development, 198–202; on learning strategies, 75–79; for measuring change, 156–160; on motivation, 85, 90–91, 110–114; "*N* of One" type of, 112–114; on peer learning group effectiveness, 204; planning, general guidelines for, 226, 227; planning, resources for, 227–228; on prerequisite knowledge, 52–56; prospectus development for, 223–224; on student evaluation of instruction, 151–160; on study methods, 71–79; in "The Captive Audience" case study, 110–114, 134–138, 151–160; in "The Challenge" case study, 207–227; in "The Leslies" case study, 52–56, 71–79, 91–92

Classroom Researchers, and methodology, 16–18

Clear goals, 102

Clinchy, B., 13, 140, 184, 185, 187–188, 192–193, 194

Closed-question instruments, 154

Cognitive learning theories, 37–38; discussion and analysis of, 218; recommended readings about, 44–45; and schema theory, 38–44. *See also* Learning strategies; Metacognition

Cognitive motivation theories, 98–105. *See also* Motivation

Cognitive skills, levels of, 136–137. *See also* Critical thinking; Intellectual development

Cohen, J., 51–52

Cohen, P. A., 142, 143, 146

Collaboration, in Classroom Research, 3, 199–202

Collaborative learning: versus cooperative learning, 173–174; learning focus versus busy work in, 181–182. *See also* Peer learning groups

Collis, K. F., 139

Commitment, goal, 103

Commitment level of intellectual development, 185

Competence, and self-confidence, 100–112

Competition: effects of, on motivation and learning, 104; and grading, 116, 120, 181; and peer learning, 1891

Comprehension monitoring, 61

Concept Mapping (CAT 16), 47–50, 56; Building Bridges modification of, 69–71

Confidence. *See* Self-confidence

Confidentiality, in Classroom Research, 78–79

Connected learning, 192–193

Context, and Classroom Research, 3, 14

Contextual knowing, 187

Controllability, 82

Cooper, J. L., 173, 174, 175, 176, 178, 180, 181, 182, 183

Cooperation, among teachers, 21–22

Cooperative learning, 21–22, 177; versus collaborative learning, 173–174, 178; guidelines for, 178–180. *See also* Peer learning groups

Corno, L., 25, 80, 85, 100

Cost, of completing task, 102

Costin, F., 153

Course design, for deep learning, 127–130

Course evaluation: design of midterm, 151–156; end-of-course telephone interview, 171–172. *See also* Student

evaluation of instruction

Course-Related Self-Confidence Surveys (CAT 32), 87

Covington, M. V., 25, 54, 82, 83, 84, 85–86, 101, 106, 116, 139

Crawford, M., 39, 40, 41, 44

Critical thinking, 183; Classroom Assessment of, 196–198; Classroom Research on, 202–204; versus connected learning, 192–193; discussion and analysis of, 219; discipline-specific, 203; and disposition, 191; elements of, 191; measurement of, 202–203; and peer learning groups, 176–177, 193–194; recommended readings on, 194–196; research and theory about, 190–194; strategies for improving, 192–194. *See also* Intellectural development.

Cromwell, L., 203

Cronbach, L. J., 12

Cross, D. R., 85

Cross, K. P., 2, 5, 7, 20, 22, 26, 45, 56, 63, 87, 91, 104, 107, 109, 133, 141, 142, 143, 149, 150, 152, 157, 188, 197, 198, 220, 222, 223, 225, 227, 228, 229

Cross, W., Jr., 185

Curiosity, 99

D

Davis, B. G., 18–19, 136, 182–183

Davis, E. A., 180, 182

Deci, E. L., 177

Deep learning, 122–127; instrument for assessing, 139; strategies for improving, 127–130

"Deep Learning, Surface Learning," 127–129

Defining Features Matrix (CAT 9), 196, 197–198

de Groot, A., 41

Demographic typing, 139–140

Descriptive studies, 71–72, 73–74

Development, zones of proximal, 177. *See also* Intellectual development

Diagnostic Learning Logs (CAT 40), 67–69, 74

Dick, W., 38

Diener, C. I., 121

Difficult goals, 102

Directed Paraphrasing (CAT 23), 222–223

Discovering the Muddiest Point (CAT 7), 223

Discovery, scholarship of, 26

Discovery-learning physics lab. *See* "The Captive Audience" case study

Diversity, in teaching talents, 25–26

Dressel, P. L., 191

Dualist level of intellectual development, 185, 188

Dweck, C. S., 80–81, 120, 121–122

E

Eble, K. E., 145

Eccles, J., 85, 100, 101

Economics course case study. *See* "The Leslies" case study

Edgerton, R., 25

Educational research, traditional, 11–18; criticisms of, 11–17; and the exception debate, 12; and the exclusion debate, 12–13; forms of, 71–74; and the impoverished debate, 14–17; for information collection about prerequisite knowledge, 50–52; methodologies of, 14–17; and scientific method, 11–12; statistical significance in, 51–52; and stereotyping, 73–74; use of, versus Classroom Research, 54–55, 76, 198–199; use of, for intellectual development research, 198–199; and the whole paradigm debate, 14. *See also* Classroom Research

Effort, 82–84

Eisner, E., 5, 11

Eison, J. A., 66, 114–116, 117–119, 120, 130–131, 133, 134, 136, 139, 203

Elaboration learning strategies, 60

Electronic Mail Feedback (CAT 42), 150–151
Elliott, E. S., 122
Entity learners, 81
Entwistle, N., 132
Epistemology, 186–187
Erikson, E., 195
Essay, end-of-term, 169–170
Evaluation, quantitative versus qualitative, 14–15
Evaluation Network (ENet), 14–15
Evaluation Research Society (ERS), 15
Exception debate, 12
Exclusion debate, 12–13
Expanding the Case, 225, 227
Expectancy-value theories of motivation, 100–101; application of, 103–104; and self-confidence, 110–112; and task value, 101–102
Expectation: instructor's level of, for students, 25, 103–104; and motivation, 100–101
Experimental studies, 72–73
Experts: assessment, 6, 10–11; educational research, 11, 14; teachers as, 4–5, 11
Extrinsic motivation, 98–100; reduction of, 105; and surface learning, 126–127. *See also* Grades; Motivation, student

F

Faculty development, 4, 5–6; defined, 18; enhancement of, with Classroom Research, 19; relationship of Classroom Research to, 18–26; and seven principles for good practice in undergraduate education, 19–26; techniques of, 18–19. *See also* Teachers
Faculty evaluation: recommended readings on, 147–148; and teacher strain, 146–147. *See* Student evaluation of instruction; Student ratings
Failure: dealing with threat of, 83, 101; and goal orientation

theories, 121–122; and motivation theories, 81–82, 100–101, 114
Failure-accepting students, 84
Failure-avoiders, 84
Feather, N. T., 100, 101
Feedback, prompt, 22–24. *See also* Student evaluation of instruction
Feedback loop, 9–10
Feldman, K. A., 20
Feminism, and educational research, 12–13, 187–188, 192–193, 194, 200. *See also* Gender differences
Ferrara, R. A., 57, 64
Fetterman, D. M., 15
Fideler, E. F., 229
Fiechtner, S. B., 180, 182
"Financial Rewards Are Ineffective for Faculty," 146
Finley, J., 140
Fischer, P. M., 58, 59
Flannery, J., 182
Flavell, J. H., 57
Focused Autobiographical Sketches, 87–90
Focused Listing (CAT 2), 220–221
Focused topic instruments, 154–155
Forsyth, D. R., 86, 104, 105, 106, 115
Fox, P. W., 24
Franklin, J., 142–143, 148
Frannson, A., 126
Free riders, 178
Freeloaders, 178
Freewriting, 221
Fuhrman, B. S., 136

G

Gagne, R. M., 38
Gamson, Z. F., 19–20, 154
Garcia, T., 77, 78
Geer, B., 122
Gender differences: Classroom Research on, 200; discussion and analysis of, 219; in learning approaches, 140; in ways of knowing, 187–188, 192–193, 194, 200

Generative learning, 60
Gentner, D., 38
Ghatala, E. S., 61
Gibbs, G., 122, 123, 129, 130, 132, 133
Gilligan, C., 13, 185, 192
Glaser, E. M., 191
Glaser, R., 41
Gmelch, W. H., 147
Goals: attributes of, 102–103; Classroom Assessment of, 107–110; identification of student, 103; mastery and performance, 81, 120–122; and motivation, 98–114; role of, 102–103; teachers', versus assessment measures, 119–120; theories about, 98–105, 120–122. *See also* Motivation
Goals Ranking instrument, 141
Goetz, E. T., 62
Goldberger, N. R., 13, 140, 184, 187
Goldman, B. A., 138
Goodsell, A., 183
Grade-oriented students (GO), 117–120, 121
Grades: Classroom Research on, 134–138; and deep versus surface learners, 122–127, 129; effects of, on student learning, 114–141; faculty attitudes towards, 119–120; gatekeeping function of, 115–116; and goal orientation, 120–122; and peer learning groups, 178–179, 181; purpose of, 115–116; recommended readings on, 130–131; research and theory about, 114–130; student orientations to, 117–120
Grading systems: criterion-based, 120; normative, 104, 120; for peer learning groups, 181
Grasha, A. F., 136
Group Instructional Feedback Technique (GIFT) (CAT 44), 109, 149–150
Group learning. *See* Peer learning groups

Group-Work Evaluations (CAT 47), 196–197, 198, 199
Guba, E., 11

H

Habeshaw, S., 132, 133
Habeshaw, T., 132, 133
Halpern, D. F., 194–195
Hamilton, S. J., 182
Hanley, M., 132
Hansen, A. J., 228
Harvard Assessment Seminars, 27, 133
Harvard students, 184–185, 186
Helms, J., 185
Heyl, B. S., 178
Hirsch, E. D., Jr., 38, 40, 41, 42–43, 44
History, analytical versus narrative approaches to, 191; Classroom Assessment of, 197–198; and peer learning, 176–177
History and Its Methods course. *See* "But Is It Working?" case study
Hodgson, V., 99–100, 105
Hoffmann, J., 142
House, E. R., 15
Housell, D., 132
How College Affects Students (Pascarella, Terenzini), 139
Hughes, E. C., 122
Hutchings, P., 21, 25, 183, 185, 189, 229
Hypothesis formulation: purpose of, 36; for "The Captive Audience" case study, 97–98; in "The Challenge" case study exercise, 216–217; for "The Leslies" case study, 35–36
Hypothesis investigation: for "The Captive Audience" case study hypothesis 1 (motivation and goals), 98–114; for "The Captive Audience" case study hypothesis 2 (grades and learning), 114–141; for "The Captive Audience" case study hypothesis 3 (student ratings), 141–160; for "The

Leslies" case study hypothesis 1 (prerequisite knowledge), 36–56; for "The Leslies" case study hypothesis 2 (study methods), 56–79; for "The Leslies" case study hypothesis 3 (self-confidence), 79–91

I

Importance of goal, 103
Impoverished debate, 14–17
Improvement of teaching and learning: approaches to, described, 4–6; assessment for, 7–11; faculty development for, 18–26; and measuring change, 159–160; scholarship-of-teaching approach to, 26–28; traditional educational research for, 11–18. *See also* Classroom Assessment; Classroom Assessment Techniques; Classroom Research; Classroom Research projects; Educational research, traditional; Faculty development; Scholarship of teaching
"Improving Student Learning," 127–129
Independent knowing, 186–187
Individualized instructional approaches, 90–91
Institutional assessment, 7, 10
Instruments: for assessing learning approaches, 132–133; for assessing learning strategies, 71–72, 76–79; design of, for midterm course evaluation, 151–156; for differentiating learning-oriented versus grade-oriented students, 117–119; for measuring critical thinking, 202; resources on, 138–139; types of, for formative feedback, 153–155; and typing schemes, 139–140; use of, in Classroom Assessment, 132–133; use of, in Classroom Research, 132, 138–141

Integration, scholarship of, 27
Intellectual development: in case study, 163–172, 183–184; Classroom Assessment of, 197–198; Classroom Research on, 198–202; collaborative research on, 199–202; discussion and analysis of, 219; effectiveness of college and, 190; epistemological categories and, 186–187; gender differences/similarities in, 187–188; levels of, 185–186; and peer learning, 177; recommended readings on, 194–196; research on, validity of for nontraditional students, 184–185; research and theory about, 183–190; and students, 189–190
Intelligence, students' implicit theories of, 80–81
Interactionists, 189–190
Interest/Knowledge/Skills Checklist (CAT 34), 107–109, 110–111
Internet, ASI/ASQ debate on, 132
Intrinsic motivation, 98–100; and deep learning, 126–127; strategies for increasing, 104, 105. *See also* Motivation
Intrinsic value, 101
Introductory courses: difficulty of, 37; fostering metacognition and learning strategies in, 62–63. *See also* "But Is It Working" case study; "The Captive Audience" case study; "The Leslies" case study
Inventories, 154. *See also* Instruments; Learning-strategy inventories
Involvement in Learning (Study Group on the Conditions of Excellence in American Higher Education), 22–23

J

Jacobowitz, T. 58
Jacobs, L. C., 136

Janzow, F., 119, 120, 130
JFK, 39
Johnson, D. W., 173, 176, 180, 183
Johnson, M. K., 41
Johnson, R. T., 173, 180, 183

K

Kalina, M., 228
Keller, G., 11
Kelly, D., 229
Kelly, D. K., 229
Kennedy, J. F., 39
Kesler, S. P., 143
King, A., 61–62, 177, 193–194, 195
King, P., 185, 191
Kitchener, K. S., 189
Knowing, ways of, 186–188, 194; and critical thinking, 192–193. *See also* Intellectual development
Kohlan, R. G., 153
Kohlberg, L., 195
Kohn, A., 208, 209–212
Kolb, D., 133
Kort, M. S., 229
Kozma, R. B., 85
Kulik, C.-L., 104
Kulik, J. A., 104
Kurfiss, J. G., 37, 185, 189, 195

L

Laboratory case study. *See* "The Captive Audience"
case study
Language learning, 42
Large classes, fostering metacognition and learning strategies in, 62–63
Latham, G. P., 102
Laurillard, D., 124–125
Learning: active, 22, 176; active nature of, 37–38; cooperative, 21–22; diversity in, 25–26; dynamic view of, 10; and feedback, 22–24; grades and, 114–141; and high expectations, 25; mastery, 90–91; peer, 21–22; problem-based, 105; and seven principles for good practice in undergradu-

ate education, 19–26; and student-teacher interaction, 20–21; students' conceptions of, 123–124; teachers' role in, 43; and time on task, 24–25. *See also* Goals; Improvement of teaching and learning; Motivation, student; Peer learning groups
Learning and Study Strategies Inventory (LASSI), 71, 72, 76–77, 79; ordering information for, 79
Learning approaches: Classroom Assessment of, 131–134; Classroom Research on, 138–141; deep, promotion of, 127–130; deep versus surface, 122–127; discussion and analysis of, 218; of grade-oriented versus learning-oriented students, 117–120; introduction to, 117; of mastery-oriented versus performance-oriented students, 120–122; questionnaires for assessing, 132–133; recommended readings on, 130–131; research and theory about, 114–130; and stereotyping, 139–140
Learning case studies. *See* "But Is It Working" case study; Case studies; "The Captive Audience" case study; "The Challenge" case study; "The Leslies" case study
Learning focus: in assessment, 6, 7–11; in Classroom Research, 2
Learning issues: in "But Is It Working?" case study, 161, 172; identification of, guidelines for, 216–220; Classroom Assessment Techniques and, 220–225, 227; identification of, 207; in "The Captive Audience" case study, 93, 97–98; in "The Challenge" case study, 207, 216–220; in "The Leslies" case study, 29, 34–35. *See also* Critical thinking; Gender differences;

Goals; Grades; Intellectual development; Learning approaches; Motivation; Peer learning groups; Prerequisite skills/knowledge; Self-confidence; Student ratings; Study methods
Learning logs, 67–69, 74
Learning-oriented students (LO), 117–120
Learning strategies: Classroom Research on, 75–79; defined, 60; development of, through instruction, 61–62, 75–79; development of, in large classes, 62–63; recommended readings on, 63–65; research and theory on, 60–61. *See also* Study methods
Learning strategy inventories, 71–72, 76–79; ordering information for, 79
Learning Styles Inventory (LSI), 133
Learning theories: cognitive, 37–38; recommended readings about, 44–45; and schema theory, 38–44. *See also* Learning strategies; Metacognition
LeCount, J., 24
Lectures: first-day, 68; versus individualized approaches, 91; and peer learning groups, 174–175; student attention to, 65–67
Leggett, E. L., 81, 120, 121–122
Lewis, K. G., 146
Light, R. J., 27, 51, 71, 133, 135, 147–148, 152
Lin, Y-G., 21, 43, 44, 60, 64, 80, 86, 193
Lincoln, Y. S., 11, 12, 13, 15, 16
Linsky, M., 228
Literature review: of critical thinking, 191–194; of goals and motivation, 98–105; of grades and student learning, 114–130; guidelines for, in Classroom Research, 222; of intellectual development, 183–190; of metacognition

and learning strategies, 56–63; of motivation theory, 79–85, 98–105; of peer learning groups, 172–182; of schemata and role of background knowledge, 36–44; of student confidence and motivation, 79–85; of student evaluation of teaching, 141–147

Litwin, G. H., 101

Locke, E. A., 102

Locus, 81–82

LOGO/LOGO II, 117–119, 133, 139, 141

LOGO F, 119

Lovrich, N. P., 147

Lowman, J., 20–21

Lowther, M. A., 102, 103

M

MacGregor, J. T., 175, 183

Magolda, M.B.B., 186–187, 188

Maher, M., 183

Making Sense of College Grades (Milton, Pollio, Eison), 114–115

Male elitist view, and educational research, 12–13. *See also* Gender differences

Mandinach, E. B., 25, 80, 85, 100

Mandl, H., 58, 59

Marsh, H. W., 143

Martinez Pons, M., 59

Marton, F., 124

Mastery goals, 81, 120–122

Mastery learning, 90–91

Mayhew, L., 191

McKeachie, W. J., 18, 21, 43, 44, 60, 64, 77, 78, 80, 85, 86, 99, 120, 136, 146, 175–176, 177, 193

McKinley, D. L., 140

McKinney, M., 173, 174, 176, 178, 180, 181, 182

McMillan, J. H., 86, 104, 105, 106, 115, 136

McNeill, J., 176

Meaningful learning, 60

Measurement experts, 6, 10–11

Measures of Personality and Social Psychology Attitudes (Robin-

son, Shaver, Wrightsman), 138

Measures of Social Attitudes (Robinson, Shaver), 138

Memory: and cognitive learning theory, 38; and schemata, 39–44. *See also learning headings*; Metacognition; Schemata

Metacognition: Classroom Research on, 78–79; defined, 57; development of, through instruction, 61–62, 78–79; development of, in large classes, 62–63; recommended readings on, 63–65; research and theory on, 56–60. *See also* Study methods

Meyer, D. K., 38, 40, 60, 64–65

Miami University, 186

Miles, C., 62

Miller, C. D., 140

Milton, O., 65–66, 114–116, 117–119, 130–131, 133, 134, 136, 139, 203

Mines, R. A., 189

Minute Case: in Classroom Research project, 225; expanding the, 225, 227. *See also* Minute Papers

Minute Papers (CAT 6), 20, 131, 133–134, 196; excerpts from history class, 170–171

Mishler, E. G., 11, 14

Moore, J. F., 228

Mosteller, F., 229

Motivated Strategies for Learning Questionnaire (MSLQ), 71–72, 77–78, 79; ordering information for, 79

Motivation and Learning course. *See* "The Challenge" case study

Motivation, student: Classroom Assessment of, 86–90, 107–110; Classroom Research on, 90–91; cognitive theories of, 98–105; and competition, 104, 116; and deep versus surface learning, 122–130; discussion and analysis of, 219–220; and goals, 102–104, 120–122; and instructional practice, 103–105; intrinsic,

increasing, 104, 105; intrinsic versus extrinsic, 98–100, 105; recommended readings on, 85–86, 106–107; and self-confidence, 79–85, 110–112; theories of, 79–85, 98–105. *See also* Self-confidence

Mueck, R., 176, 180

Multiplicity level of intellectual development, 185, 188

Murray, H. G., 145, 153

N

"*N* of One" research, 112–114

Namenwirth, M., 13

Nation at Risk, A (National Commission on Excellence in Education), 4

National Center for Research to Improve Postsecondary Teaching and Learning (NCRIPTAL), 77

National Commission on Excellence in Education, 4

National Governors' Association, 8

National Grade Survey, 115–116

Naveh-Benjamin, M., 43

Nelson, C. E., 176–177, 179, 182

Newble, D. I., 105

1980s, student learning outcomes assessment in, 4, 6

1990s, and scholarship of teaching, 4

1970s, faculty development in, 4, 5–6

1960s, educational research in, 4, 5

Norman, D. A., 38, 45

O

Obler, S., 67

Omelich, C. L., 83, 86, 101, 116

Open-ended instruments, 154

Organization learning strategies, 60–61

Osborne, L., 138

Oseroff-Varnell, D., 142

O'Sullivan, J., 61

Outcalt, D. L., 23

Overall, J. U., 143

Overstrivers, 84

Ownership of goal, 102–103

Oxford Centre for Staff Development, 127–129

P

Pascarella, E. T., 27, 91, 138–139, 160, 185, 186, 189, 190–191, 193, 195–196, 202
Peer learning groups, 21–22; assigning students to, 180; benefits of, 176–177; in case study, 163–172; Classroom Assessment of, 198; Classroom Research on, 204; and critical thinking development, 176–177, 193–194; as effective use of class time, 174–176; explicit role structuring in, 179; features of, 173–174; guidelines for, general, 180–182; guidelines for structured, 177–180; individual accountability in, 178–179; positive interdependence in, 178; rationale for, 173; recommended readings on, 182–183; research and theory about, 172–182; teamwork skills in, 179–180. *See also* "But Is It Working" case study; Cooperative learning
Peer questioning, 177
Peer review, 5
Peer teaching, 177
Performance goals, 81, 120–122
Perry, W. G., Jr., 184, 185, 186, 187, 188, 189, 190, 196, 198
Photographic memory, 40
Physics lab case study. *See* "The Captive Audience" case study
Piaget, J.-P., 195
Pintrich, P. R., 21, 40, 44, 58, 60, 64, 77, 78, 80, 85, 86, 99, 101, 106–107, 121, 193
Pollio, H. R., 66, 114–116, 117–119, 130–131, 133, 134, 136, 139, 203
Portfolios, teaching, 25
Positivism, criticisms of, 12–17. *See also* Educational research, traditional
Practicality, and Classroom

Research, 3
Premed students in physics lab. *See* "The Captive Audience" case study
Prerequisite knowledge/skills: Classroom Assessment of, 45–50, 107–109; Classroom Research of, 52–56; discussion and analysis of, 217–218; hypothesis of, in case study, 36; lack of, 34–35; literature review for, 36–44; and mastery learning, 91; recommended readings for, 44–45; traditional educational research of, 50–52. *See also* Schemata
Pressley, M., 61
Problem-based learning, 105
Problem-solving tasks, student approaches to, 124–126
Problematic level of intellectual development, 185
Process, and Classroom Research, 4, 12
Prospectus development, for Classroom Research project (CAT 27), 223–224
Punctuated Lecture (CAT 38), 66–67

Q

Qualitative versus quantitative methodology, 14–17
Qualitative-Quantitative Debate: New Perspectives, 14
Quinlan, K., 25

R

Rallis, S. F., 11, 14
Ramsden, P., 105, 122–123, 124, 125, 131, 132
Rau, W., 178
Reading comprehension: and deep versus surface learning, 124, 126; and metacognition, 58–59; and schemata, 42–43
"Received knowledge" level of intellectual development, 188
Recommended reading: on case studies, 227–228; on Classroom Assessment, 227–228;

on Classroom Research, 227–228; on cognitive skills, 194–196; on faculty evaluation, 147–148; on grades and learning, 130–131; on intellectual development, 194–196; on metacognition and learning strategies, 63–65; on motivation and goals theory, 106–107; on motivational theory, 85–86; on peer learning groups, 182–183; on schemata and role of background knowledge, 44–45
Rees, E., 41
Rehearsal learning strategies, 60
Reichardt, C. S., 11, 14
Relational studies, 72
Relevance: in Classroom Research, 3, 15–17; and intrinsic motivation, 99–100
Research and development (R&D) centers, 4, 5. *See also* Educational research, traditional
Research design: in Classroom Research, 74–75; traditional forms of, 71–74
Resnick, L. B., 37, 38, 43
Resource management strategies, 61
Rest, J. R., 190
Rewards, faculty: extrinsic, and assessment-for-accountability, 9; extrinsic versus intrinsic, 146; intrinsic, and assessment-for-improvement, 9
Rio Hondo College, 67
Robinson, J. P., 138
Robinson, P. R., 173, 174, 176, 178, 180, 181, 182
Rossi, P. H., 14, 16

S

Saari, L. M., 102
Saljo, R., 123, 124, 125
Sampling, 113
Schemata: and academic performance, 43; assumptions of, 39–44; and background knowledge, 40–44; and cog-

nitive learning strategies, 70; and cognitive learning theories, 37–38; defined, 38; discussion and analysis of, 217–218; literature review of, 36–44; and memory, 39–41; recommended reading on, 44–45; theory of, 38–44. *See also* Prerequisite knowledge/skills

Schenk, S. M., 123–124

Scholarship, and Classroom Research, 3

Scholarship of application, 27

Scholarship of discovery, 26

Scholarship of integration, 27

Scholarship of teaching, 1–2, 4; relationship of Classroom Research to, 26–28

Scholarship Reconsidered (Boyer), 1, 4, 26–28

Schön, D. A., 15, 192

Schunk, D. H., 99, 106–107, 121

Scientific method, 11–17. *See also* Educational research, traditional

Sechrest, L., 15

Self-confidence, student: Classroom Assessment of, 86–90; Classroom Research on, 90–91, 110–112; and expectancy-value motivation theories, 100–101, 110–112; lack of, 35, 79, 79; and motivational theories, 79–85, 100–101, 110–112; recommended readings on, 85–86

Self-Confidence Surveys, 87

Self-efficacy theory, 80–81

Self-initiated inquiry, 22

Self-paced instruction, 90–91

Self-regulatory strategies, 59–60, 61

Self-worth models of motivation, 82–84; and grades, 116

Semb, G., 119

"Seven Principles for Good Practice in Undergraduate Education," 19–26, 154

Sharan, S., 179

Shaver, P. R., 138

Shaw, K. N., 102, 103

Short-term memory, 38

Shulman, L. S., 5

Silverman, R., 229

Singer, J. D., 51, 71, 135, 147–148, 152

Skinner, B. F., 213

Slavin, R. E., 176, 183

Small Group Instructional Diagnosis (SGID), 149–150

Small-group learning. *See* Peer learning groups

Smith, B. L., 175, 183

Smith, D., 193

Smith, D.A.F., 21, 44, 60, 64, 77, 78, 80, 86

Smith, K. A., 173, 180, 183

Smith College, 192

Sorcinelli, M. D., 20, 24, 25

Specific goals, 102

Spencer, R., 119

Spilich, G. J., 40

Stability, 82; of goal, 103

Stark, J. S., 102, 103

Statistical analysis, 16–17, 50–52. *See also* Educational research, traditional

Statistical significance, 51–52

Steadman, M. H., 24, 77–78, 147, 157, 229

Stereotyping: in descriptive research, 73–74; and use of instruments, 139–140

Sternberg, R. J., 61

Stevens, A., 38

Stone, O., 39

Structure of the Observed Learning Outcome (SOLO) taxonomy, 139

Student-centered methods, 21

Student evaluation of instruction: Classroom Assessment of, 148–151; Classroom Research on, 151–160; end-of-course, 171–172; impact of, on teaching improvement, 145–146, 157–158; midterm, design of, 151–156; recommended readings on, 147–148; research and theory about, 141–147. *See also* Student ratings

Student ratings: design of

midterm, 151–156; of difficult courses, 25; effectiveness of, 23, 145–146, 157–158; faculty attitudes toward, 94, 95–96, 141–143; guidelines for constructing instruments for, 152–153; recommended readings on, 147–148; research and theory about, 141–147; and student attitudes, 158–159; summative versus formative, 144–145; uses of, 144–145. *See also* Student evaluation of instruction

Student-teacher interaction, 20–21

Students: assessment of, as learners, 9–10; attention behavior of, 65–66; attitudes of, improvement of, 158–159; cooperation among, 21–22; role of, in peer learning groups, 175–176. *See also* Assessment of students; Learning approaches; Motivation, student; Peer learning groups

Study Group on the Conditions of Excellence in American Higher Education, 22–23

Study methods: Classroom Assessment of, 65–71; Classroom Research on, 71–79; hypothesis of ineffective, 35, 56–57; inventory instruments for assessing, 71–72; literature review of, 56–63; recommended readings on, 63–65. *See also* Learning strategies; Metacognition

Subjectivism, 188

Success: increasing expectations for, 103–104; and motivation theories, 81–82, 100–101

Success-oriented students, 83

Surface learning, 122–127

Surveys, 71; Course-Related Self-Confidence, 87. *See also* Instruments

T

Tarule, J. M., 13, 140, 184, 187

Task value, 100–102

Taxonomies, 139

Teachers: and assessment models, 9, 11; attitudes of, towards grades, 119–120; characteristics of effective, 20–21; cooperation among, 21–22; versus educational research experts, 4–5; and faculty development, 5–6, 18–26; feedback for, 23–24; as judges of effectiveness, 24; role of, in cooperative learning, 175; role of, in learning, 43; seven principles for good practice applied to, 19–26; strain on, 146–147. *See also* Faculty development; Student evaluation of instruction; Student-teacher interaction

Teacher–directed research, 2–3, 13–14

Teaching: diversity in, 25–26; enthusiasm in, 100; seven principles for good practice applied to, 19–26; student evaluation of, 141–160. *See also* Improvement of teaching and learning; Scholarship of teaching

Teaching Tips (McKeachie), 18

Teaching Tools (Davis), 19

Teamwork skills, 179–180. *See also* Peer learning groups

Technical rationality, 192

Telephone interviews, end-of-course, 171–172

Temporality of goal, 102

Terenzini, P. T., 27, 91, 138–139, 160, 185, 186, 189, 190–191, 193, 195–196, 202

Test design, 135–138. *See also* Assessment of students

Testing. *See* Assessment of students

"The Captive Audience" case study: case analysis of, 97–98; hypotheses formulation for, 97–98; hypothesis 1 (motivation and goals) of, Classroom Assessment of, 107–110; hypothesis 1 (moti-

vation and goals) of, Classroom Research on, 110–114; hypothesis 1 (motivation and goals) of, investigation of, 98–114; hypothesis 1 (motivation and goals) of, literature review, 98–105; hypothesis 1 (motivation and goals) of, recommended reading, 106–107; hypothesis 2 (grades) of, Classroom Assessment of, 131–134; hypothesis 2 (grades) of, Classroom Research on, 134–138; hypothesis 2 (grades) of, investigation of, 114–141; hypothesis 2 (grades) of, literature review, 114–130; hypothesis 2 (grades) of, recommended reading, 130–131; hypothesis 3 (student ratings) of, Classroom Assessment of, 148–151; hypothesis 3 (student ratings) of, Classroom Research on, 151–160; hypothesis 3 (student ratings) of, investigation of, 141–160; hypothesis 3 (student ratings) of, literature review, 141–147; hypothesis 3 (student ratings) of, recommended reading, 147–148; presentation of, 93–97

"The Challenge" case study: analysis and discussion of, 216–217; identification of learning issues in, 216; presentation of, 207–216; reader's challenge in, 216–217; reading assignment in, 209–212

"The Leslies" case study: case analysis of, 33–36; hypothesis formulation for, 35–36; hypothesis 1 (prerequisite knowledge) of, Classroom Assessment of, 45–50; hypothesis 1 (prerequisite knowledge) of, Classroom Research on, 52–56; hypothe-

sis 1 (prerequisite knowledge) of, investigation of, 36–56; hypothesis 1 (prerequisite knowledge) of, literature review, 36–44; hypothesis 1 (prerequisite knowledge) of, recommended reading, 44–45; hypothesis 1 (prerequisite knowledge) of, traditional educational research approach to, 50–52; hypothesis 2 (study methods) of, Classroom Assessment of, 65–71; hypothesis 2 (study methods) of, Classroom Research of, 71–79; hypothesis 2 (study methods) of, investigation of, 56–79; hypothesis 2 (study methods) of, literature review, 56–63; hypothesis 2 (study methods) of, recommended reading, 63–65; hypothesis 3 (self-confidence) of, Classroom Assessment of, 86–90; hypothesis 3 (self-confidence) of, Classroom Research of, 91–92; hypothesis 3 (self-confidence) of, investigation of, 79–91; hypothesis 3 (self-confidence) of, literature review, 79–85; hypothesis 3 (self-confidence) of, recommended reading, 85–86; learning issues in, 29, 34–35; presentation of, 29–33

Theall, M., 142–143, 148

Time on task, 24–25

Tinto, V., 183

Tobias, S., 104, 107, 192

Transitional knowing, 186

Tucker, D. G., 43

Turnbull, W., 8

Typing schemes, 139–140

U

Underwood, V., 62, 63, 65

University of California, 23

University of California, Berkeley, 20

University of Texas, Austin, 62
Utility value, 102

V

Value, task, 100–102
Van Rossum, E. J., 123–124
Vicarious experience, 100
Voss, J. F., 40
Vygotsky, L., 177

W

Watson-Glaser Critical Thinking Appraisal, 202
Webster's New World Dictionary, 11
Weimer, M., 21, 23, 144, 148, 149, 150, 152, 153
Weiner, B., 81, 82
Weinstein, C. E., 38, 40, 60, 62, 63, 64–65, 76
Wellman, H. M., 57
Welty, W., 229
What Matters in College? Four Critical Years Revisited (Astin), 176
Whole paradigm debate, 14
Wigfield, A., 100, 101
Wilke, P. K., 147
Wilkerson, L., 229
Willett, J. B., 51, 71, 135, 147–148, 152
Wilson, R. C., 20
Wittrock, M. C., 60
Women: and intellectual development research, 184–185; learning approaches of, 140. *See also* Gender differences
Women's Ways of Knowing (Belenky, Clinchy, Goldberger, Tarule), 187
Wrightsman, 138

Y

Yussen, S. R., 57

Z

Zimmerman, B. J., 59